PILGRIM
ROUTES
of the
BRITISH
ISLES

PILGRIM
ROUTES
of the
BRITISH
ISLES

EMMA J. WELLS

ROBERT HALE

First published in 2016 by
Robert Hale, an imprint of
The Crowood Press Ltd
Ramsbury, Marlborough
Wiltshire SN8 2HR

enquiries@crowood.com

www.crowood.com

This impression 2021

British Library Cataloguing-in-Publication Data
A catalogue record for this book is available from the British Library.

ISBN 978 0 7198 1707 6

Photograph previous page: Pilgrims journeying across the Causeway
from Lindisfarne/Holy Island.

Typeset by Eurodesign

Printed and bound in India by Parksons Graphics Pvt. Ltd., Mumbai.

Contents

Acknowledgements

Many people have helped to shape this book – whether through their time or knowledge – into what it has become, and I would like to express my gratitude to each and every one. Above all, I am indebted to Jim Brightman for his endless generosity and hard work in creating the map illustrations that structure the entirety of the routes and complement them most beautifully. Without his creativity, imagination and kindness, the end result would not be a patch on what it is. Also, to Alexander Stilwell of Robert Hale, for initally suggesting to me that I write the book, and for his encouragement, patience and help along the 'Way(s)'.

Although writing this book has been an extremely enjoyable and rewarding experience, several acts of bad luck have led to some of the greatest acts of kindness. My sincere thanks to 'Caractacus Potts' (Steve Dunn) for going out of his way to help capture some of the fantastic images of Our Lady of Caversham Way and the Pilgrims' Trail; to Louise Hampson of the University of York (and the Centre for Christianity and Culture) who helped in sourcing the best images possible; to Matt Champion for lamenting my cause and helping in any way he could; to Dr Martin Locker for kindly allowing me a copy of his thought-provoking manuscript prior to its publication and for the use of his images; to David Ross of Britain Express (www. britainexpress.com) whose stunningly magnificent images are featured throughout this book; to Oliver Howes, creator of the informative and beautifully illustrated website www.oliverscornwall.com, for his fantastic images of the Cornish sites; to Martin Crampin for his images of the Welsh sites; and to all other individuals who kindly allowed me to use their images. To you all, I am forever indebted!

This book could not have been written without a great many people, and to them I am truly appreciative. To my friends, family and colleagues – thank you, simply for your support.

Any remaining inconsistencies and errors are thus my own, but every effort has been made to verify facts, where possible. So, too, is the judgement about which of Britain's many, many pilgrimage routes to include. Some of my own, and no doubt many readers' favourites, had to be relegated – but this is the nature of such a vast and interesting subject.

Emma Wells
Yorkshire, March 2014

To my parents, grandparents and to all those
who have aided the journey(s) along the way.

Preface

Give me my scallop-shell of quiet,
My staff of faith to walk upon,
My scrip of joy, immortal diet,
My bottle of salvation,
My gown of glory, hope's true gage;
And thus I'll take my pilgrimage.

from *The Passionate Man's Pilgrimage*
by Sir Walter Raleigh, *c*.1603

Wandering the many gigantic cathedrals, quaint parish churches and ancient landscapes of Britain has been a lengthy pastime of mine, no doubt a result of growing up in the heart of North Yorkshire surrounded by the many religious institutions that our modern faith was built upon. Many stand as ruins, empty reminders of an era of religious life so grand yet so ephemeral; decaying fragments in the landscape silencing the familiarity of the past. Yet they once housed what can be argued as the main pillar of the religion of our past: the relics and tombs of the saints. And to them virtually every level of society journeyed. This was known as pilgrimage.

While the majority of the shrines that once housed the saints are now gone, forever lost to history, many of the routes leading to them still survive and have resonance with pilgrims and tourists to this very day. But their authenticity as historical routes is very much in question and may be more attributed to popular folklore than fact. Several are believed to be ancient prehistoric trackways and therefore long pre-date their inception or the medieval era when pilgrimage was at its height in this country. Rather, modern-day pilgrims are most often invited to follow byways which pass through outstanding landscapes or by tourism hotspots, rather than the trails followed by pilgrims past.

Nevertheless, it is the links with the histories of the walks that still resonate with people, and the connections with such a plethora of human travel over the course of such a long period of time, however trivial, undoubtedly act as primary catalysts in drawing so many to come and walk them year upon year, from all over the world. And it is these extricable links with the past that this book aims to uncover: the ingrained memories that still survive in both the landscapes and the architecture encountered. It is somewhat of a reappraisal of the paths and their accompanying sites, delving further into their histories whilst allowing the reader to connect with and experience their own journey through a renewed understanding of all aspects that such journeys comprise.

As Robert Macfarlane wrote: '*For paths run through people as surely as they run through places*'. And, thus, let's take our pilgrimage…

Timeline of Architectural Styles and Periods

Paleolithic/Mesolithic/Neolithic: c.70,000–2500BC

Bronze Age: 2500–800BC

Iron Age: c.800BC–43CE

Roman Era: 43–410CE

Anglo-Saxon era: 410CE–1066

    Viking: 8th–11th century

    Norman: 11th/12th century

Medieval: 1066–1485

    Gothic: 12th–16th century

    Early English: c.1180–c.1250

    Decorated: 13th–14th century

    Perpendicular: 1320s–early 16th century

Tudor: 1485–1603

    Renaissance: c.1450–1550

    Henrician: 1509–1547

    Elizabethan: 1558–1603

Stuart: 1603–1714

    Jacobean: 1603–1625 (but largely until mid-17th century)

    Commonwealth: 1640–1660

    Restoration: 1649–c.1680

    William and Mary: 1689–1702

    Queen Anne: 1702–1714

Georgian: 1714–1810

    Baroque: c.1660–1720

    Palladian/Neo-Classical: c.1715–1830s

    Rococo: 1730–1780

Regency: 1811–1830

Victorian (includes Baroque/Gothic): 1837–1901

Arts and Crafts/Art Nouveau/Art Deco: 1880–1940

Edwardian: 1901–c.1914

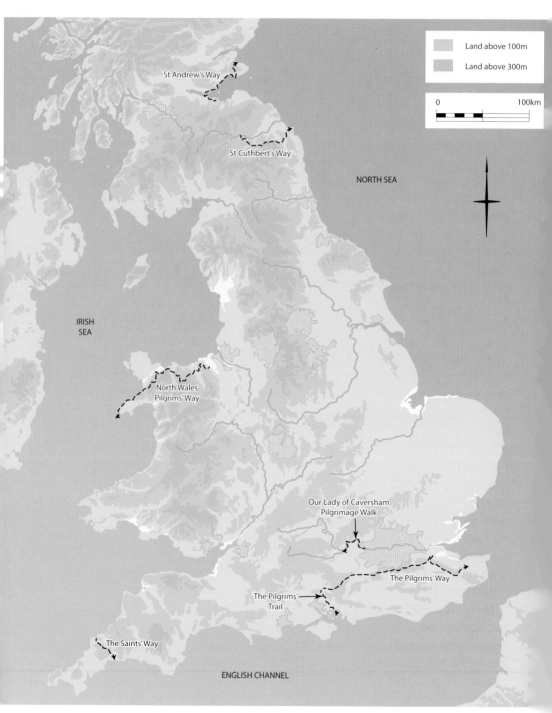

Map showing location of all seven routes in Britain. JIM BRIGHTMAN

Introduction: A History of Pilgrimage

Open a book and you're a pilgrim at the gates of a new city.
Hebrew proverb

Throughout contemporary and medieval literature, the concept of 'pilgrimage' is thought to have acquired different meanings for different cultures, eras, levels of society and even religions. Accordingly, a precise definition of the term has often eluded scholars but, in essence, historical pilgrimage involved any journey undertaken for a specifically religious purpose and which involved an overnight stay at a pilgrimage centre, particularly the latter. Canon law defined it as a mandatory journey imposed as penance for wrongdoing, or a voluntary act which involved a preliminary vow – and both had to be undertaken in the appropriate manner, that is, carrying the pilgrim insignia of scrip and staff. Derived from the Latin *peregrinatio*, or wandering/travelling around, pilgrimage journeys thus usually have a specific underlying religious intention. On the other hand, the *Middle English Dictionary* attributes a wide range of meanings to the term 'pilgrim', from the Latin word *peregrinus* (*per*, through, and *ager*, field, country, land), including: a traveller to a holy place; a wayfarer; an alien/foreigner/stranger/sojourner/exile for the Christian faith; or man or soul as an alien, especially one whose home/destination is heaven.

The zenith of pilgrimage to these blessed sites in Britain was from the mid to late Middle Ages. The acquisition of relics was vital to the income of a church, and it was believed that the possession of saintly relics increased a church's spiritual authenticity. Parish churches, monasteries and cathedrals all vied for pilgrims' custom with sacred relics or, failing that, a locally associated saint was very much an in-demand entity. People would travel far and wide just to get a glimpse of the shining beacons of their faith: the shrines of saints, due to their promises of hope and the ridding of sins. And in addition to an historical form of tourism – a sort of 'been there, done that' – it is this penitential hope, the quest for penance of one's sins, that motivated most and forced some to direct others to go on their behalf both in life and, making suitable provision in their wills, also after death.

Many faiths still believe in pilgrimage as an act of penance or spiritual cleansing. Yet, although there is penitential motivation in subjecting the body to the rigours of the journey to rid oneself of past sin, Christianity required pilgrims to endeavour upon such journeys as a form of insurance in order to gain indulgences that would release them from time spent in Purgatory. It was, it could be argued, the desire to obtain indulgences that populated the idea of pilgrimages. Controlled by the medieval Western Church, indulgences were used to encourage visits to shrine sites, and ultimately led to the idea of 'buying salvation'. Both popes and bishops granted indulgences, perhaps equally for the intentions of the pilgrim's soul and for the prosperity of the shrine or associated site.

The rituals of venerating saints and following paths 'in their footsteps' is by no means a new phenomenon and rather has been practised for thousands upon thousands of years. And while pilgrimage was ubiquitous in the Anglo-Saxon and medieval periods in Britain, pilgrimage is still, to this day, a powerful and resonant act of worship. Many of the most visited and revered of these medieval shrines have faced a modern revival, with pilgrims creating their own paths to them loosely based on the ancient routes of the past. While some are attempting to evoke the experience of the Middle Ages, others are keen to uncover these routes and sites, some from a purely anthropological perspective, and some simply out of mere curiosity for our history and landscape.

The concept of physical travel to a sacred place for varying kinds of religious belief is not exclusive to Christianity. Journeying in search of enlightenment, salvation or hope was, and still is, a common practice of virtually every culture and faith. The majority have adopted an idea of pilgrimage, and for many it is, or has been, an important aspect of religious life. In Britain, pilgrimage began even before there were Christians! Prehistoric trackways are a 'lore unto themselves' and have shown the way to our ancestors for millennia. The chalky trails of the English Downs, for example, can still be traced and are still walked upon, continuing their existence as subtle landmarks, chains across our landscapes, ingrained with the mysticism of the past as they have been for so long. Muslims have also travelled to Mecca and Jews to Jerusalem: where even, as a boy, Jesus travelled with his family for the High Holy Days. In the 2,000 years since his crucifixion, Christians have been eager to follow in his footsteps.

The archetypal pilgrimage for Christians is to the Holy Land or simply Jerusalem, and it is this journeying to the places where Christ lived and died that began such tourism for faith. Since the second and third centuries CE, evidence survives of pilgrims' desires to discover and learn about the biblical lands, and of their visiting both the holy sites associated with them and the Christians who lived there. However, it was the early fourth century that marked a major shift in Christian attitudes. When Emperor Constantine was converted to Christianity in 313CE, he brought with his new faith the concepts of sacred places and buildings derived from Roman and Greek pagan religion. This led to the construction of churches on the site of the 'rediscovered' tomb of Christ, on the Mount of Olives and in Bethlehem, which therefore became focuses for the Christian 'Holy Land'. With them, a new sacred geography was born, enabling spiritual tourism through journeying.

At a similar time, particularly from the fourth century onwards, places were beginning to be viewed as inherently holy if they featured an association with the Trinity, or with a person whose closeness to God had given them a comparable holiness (either through martyrdom or the leading of an exemplary Christian life). The development of these saintly cults was crucial to the growth of place-orientated pilgrimage. The actual presence of the saint, through their existing relics or body, or their association with a particular place in life or death, drew pilgrims and helped to establish a new sacred geography across the whole of Christendom, as relics were transferred from one place to another and new local saints emerged. In essence, anywhere or anything that had been in contact with a saint or his shrine was instilled with a sacred quantity.

Unfortunately, it was this absence of any rational criteria for assessing the authenticity of relics that ultimately led to Reformation consternation towards them, as several churches laid claim to the same relic (a common occurrence) while others were accused of fraudulently substituting saintly bones for those of animals – think the Pardoner in Geoffrey Chaucer's Prologue to the *Canterbury Tales* (*c*.1385–1400), who we are told is carrying among his relics a jar full of pig bones, and that with them, he is able to cheat a poor parson out of two months' salary! The rapid expansion of pilgrimage seen in the fifteenth century largely encouraged these frauds and sat at the heart of the criticisms put forth throughout the sixteenth-century English Reformation and Break with Rome.

During the centuries when the Holy Lands were inaccessible or too dangerous to visit, many Christians sought out reproduction pilgrimage practices such as walking labyrinths in the grounds of cathedrals, journeying to European sites, or simply visiting shrines closer to home. The primary pilgrimage site in Europe was St Peter's in Rome, the home of the earthly remains of the Apostle Peter. The second most visited contained the remains of the Apostle James at Santiago de Compostela in Spain, and it was his emblem of the scallop shell that became the universal attribute of the pilgrim. During the journey, this symbol played an important role in signifying that the wearer was a pilgrim, and granted them special protection. After their pilgrimage had been completed, the badges (which were often collected at each station or shrine site) became emblems of their faith and devotion, a relic of their transformation as well as proof of their journey – many would often be thrown in wells or hidden within the home in the hope of continuing their thaumaturgical powers.

England's most famous site began as St Cuthbert's shrine at Durham Cathedral (Cuthbert died on Lindisfarne in 687AD) but, following the martyrdom of Archbishop Thomas Becket in 1170 on the order of Henry II within the confines of Canterbury Cathedral, Durham was then eclipsed as thousands flocked to the city that housed the tomb and later the embellished shrine of the murdered holy man. The popularity of the site, which drew tens of thousands every year, was immortalized by Chaucer's *Canterbury Tales*, the story of twenty-nine erstwhile pilgrims ostensibly seeking healing and transformation.

Evidence suggests that many journeys were actually very short (a few days, like Chaucer's pilgrims took), and so long-haul pilgrimages were seen as the exception rather than the rule. However, many think of pilgrimage as involving tortuous and arduous journeys lasting months on end in all weathers and often crossing oceans. This stereotype has originated from both modern and medieval literature. But, in fact, it was not the most common form of pilgrim journey, even in the medieval period. The majority were simply taken to a local saint's shrine, which may even have been within the city walls in which one lived. This is the reason for the differences between the routes featured within this book – they are diverse, just like the journeys taken by the historical pilgrims themselves. In addition, the majority of pilgrims did not go on many pilgrimages during their lifetime; some may have journeyed to a site only once, whilst cult churches often restricted the days on which pilgrims could visit. These were often the major feast days.

Pilgrimage was still considered pilgrimage so long as the concepts of self-abnegation and abandonment of everyday life or familiar ties were present, even in small form. Any durational length could earn a pilgrim penance or an indulgence, and for any purpose ranging from cures to hopes for better harvests or even simply to have a day out! In general, most pilgrims did not seek to make pilgrimages in expectation of miracles, but for more everyday eases and cures in a world without medicine.

And what happened when they reached their destinations? Upon entering into the sacred environ of a pilgrimage church today, for example, I am often struck by how little of the medieval elements of the shrine and its sacred locale the modern-day visitor encounters. This book attempts, as far as is possible, to understand and reconstruct just what the pilgrims of the past were exposed to, and how this differs from our experiences in the modern world.

Pilgrimages Today

There is little difference between the reasons why people set out on pilgrimages today and why they did so in the past. Yet, the dividing line between tourists and pilgrims is becoming increasingly blurred: tourists return with souvenirs, while pilgrims return with blessings. Victor and Edith Turner claimed that 'a tourist is half a pilgrim, if a pilgrim is half a tourist'. Both in the medieval past and in the present day, it can be argued that some tourists utilize religious traditions and sites for multiple purposes, not simply ascetic practices. In the modern world religious belief is not at the forefront of pilgrim travel, and many who journey to Walsingham, Canterbury or Durham, for example, desire to sightsee and appreciate the historical locale, or even to participate in the religious customs/ceremonies, whether this be as part of a spiritual mission or simply as recreational entertainment. Above all, in terms of pilgrimage, experience is often the overarching and underlying yearning.

But is there really a difference: is a pilgrim badge from Canterbury Cathedral still not considered a souvenir? Is the encouragement of all pilgrims travelling the St Andrew's Way to display the official 'badge' and Way Card of the route not embedded with the same principle of displaying one's status during a pilgrimage?

Furthermore, the idea of undertaking liminal activity – 'time out' from ordinary life – is just as relevant, if not more so today than it was in the medieval period. Today's pilgrims, who trudge across often arduous landscapes in their desire to reach a sacred end, are following in the footsteps of their pilgrim ancestors, who also journeyed in the hope of a miracle. Thus, the identity of the modern pilgrim may be defined in broader terms than that of the medieval pilgrim who piously journeyed towards the shrine of a saint, and yet the term 'modern' has been applied to any pilgrimage that is post-medieval or post-Reformation, which is broad enough to account for the kind of pilgrim seen today.

Pilgrimage walks are marching their way back and enjoying an extraordinary revival across Britain. A 2012 *Guardian* article by Robert MacFarlane noted that 'More and more people are setting out on pilgrimages, for religious, cultural or personal reasons', while Jane Alexander of *The Telegraph* concurred: 'While figures for churchgoing continue to fall across Europe, the number of those making pilgrimages is steadily rising. Many people uncomfortable about sitting in pews and uneasy with institutionalised religion find it easier to walk rather than talk their faith.'

Essentially, the 'walk of faith' is an increasingly fashionable approach to modern religion. While many churches of the Christian world remain rather empty, pilgrims from all walks of life are flocking to pilgrimage sites, seeking something beyond what they are receiving in their mother institutions. Walking both national and ancient trails is becoming a favourite pastime of not only the frequent hiker but also of those simply interested in discovering the hidden gems and tales of our countryside. And it appears this is a growing international phenomenon. In 1985, 2,491 people received the certificate of completion to Santiago de Compostela, Spain, known as *la autentica*. Since it became a UNESCO World Heritage Site, it has seen a staggering rise in visitor numbers, with more than 270,000 in 2010. A quarter of a million pilgrims also now converge each year on the north Norfolk village of Walsingham, site of the eleventh-century shrine of the Virgin Mary and self-branded 'England's Nazareth'.

But how much is really known of these well-trodden paths, and how have they survived in our memory? Saints and their associated sites of pilgrimage are a staple of Britain's historical past – some of which are as much as, or more than, a thousand years old – and have helped shape the country's natural and architectural landscape. Today, the systems of trails and roads carved by these spiritual pilgrims are now being revived as some of the most popular routes in the country. Many argue they were born as the toll-road system developed. A 1663 Act of Parliament was the first legislation to allow Justices of the Peace to levy tolls on roads in order to contribute to their upkeep. To avoid paying fees to use the toll roads, many travellers reverted to using ancient trackways whilst also following the old trade routes which, over time, became accepted ways for travellers and pilgrims alike. They also tended to follow byways, as many highways were unoccupied and may therefore have been unsafe in some areas, while others graced uncultivated land so they could pass without trespassing on tilled land.

This led to side routes and hidden tracks over time becoming repeatedly used and thus ingrained within the landscape. Furthermore, in bad weather, well-trodden paths may have suffered surface damage, making them difficult to walk or ride on. Think how different the journey medieval pilgrims would have faced when travelling to the Feast of St Thomas at Canterbury on 29 December in comparison to those travelling to his Feast of Translation on 7 July! It is likely that the former sought out the well-worn tracks, which meant their journeys were as quick, passable and secure as could be. It is possible to trace pilgrim routes and related sites from the Middle Ages onwards in this way, by noting which monasteries, churches and chapels offered hospitality and opportunities for worship along these routes, and by identifying the holy wells and sites that pilgrims would have bypassed en route to their final sacred destinations.

Modern-day wayfarers are now following in their footsteps, eager to learn more about the treasure troves of shrines, standing stones, chapels, churches and holy wells that connect these routes, and which combine to form some of the most extraordinary landscapes the country has to offer, all of which beg for inspection and reflection.

The subject of pilgrimage routes and the association between the physical act and the places encountered along the way has generally been overlooked, yet pilgrims often visited a number of shrines or interesting/sacred sites en route to the principle shrine. The role of such sites has often been sidelined in favour of individual, prominent centres of pilgrimage, ritual settings, shrine monuments and, above all, the journey itself, perhaps due to the exciting prospect of reconstructing such past historical practices and experiences. This is easy to understand considering that our modern methods of travel consist largely of planes, trains and automobiles, all of which were out of bounds to the bygone pilgrim – and rightly so, as enduring the journey was an inherent part of the process. However, while the route may have been taken at a much slower pace, modern-day pilgrims also travel them (although perhaps using different modes of transport) in the hope of moving past and towards many significant architectural sites. And it is encounters with such structures and buildings found along the way which have been largely neglected.

What we tend to forget is that these monuments and structures represent the key points of these spiritual journeys, and are therefore fundamental parts of the overall pilgrimage. They are as much a site, an event and a sign in themselves. Moreover, at least one of them forms the climatic event of the pilgrimage itself. They are not simply stop-offs as one moves across these historical landscapes, but rather cumulatively form the settings for intense experiences. In fact, visits to the smaller sites along the approach to the major destination were often thought to increase the devotional power of a cult: they were rewards of the endurance encountered throughout; the appetizers and motivators for the pilgrim to reach his/her goal along the way towards the object of devotion, such as the shrine of Our Lady at Walsingham or the site of St Thomas Becket's martyrdom at Canterbury. Their importance cannot be overlooked.

How to 'Read' this Book

This book is the first study of several of Britain's most important and richly evocative pilgrimage routes in one single publication. It is intended to give the reader a foundational understanding and informative experience of the history, significance and practices surrounding these sacred paths and sites. It will feature detailed studies of the historical formation and development of the routes themselves, as well as analyse the complex religious and secular landscapes of the sites, monuments and buildings found along them. The origins of the routes will also be explored in contrast to the paths of the modern courses many now follow, and which have been altered for myriad reasons since their historical inception. The ultimate aim is therefore to unite the isolated features of pilgrimage in the spiritual, historical and physical sense.

Having emphasized that the focus of this book is Britain (in the modern sense of the word) or, more precisely, England, Scotland and Wales, and with a concentration on Christian sites which largely proliferated or were established in the medieval period, a few caveats must be highlighted. It is not possible to recover every detail of each pathway that past pilgrims walked upon. Holy places were often identified simply through the belief of the pilgrim, and only over time did some sites become institutionalized through increasing devotion or repeated visits. Linked to this, many sites may have arisen out of the propagation of miracle accounts that were localized rather than known of nationally. Moreover, modern historic and archaeological evidence often sits in direct conflict with historical pilgrim routes, as they were predominantly travelled via following long-lost scripture, word of mouth or other geographical practices. Certain relics may also have been hidden along the paths to protect them from mass devotion or simply theft and, accordingly, such sites are forever lost to history. In fact, a significant majority of these routes are based on those sites that, for whatever reason, generated some sort of demand for pilgrimage and contained associative sites along the way.

Also, we cannot be sure that a route followed in the fourteenth century had not been entirely changed by the fifteenth, and some of these routes have actually only become popular with modern-day pilgrims through recent research that has established links between them and their saints. But the key to experiencing these routes is to understand them, even from a modern perspective. The only context we have to connect with the past is our own experience, and it is this idea that embodies many of the pilgrims walking in the footsteps of their forebears today.

Thus, this book is a clear and concise step-by-step guide combined with a definitive study of the pilgrimage routes and landscapes of Britain for pilgrims, hikers, or simply the interested historian or prospective traveller. It is organized geographically, leading the reader from the north to the south of the British Isles, to uncover the ecclesiastical and secular art, architecture, historical narratives and terrains encountered along the ways. Each chapter focuses on one of seven different pilgrimage routes of significant historical origins, and which culminate at the shrine site of a notable (largely Anglo-Saxon/medieval) saint. The routes included are:

- St Andrew's Way
- St Cuthbert's Way
- The North Wales Pilgrim's Way (Holywell to Bardsey Island)
- Our Lady of Caversham Pilgrimage Walk
- The Pilgrims' Way (beginning as St Swithun's Way)
- The Saints' Way, or Forth an Syns
- The Pilgrims' Trail (Hampshire to Normandy)

The book is designed to be a companion both to the voyager of these routes and to the visitor of past pilgrim sites. Detailed maps are provided for each chapter based on the modern courses, which identify all major sites of historical significance, as well as those of additional interest, as many modern-day routes have deviated from their original paths for numerous reasons including, as noted, tourism, the growth of towns/ cities, and modern transport means.

Each chapter therefore discusses each significant site encountered on the journey in a geographical manner. Visits to the supplementary sites may be undertaken as part of the journey by making separate detours along the way; however, overall, the chapters are structured so that the most interesting sites may be followed in the order they appear in the landscape. Accordingly, to follow these routes, modern pilgrims should use the illustrated maps for reference as the chapters do not provide detailed instructions of every twist, turn and path to be taken. Focus is on the sites themselves, with short prefaces to how they are reached. Some chapters provide more details of the main route than others (for example, the North Wales Pilgrim's Way), simply because, in some places, the journey stretches across open countryside with few connecting points of reference; other chapters simply move from site to site as so many are encountered along the route.

The organization of the book itself also follows a journey of its own: it is structured geographically (approximately) based on the locations of the routes, starting in the north (Scotland) and ending, with Chapter Seven, at the very southerly point of England. This was the primary principle in deciding which routes to include and those not to. The geographical diversity of England, Scotland and Wales had to be covered, but this decision was also made by the locations of the shrine sites themselves, many of which were housed in the most notable towns and cities of the Middle Ages. Today, some of the routes have been significantly altered from their medieval beginnings in order to accommodate modern-day tourism, as many towns and villages vie for a place along such routes in the hope of economic prosperity on the back of pilgrimage promotion. Perhaps this is no different to the mentions of Rochester or Deptford in the *Canterbury Tales*, which no doubt saw a great many more visitors following its publication. Ireland was not included simply because pilgrimage there is distinctive in itself, and would have required a further publication of its own. In addition, the pilgrimage experiences formed throughout England, Scotland and Wales are generally linked, or include associations, with some notable cults stretching the borders of at least two countries.

Yet any attempt to focus on the historical pilgrim routes of Britain has to leave out some that many readers may consider especially notable – but there is reason in the choice, and the following explains the criteria by which the routes made it into this book. The first principle was that each had to culminate in a shrine of some historic significance. While not every pilgrimage site has been preserved, so many great shrine sites and associated structures and monuments do survive, many of which are sited off the beaten track or simply in ruinous states, and so for abundant reasons are not as celebrated as Canterbury, Lourdes, Santiago or Walsingham. And yet their histories are just as fascinating. I therefore wanted to take the reader on a journey of the undiscovered sites encountered along the routes, and the histories that likely would be lost without this guide.

Some of the sites featured are therefore simply ruins or earthworks, but they are evocative, important sites that should not be overlooked, such as the Cornish site of Tywardreath Priory, which was dissolved and demolished in 1540, with many of its stones reputedly used to build Angers Abbey in France. It was for this particular reason that I chose not to include one of the most popular pilgrim attractions in England, which culminates the 67-mile (108km) 'Walsingham Way': the route from Ely Cathedral to the Slipper Chapel, where the shrine and relics of the Virgin were housed in the small Norfolk village of Little Walsingham.[1] For the benefit of the reader, however, a brief summary and history of the route is provided.

The Way begins at the site of the original shrine of St Etheldreda within Ely Cathedral (which features great evidence of Reformation destruction, if nothing else), passes by the ruins of Castle Acre Priory, the first Cluniac monastery in England, and culminates at the village of Little Walsingham, located halfway between the city of Norwich and the town of King's Lynn. In 1061 the widow of the lord of the manor of Walsingham Parva, Richeldis de Faverches, had a vision of the Virgin Mary. Mary took Richeldis in spirit to Nazareth to show her the place where the Angel Gabriel had appeared to her. Richeldis was told to take note of the measurements of the Holy House and build a copy of it in Walsingham. Her son, Geoffrey de Faverches then left instructions in his will for a priory to be built around the Holy House, which was undertaken by the Augustinians in the mid-twelfth century.

In addition, the Slipper Chapel, located about a mile south of Walsingham in Houghton St Giles, is the primary Catholic shrine at Walsingham. It was built around 1340 as the last pilgrim chapel before the village, and is the only surviving station of many that once marked the pilgrimage route. Its unusual name derives from the pilgrims who would remove their shoes here to walk barefoot the rest of the way to Walsingham. The church was restored and reconsecrated by the Roman Catholic Church in 1938 and became the Catholic National Shrine of Our Lady. Then, the first building encountered upon entering the village of Little Walsingham was the Franciscan Friary, established by Elizabeth de Burgh, Countess of Clare, in 1347.

By the fourteenth and fifteenth centuries Walsingham and Canterbury were the two premier places of pilgrimage in England. Suppressed at the Reformation, the Walsingham shrine was revived in 1921 by Friar Patten, the vicar of Walsingham,

---

[1] There is also a further route from King's Lynn to Walsingham – *see* John Merrill's 2003 guide in Further Reading. For the main Ely route, *see* the Long Distance Walkers Association (LDWA) for full details: https://www.ldwa.org.uk/ldp/members/show_path.php?path_name=Walsingham+Way+-+Ely+to+Walsingham, and John Merrill's 2003 guide, again in the Further Reading section.

who reignited the medieval pilgrimage among Anglicans. He commissioned a new statue of Our Lady of Walsingham, based on the image shown on the medieval seal of the priory. The statue was placed inside a replica of the Holy House (thus resembling the original shrine) within Little Walsingham's parish church in 1922, and the first organized Anglican pilgrimage took place in 1923. Its crypt contains the Holy Well, which was discovered during the construction of the church and is believed to have healing properties.

The shrine site of Our Lady of Walsingham actually consists of several shrines and chapels of various denominations that are scattered around the village, including the Roman Catholic Church of the Annunciation (*aka* New Parish Church), dedicated in 2007; the Shirehall Museum, which includes an exhibit on the history of the pilgrimage to Walsingham; the Parish Church of St Mary, where the modern statue was originally placed; and the ruins of the Franciscan friary. Also, in 1938, the Roman Catholic Chapel of the Holy Spirit was added adjacent to the National Shrine of Our Lady to provide more room for pilgrims. The small chapel contains votive candles and a fine modern mosaic by Anna Wyner called 'Descent of the Holy Spirit at Pentecost – Our Lady in the Midst of the Apostles' (1988). Finally, 1982 saw the completion of the Chapel of Our Lady of Reconciliation to replace an open-air altar.

There is an abundance of literature written on this particular site of pilgrimage, largely as it is the most salient English site visited by pilgrims from across the globe to this day – around 250,000 pilgrims each year, as individuals or as parish groups accompanied by their priest. However, the route between Ely and Walsingham is a rather new creation and, in fact, much scholarship has discovered that the majority of medieval pilgrims made their way to the shrine from their own doorstep – there was no single prescribed route. As many of the associated chapels and sites in the area were largely eradicated during the Dissolution, it was felt that the other routes chosen provided much more to see in visual and spiritual terms, which fitted with the objective of this book.

Other routes to Walsingham included those from London via Waltham Abbey, Newmarket, Brandon, Swaffham, Castle Acre Priory and East Barsham; from the north, pilgrims crossed the Wash near Long Sutton and came through King's Lynn (then called Bishop's Lynn), Flitcham, Rudham and Coxford; and from the east the route ran through Norwich and Attlebridge. In addition, many of the relics and shrine sites were created in the twentieth century and so, in part, are more 'modern attractions'. Add that to the fact that very few interesting historical sites for the purposes of a pilgrim route are encountered along the Walsingham Way, I felt that others were more worthy of inclusion.

Thus, not all sites included in this publication are simply 'buildings'. Pilgrim stations or sites can be divided into categories, including tomb and shrine sites (for example, monasteries or churches serving as the final destination); holy wells and springs; chapels and parish churches visited along the way and/or attributed to the hagiography (or stories) of a saint; topographies; and finally, monuments and stones. The latter are often places that no longer contain any remnants of the saint but are still considered sacred. In fact, some sites are considered sacred simply due to their popularity and the inherent spirituality the particular site has afforded pilgrims over the years. They may not necessarily have any deep or meaningful association with the life or death of a saint, but their notoriety has built up simply due to the regularity of pilgrim visitations. In essence, places 'gather' meaning through human interactions with sites. It is therefore worth retaining the question throughout: what makes a place holy?

In tandem, parts of the routes are simply beautiful landscapes. While I am an avid purveyor of things to see at historic sites, there are occasional entries where little remains associated with the cult, yet they simply embody or evoke a striking feeling and therefore form an inherent part of the overall experience of the journey. For example, many of the sites along St Cuthbert's Way are associated with the saint because his body was hidden at the locations during the Viking raids of 875CE – even Lindisfarne Priory is empty of any relics as Cuthbert's body was taken to Durham Cathedral. But this, in some respects, provides us with a more valuable experience, as including only the 'best bits' would feel somewhat contrived and sterile. I hope that you feel instead a sense of truly walking in the footsteps of bygone pilgrims, equally experiencing the exciting and mundane aspects of such journeys.

A further principle for the decision of which routes to include was the associated cult itself. The attempt was to feature routes with fascinating tales about interesting saints, and sites associated with the accounts of their lives and deaths. Indeed, the journeys that human beings undertake leave tracks, and the destinations they seek out are inscribed by the cultures that visitors bring with them. But this is also where problems lie, because many of the modern-day routes with apparent historical origins are in fact what David Brown has termed 'genuine fakes'. What many actually offer is a sequence of carefully constructed sites and spectacles that provide both factual and manufactured encounters with the cult. The majority of these trails have been created in the modern day to showcase the best aspects of the countryside that Britain has to offer, rather than being formed or derived from historic connections to the landscape. A multitude of other attractions are given equal standing alongside the landscape and genuinely medieval cult sites.

Such pilgrim stations (or stops) may be better termed 'sights and attractions', because while many are fundamentally connected with the saint in some way, genuine sites may be bypassed in favour of ones closer to the route's trail (important sites that deviate too far from the main route or are difficult to access are often overlooked in favour of those that are closer) or because they are largely unknown, or possess little history. Returning to St Cuthbert's Way, Melrose Abbey is a significant station along the modern route and yet the monastery Cuthbert entered as a novice monastic in 651AD was in fact Old Melrose or 'Mailros', and not Melrose where the beautiful twelfth-century ruined Cistercian abbey stands today.

Perhaps the main reason for this is that many of these routes were created by the tourism industry in the twentieth century, effectively *borrowing* from the original stories. St Cuthbert's Way was created in 1995 by Roger Smith and Ron Shaw (who worked for the Scottish Borders tourist board) in the hope that after 1,300 years, the new route would become a modern pilgrimage in Cuthbert's memory. By comparison, the trail known as The Pilgrim's Way between Holywell and St David's in Wales, was not even recorded until John Ogilby mapped it in 1675. Whereas the latter may not be described as a particularly 'modern' invention, it is certainly not a comparatively historical route.

This book will use modern guidebooks for reference, but many types of source material have been used in the research. Contemporary primary sources for pilgrimage are minimal, although a handful of early pilgrim journals and guidebooks are extant, such as *The Book of Pilgrims* published in 1486 and Domenico Laffi's seventeenth-century diary of his pilgrimage from Bologna to Santiago, as well as royal inventories that provide candid evidence of the routes that monarchs took and the places they visited. The abundance of evidence has derived from the architecture encountered along them – the churches, monasteries, monuments, shrines, wells, chapels, stones, crosses – and the ever-expanding literature about them, which provides a wealth of information. In some cases, cartographic evidence and place-name studies also complement the architectural records, and so routes can be pinpointed by analysing where sites are situated in relation to old roads and pathways.

It will act as an informative guide to some of the most notable, as well as the less familiar, pilgrim routes of Great Britain, providing somewhat of a journey of discovery with a practical commentary on the shrines, architecture and art encountered, in addition to observations on the wider secular landscape and history of the pathways.

It will seek to include the most notably associated cult sites, even if they are off the beaten trails or largely unknown to modern-day walkers. In addition, within each route, both the selected starting point for the pilgrimage – typically a site confirmed in the historical record as linked to the pilgrim destination, or a settlement of some significance within the local area and thus well connected to the route network – and the culminating site of the journey, the saint's shrine site, remain constant stops.

However, it is *not* a clear substitute for a comprehensive guidebook to each and every monument and/or site across the ages and so, at the end, I have provided full cartographic details and links to further information on tracing the routes.

Through a diverse mix of subjects, it is hoped that this book will force you to think more deeply about the history of these sites, and therefore show you how to subsume yourself within the palimpsest of layers that each holds. It will act as your acquaintance as you take every step and look upon every ancient monument or historical landscape through the eyes of pilgrims past. My ultimate hope for this book is therefore that by walking in their footsteps, you may dispel L. P. Hartley's claim that 'the past is a foreign country' – but the modern pilgrim must devise his own path to discover it.

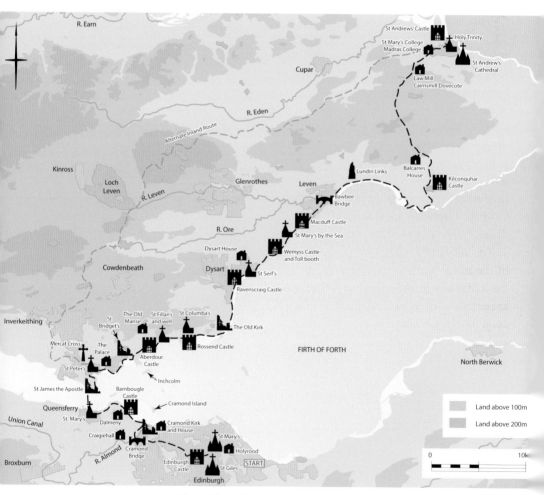

Map of St Andrew's Way. JIM BRIGHTMAN

CHAPTER ONE

St Andrew's Way

This Scottish pilgrimage commemorating the patron saint of Scotland, and the town in which his relics were contained, can very much be classified as a revived version of a 1,000-year-old route. Recent campaigns have sought to revive interest in the Christian origins and tradition of the town of St Andrews in an attempt to turn it back into a major centre of pilgrimage rivalling that of Santiago in Spain. With the support of Fife Council and its museum, the Cathedral Project began a series of exhibitions and walks which sought to stimulate knowledge and promote the embedded history of their town. This began in September 2000 with a four-day pilgrimage from St Andrews to Edinburgh, following, as much as was possible, the medieval route to North Queensferry but going in the reverse direction. This walk revived great interest in the authenticity and history of the route, and led to Fife Council reopening and officially waymarking the main medieval pathways across the region so modern-day pilgrims could walk in the footsteps of their forebears.

The Way of St Andrew was officially launched in July 2012, and is perhaps one of the most 'authentic' routes included in this book. In order to fully experience the route, an official badge may be purchased to show your pilgrim status, on your knapsack, or on your clothes. The current design features the scallop shell emblem upon the Scottish flag.

The History of St Andrew

The route is 71 miles (115km) in distance, and follows a modern restoration of a medieval pilgrimage walk from central Edinburgh across the Forth Road Bridge to St Andrews. The desire to revive the historical pilgrim links at St Andrews is not surprising given that the majority of the town's development derived from its religious associations. Firstly, the cathedral of St Andrews was built to house the relics of the saint as the town became the focus of pilgrimage, and therefore a site that was fitting for his growing popularity was demanded. As such, the original name of the town was changed from Kilrymont (or 'Church on the King's Hill') – named after St Kenneth, who was thought to have established a site for the church in c.570CE – to St Andrews, after the relics were brought to the town in the Middle Ages.

According to legend, in 345CE St Regulus or Rule had a vision whereby he was told to bring the relics of St Andrew (of which he was the guardian) from Patras in Greece and move them to Constantinople, to the outer limits of the Empire; it is said he was shipwrecked at Kilrymont. Another legend states that Bishop Acca came north from Northumbria in around 746CE bearing the relics of the apostle Andrew. The more likely story is that the relics were brought to the town by the Northumbrians in an effort to promote St Andrew over St Columba and, in doing so, lessening the influence of the Gaels.

Although the current cathedral of St Andrews dates from the medieval period, there were previous churches built on this site. The relics – an arm bone, three fingers, a tooth and a kneecap – were first kept in a shrine in the Romanesque St Rule's church of which the tower and choir are still extant. However, a more ancient Christian site lies to the east, outside the cathedral precinct wall, between it and the sea. Known as St Mary on the Rock, the cruciform church's foundations can still be made out in the ground. The earthworks that remain date back to the twelfth century, and were only uncovered in 1860 after being lost for centuries – yet the site and church date back to the eighth century. Fragments of crosses discovered there, now in St Andrews Museum, suggest the church may have been built for the Culdee community, who were a group of Celtic monks ousted by Augustinian canons who took residence there when St Andrews Cathedral was built.

The cathedral, now ruined, was founded in 1162, completed in 1318, and consecrated in the presence of King Robert the Bruce. Forty feet (12m) longer than any other cathedral in Western Europe of great pilgrimage status, it was also the largest building in medieval Scotland, providing more accommodation than was afforded by the older church of St Rule. As such, it dictated the layout of the town in various ways. When the Picts and Gaels united to form the Kingdom of Scotland under Kenneth MacAlpin in the ninth century, St Andrews Cathedral became the focus of pilgrim routes from Scotland and abroad. This was aided by Queen Margaret in the eleventh century, who developed the route of pilgrimage from South Scotland to St Andrews when she established the ferry from South to North Queensferry, giving her name to the settlement and establishing various pilgrim hospices there.

It is important to note here that in the medieval period there was no distinction between a hostel, a hospice and a hospital. This arose from the monastic *hospitium* or, more generally, the *hospitalis domus* – a place for guests – being shortened to *hospitale*, hence the modern term. They were ultimately based on the duty to support travellers and the sick. Thus, their role was to provide care and assistance to pilgrims, which was not necessarily medical. It was not until much later that the limited medical meaning was given to the term we use today.

When Queen Margaret died in 1093 her body was laid to rest in Dunfermline Abbey and her tomb became a site of pilgrimage itself – in fact, upon her canonization in 1251, the Pope declared that the Queen's shrine should be determined as a station along the route. This declaration was specifically designed, however, to carry the increasing number of pilgrims from the south to St Andrews. Those journeying from the west took a ferry across the River Tay, while those coming from the north had to cross the Tay estuary via Dundee and Tayport. The latter two routes had to converge where the modern village of Guardbridge is now sited (the clue is in the name, as many translations note the location origins as the last hospice station where pilgrims would assemble before travelling to St Andrews in procession) in order to cross the River Eden, which lies 5 miles (8km) north of St Andrews.

The pilgrim population of St Andrews had become so enormous by the fifteenth century that, upon arrival, pilgrims had to be taken to a holding station on the outskirts of the town. They then made their way towards the cathedral down South Street. After venerating at the relics, they would finally proceed in a one-way system up North Street. The layout of the town centre thus derives from the need to contain these grand pilgrim processions along the streets to the shrine, and a major part of the centre was used to serve the needs of the pilgrim trade – along Market Street, between North Street and South Street, traders and shops sold badges, souvenirs and provisions.

The main digression from this original route arises when considering *how* one journeys from A to B. While the modern route is fairly close to one of the initial tracks, the revised version accounts for large and busy roads, and has to find alternative routes for safety purposes. The Great North Road is joined near Keltybridge but the medieval routes are either followed via their modern counterparts or simply in the general direction of where they were originally located. In addition, the Forth Bridges are part of the current route to Queensferry, but medieval pilgrims would have had to cross the river by boat. They would have taken one of two ferries: an eastern crossing from North Berwick to Earlsferry, or a western route from Queensferry to North Queensferry, as established by Queen Margaret. The ferries lasted until 1964 when the bridge was opened.

An Overview of the Route

Starting at either St Mary's Roman Catholic Cathedral or the twelfth-century High Kirk of St Giles, the route descends down through Edinburgh to the sixteenth-century Cramond Brig. It then follows the shore of the Forth estuary to reach South Queensferry and across to North Queensferry.

However, there are two possible routes for this pilgrimage: one takes you from North Queensferry, across country towards Loch Leven and then east, and the second, modern route, heads straight towards Kirkcaldy and up to St Andrews. The latter route is covered in this chapter, as it is the current way authorized and most recently created (partly due to safety); however, a summary of the inland route is provided below as it is an interesting alternative, providing stops at many important historic sites.

INLAND ROUTE

After crossing the Forth Road Bridge into North Queensferry, the route heads out into the country and across several hills, including Muckle Hill. Rosyth is the next place to be encountered, then on to Dunfermline by the banks of Towere Byrn, and up past the ruins of Queen Margaret and King Malcolm Canmore's house. From there, the route passes through Kingseathill, and then over wooded Town Hill to Kingseat. The hamlet of Lassodie begins the next section of the route, which carries on round the east end of Loch Fitty before ending in the village of Keltybridge – the bridge here originally carried the main road north for the route, now the B996, but previously the former Great North Road, the line of which can be seen a few fields beyond.

Harren Hill is then traversed, followed by Benarty Hill, and a descent down to the top of Vane Hill: here you can overlook Loch Leven, where Mary, Queen of Scots was imprisoned on Castle Island in the 1560s – the island may be visited by a short detour.

The route follows the road, bypassing Loch Leven Sluice House, and on to Scotlandwell. It makes a long ascent towards Munduff Hill and across the plateau of the Lomond Hills, and then, between West Lomond and East Lomond, it drops down Maspie Den towards Falkland and its palace.

The next section begins on a flat level, along the River Eden until past Kingskettle; then from Balmalcolm, it ascends again to the slopes of Down Law and Cults Hill. Heading up to Coaltown of Burnturk the landscape is punctuated with mining history, and the views look out over the Eden Valley as you head out on the road to Chance Inn, Craigrothis. This section culminates at Ceres and its war memorial marking the Battle of Bannockburn.

The final section of the route passes over the old packhorse bridge in Ceres, and up towards and over Kininmouth Hill. It passes Arnsheen then Denhead, and on through Craigton Country Park by way of Lumbo Den, finally feeding down into the Lade Braes Walk and town.

This brings you into St Andrews. The town is entered via the ancient West Port from Lade Braes Walk, which follows the route of the Kinness Burn and up South Street towards the cathedral, where it ends.

THE MODERN COASTAL ROUTE

After crossing the Forth Road Bridge, the Way descends into North Queensferry where, directly underneath the railway bridge, it joins Fife Coastal Path. The signposted path hugs the Path and national bike route, continuing along this until the island of Inchcolm comes into sight. It then passes St Bridget's church, carries along into the pretty fishing village of Aberdour, and down to the harbour. It then continues along the Fife Coastal Path and woodland tracts to the town of Burntisland.

Leaving Burntisland, the Way passes Kinghorn and carries on to Kirkcaldy. It then descends abruptly to the beach, and follows the signposted Fife Coastal Path to Lundin Links and Leven. Take the beach or the path to the village of Largo, and on to Largo Bay through dunes to Earlsferry.

After Earlsferry, the Way strikes north off the Fife Coastal Path, continues along quiet roads and tracks until Largo Ward, then to Radernie, where it is signposted to Cameron Reservoir. After the reservoir it passes through Denhead and the golf clubhouse at Craigtoun, before descending along the picturesque burn and forest track of Lumbo to

St Andrews. It enters the town bypassing Lade Braes Walk to the east, following the route of the Kinness Burn and up South Street towards the cathedral, where it ends.

Addendum: Additional Routes

In addition to the primary Way, in 2013 two new popular routes were established. These were named St Columba's Way, which runs from Iona to St Andrews, and St Duthac's Way, from Aberdeen to St Andrews. These sit alongside additional start-point locations including the Ladywell Way (from Motherwell), St Wilfrid's Way from Hexham, St Duthac's Way from Aberdeen, and St Margaret's Way from Edinburgh. Further smaller extensions within the main route to St Andrews have also been created and subsequently revised, such as St Margaret's Loop (North Queensferry to Dunfermline), Rosslyn Chapel Way (via Rosslyn Chapel), and St Margaret's Elbow (Earlsferry via Crail).

Start of the Route: Edinburgh

The route begins at Eduardo Paolozzi's giant foot of bronze at the top of Leith Walk by St Mary's Roman Catholic Cathedral. The Manuscript of Monte Cassino, *aka* the 'Big Foot', is a three-piece sculpture outside St Mary's. The sculpture is an allegory of a pilgrimage – the foot that travels, and the connecting ankle and hand receiving alms or hospitality.

ST MARY'S ROMAN CATHOLIC CATHEDRAL

St Mary's is the Cathedral Church of the Archdiocese of St Andrews and Edinburgh. Bishop Hay, Vicar Apostolic for the Lowland District, chose the site in 1801. After his Chapel in Blackfriars' Wynd was burnt down by a mob, he hoped the new site would be a more protected, sheltered spot. But it was Bishop Cameron who actually opened the Chapel of St Mary's. Designed by the prominent ecclesiastical architect James Gillespie Graham in 1814, under successor Bishop Cameron the church was considerably embellished, and upon the restoration of the Scottish hierarchy in 1878 it became the pro-cathedral of the new Archdiocese of St Andrews and Edinburgh. At the request of Archbishop William Smith it was named the Metropolitan Cathedral on 5 July 1886.

When St Mary's was first built it was merely a rectangular building with a shallow apse masked by a perpendicular Gothic facade, conveying the impression of a nave with flanking aisles, an example of neo-Gothic. In 1841 Bishop Gillis enlarged the sanctuary and had a new pulpit installed. Bishop Strain then had a cloister chapel built in 1866, where the Lady Aisle is now located.

Canon Donlevy was then responsible for major changes, some of which were made necessary by the 1853 fire in the adjoining Theatre Royal, which included having the side walls of the church made into arches, with aisles of considerable size on either side. The new aisle on the Lady Altar side replaced the separate cloister chapel and the sanctuary was extended to the full width of the nave, while a baldacchino was built over the altar. In 1932 the roof of the cathedral was raised.

The portion of the shoulder of the Apostle Andrew given by the Archbishop of Amalfi and a second relic given by Pope Paul VI in 1969 are placed in the altar to the north of the High Altar. The chapel, originally dedicated to the Sacred Heart, now serves as the National Shrine to St Andrew, successor to the shrine destroyed in 1559.

ST GILES' CATHEDRAL

St Giles' was founded in the 1120s when the Scottish royal family, the sons of Queen (St) Margaret and King Malcolm Canmore, made strenuous efforts to spread Catholic Christian worship throughout the Scottish lowlands. This church was a small Norman building, yet few traces of it survive in the present building.

In 1385 a larger Gothic church was partially burned. No record has been found of the rebuilding work of this second church, primarily as it was quickly repaired.

Many chapels were added throughout the next few centuries, including, most notably, a chapel for a relic of St Giles and the Chapel of the Order of the Thistle. William Forbes became the first bishop of the new diocese of Edinburgh in 1635, with St Giles' as its cathedral – it is due to this period that St Giles' is commonly called a cathedral although bishops were abolished in 1690.

EDINBURGH CASTLE

The site of Edinburgh Castle was occupied as early as 900BC. When the Romans visited in 80CE and 139CE it was an important fort of the Votadini people, later known as the Gododdin, who called it Din Eidyn. Din Eidyn was captured by the Angles in 638CE, and they anglicized the name to Edinburgh.

The castle was developed into a royal fortress during the reign of David I from 1124 to 1153. The Scots and English then struggled for control of the castle during the Wars of Independence throughout the fourteenth century.

It was then greatly extended by the Stewart dynasty, and in particular James III, who ruled from 1460 to 1488. James started the development of the palace buildings around Crown Square, culminating with the completion of the Great Hall by James IV in 1511. In the 1600s, the castle became a military base. Buildings were rebuilt and others were constructed to accommodate a large garrison as well as a secure jail for prisoners of war.

A large portion of today's castle dates back to the threat of Napoleon at the end of the 1700s. The greatest addition, the seven-storey 'New Barracks', finished in 1799, dominates the castle's western end and was intended to accommodate 600 troops.

In 1818 Sir Walter Scott uncovered the Honours of Scotland (the Crown Jewels) in a locked room in the bowels of the castle, where they had been placed in 1707. They remain on view today.

During the Victorian era a number of developments took place, including the rebuilding of the gatehouse in 1888 and the restoration of the Great Hall in 1891.

Edinburgh Castle. DAVID ROSS

Palace of Holyroodhouse. DAVID ROSS

The castle's inhabitants have included Queen Margaret (St), who died there in 1093, and Mary, Queen of Scots, who gave birth to James VI in the Royal Palace in 1566.

THE PALACE OF HOLYROODHOUSE

Others may also want to begin their pilgrimage journey at the Palace of Holyroodhouse: founded as a monastery in 1128, the palace is now the current sovereign's official residence in Scotland, situated at the end of the Royal Mile. Mary, Queen of Scots, lived there between 1561 and 1567, while successive kings and queens have made the Palace of Holyroodhouse the premier royal residence in Scotland.

Cramond

The route then leads down towards and along the hidden green space or secret garden of Rocheid Path by the Waters of Leith. It travels out of Edinburgh and towards Cramond.

CRAMOND KIRK

The origins of Cramond Kirk date back to the Roman fort that supported the invasion of northern Britain by Emperor Septimius Severus in 208CE. The Romans abandoned Cramond, and Scotland, in 212CE, leaving the settlement behind for the local population. By c.600CE a building on the site was being used for Christian worship.

The earliest part of the present church is the tower at its west end, which is thought to date back to the 1400s. The medieval church on the site had fallen into ruin, and was doubtless ill suited to the needs of the Presbyterian kirk and its differing forms of worship. The result was its near complete rebuilding. In 1828 the architect William Burn altered it again, and further major changes took place in 1911–12, which included the near-total remodelling of the interior.

CRAMOND HOUSE

Near the kirk stands Cramond House. Its core dates from the late seventeenth century, the classical front was added in 1778, while the rear was completed in 1820. Queen Victoria visited while residing at Holyrood. It has been claimed as the possible original of R. L. Stevenson's 'House of Shaws' in *Kidnapped*.

CRAMOND ISLAND

If the tide is out it is also possible to take a walk of just over three-quarters of a mile along the tidal causeway to Cramond Island. The island is uninhabited but is believed to have been used by the Romans, although nothing has been found to confirm this. On the west coast of the island are the remains of a stone jetty, likely dating to the 1800s. Nearby is the ruin of the duck house. There are also military defences, notably an emplacement for a 75mm gun intended to guard the gap between the island and the south shore of the Firth of Forth.

CRAMOND BRIG

The route then crosses over the historic Cramond Brig. Built *c*.1500, the bridge comprises three arches with large triangular cutwaters, and carries a narrow carriageway between low parapets. It once crossed the divide between Edinburgh and West Lothian. The bridge was rebuilt between 1617 and 1619, and was subject to further extensive repairs throughout the seventeenth and nineteenth centuries – all the dates appear on the bridge itself.

In *Tales of a Grandfather*, Sir Walter Scott records the traditional tale of how James V (1512–42) was attacked while walking across the bridge, and rescued by a local tenant farmer, Jock Howieson (Howison or Houison). The King asked in return that Howieson and his descendants should wash the monarch's hands, either at Holyrood Palace or when they passed by Cramond Brig.

Craigiehall

To the west, across the A90, is Craigiehall, a late seventeenth-century country house which served as the headquarters of the 2nd Division of the British Army until 2012. Craigiehall House was designed by Sir William Bruce, with input from James Smith, and was completed in 1699 for the Earl of Annandale. A good surviving example of one of Bruce's smaller houses, it set a pattern for such eighteenth-century villas in the Edinburgh area. Upstream there is also a bridge, grotto and bath house, built in a similar style and presumably by the same architect. An avenue of oak trees runs up Lennie Hill from the grotto bridge. At the summit is an ornamental temple built in 1759, commanding wide views of the expanded estate and beyond.

Dalmeny

Next, the route enters Dalmeny. It is said that Dalmeny means 'many hills', which is not surprising given the undulating topography encountered just to the east – for example, Mansion Hill and Mons Hill.

Dalmeny House can be visited by making a short detour to the east of the route, before it turns west to the village. The house was built in the neo-Tudor style by William Wilkins between 1814 and 1817.

Whilst here, you should also walk to the projecting rock terrace on the shore to see Barnbougle Castle. The first building was a thirteenth-century tower house, constructed by Philip Mowbray. In 1774, a plan for rebuilding the castle was drawn up by the notable architect Robert Adam (1728–92); his proposal was for a triangular building with the original tower at its seaward corner, but it was never executed. However, by the early nineteenth century the castle had become dilapidated – there is a tale of a wave washing into the dining room during supper! The 4th Earl of Rosebery had Dalmeny House constructed on the estate, and the family moved in upon its completion in 1817. Unfortunately, Barnbougle was also used to store explosives, and after being damaged in an accidental explosion, was subsequently left as a ruin.

In 1881 the castle was entirely reconstructed according to plans by James Maitland Wardrop in the Scots Baronial style. The older fabric of the north side was incorporated into the new building, which was primarily built to house the private library of Archibald Primrose, 5th Earl of Rosebery (1847–1929); Rosebery became the British Prime Minister in 1894.

South Queensferry

The route then travels through South Queensferry, on the southern shore of the gaping Firth of Forth. As an obvious place to cross the river when heading into Fife from Edinburgh, it is likely that settlements on each side of the river here, and ferries between them, date back to the medieval period, and perhaps even earlier.

As noted earlier, the name 'Queensferry' derives from Queen Margaret, the wife of Malcolm III who founded a church in Dunfermline, where they had married in 1070. The site became a place of pilgrimage, which led to an increasing demand for transport across the Forth Estuary. The Queen's Ferry, paid for by Margaret and operated by monks from Dunfermline, was the result. With no fixed southern terminal, it used a variety of landing places in or near the village, depending on the tide and the weather.

The two large bridges that traverse the Forth to Fife now dominate the town. The Forth railway bridge is a magnificent feat of engineering. It was built between 1883 and 1890 by Sir John Fowler and Benjamin Baker, and is designed on the cantilever principle with three towers, each 340ft (104m) high, and is 2,765yd (2,528m) long.

Work began on the Forth Road Bridge in 1958, and it opened in 1964. This suspension bridge is 2,000yd (1,830m) long, with a main span of 3,300ft (1,006m), making it the tenth longest in the world.

Queensferry offers an interesting collection of buildings. The earliest is St Mary's Church, dating from 1441. 'Black Castle' is the oldest dwelling, built on the High Street in 1626. When its original sea captain owner was lost with his ship, his maid was accused of paying a beggar woman to cast a spell on him. Both women were burned for witchcraft. The nearby Tolbooth was built in the 1600s, though the tower dates back only to 1720.

North Queensferry

Crossing the Forth Road Bridge, the Way then descends into North Queensferry where, directly underneath the famous railway bridge, it joins the Fife Coastal Path. The town sits at the tip of a rocky promontory extending south from Fife into the Firth of Forth. The Gaelic name of the original settlement here was Ardchinnechenan, then 'North Ferrie', before its association with Queen Margaret was firmly established.

Most interesting is the fourteenth-century ruined Chapel of St James the Apostle (the patron saint of pilgrims). Founded by Robert the Bruce (1306–29) and controlled by Dunfermline Abbey, it was abandoned following the Reformation. The chapel would have been the first important building seen from this landing point. A manse was also attached to the chapel with a garden to the north. The remnants of the doorway by which the chaplain left the chapel to the manse can still be seen. A stone set into the outside of the wall near the gate is inscribed, 'This is done by the sailors of North Ferrie 1752', and commemorates the many sailors who drowned during storms on the Forth.

The signposted path then hugs the coast, dominated by great bluffs of magma – reminders of Scotland's volcanic past – passing Inverkeithing and on to Dalgety Bay.

Inverkeithing

A short detour into Inverkeithing is worth making, as the town was originally founded as a port and thus has very ancient origins; some claim that these date back to Agricola's Roman adventure into Northern Scotland in 83CE. It certainly seems that the area was settled by the 400s, when a church was founded here by St Erat, a follower of St Ninian. In the medieval period the town was walled, with four ports or gates. The walls were removed in the 1500s, but a number of structures from this period still stand today. While the nave of the parish church, also known as St Peter's, dates back only to 1827, the tower was originally built in the 1300s. After a fire in 1825, the church was then reconstructed in the neo-Gothic style. It houses a hexagonal, elaborately-sculpted font – one of the finest in Scotland.

At the north end of the market area is the Mercat Cross – the pillar dates back to *c.*1400.

Near the south end of the High Street is a building variously known as the 'palace' or hospitium of the Grey Friars Franciscan friary; it dates mainly from the fourteenth century, with seventeen-century remodelling.

Dalgety Bay

Keeping to the Fife Coastal Path, the Way continues along quiet roads and forest paths and through St Davids to Dalgety Bay.

Construction of this new-enterprise town began in about 1962. The land surrounding the town was formerly part of the estate owned by the earls of Moray, who built Donibristle House as their residence (scene of the killing of James Stewart, 2nd Earl of Moray in 1592), but towards the end of the eighteenth century, the settlement was removed by order of the earls.

The bay was named after this original village of Dalgety, but the ruins of the twelfth-century St Bridget's Kirk are all that now mark the site. St Bridget's was built in the 1100s and continued to serve the parishioners after the Reformation of

1560, leading to it being significantly altered so that it was suitable for Protestant worship. The only features remaining from the medieval church are the piscina (stone basin) and credence (niche) in the south-east corner of the south wall, close to where the altar stood. The two-storey, roofless Seton Aisle dating from the 1600s features one of the best preserved laird's lofts in Scotland. The church is a real ruinous gem.

Worship continued at St Bridget's until 1830. By this date most parishioners were living over a mile away in the new mining village of Fordell, where a new kirk had been built.

Inchcolm

Carrying on along the coastal path, the famous island of Inchcolm then comes into sight – if journeying the Way in the summer months, a detour boat trip out to the island is a must!

David I established a priory here, which then became an abbey in 1235; it is now the best-preserved group of monastic buildings in Scotland. Inchcolm means 'Columba's Isle', although the 'Iona of the east' has no known link with St Columba.

The island was home to a hermit in the medieval era, and its oldest relic is a tenth-century hogback tombstone. In 1123, Alexander I sheltered here during a storm, and resolved to build a monastery in thanks for his deliverance. But he died in 1124 before being able to keep his promise. It was left to his brother, David I, to invite Augustinian canons to establish a priory on the island; as mentioned, it was raised to full abbey status in 1235.

The twelfth-century abbey church was enlarged eastwards around 1200. The original church was converted into the abbot's residence, and the later church is now mostly wall footings. However, a remarkable thirteenth-century fresco painting of a funeral procession survives in a tomb recess. Also interesting are the stone screens dividing the choir from the nave. The cloister is the most complete in Scotland, and three covered cloister walks survive. The octagonal chapter house dates to the thirteenth century and features a fine warming room above it, while the dormitory, refectory and other rooms also survive roofed.

The island's location in the Firth of Forth made it a target for English naval raids throughout the wars with England from the fourteenth to the mid-sixteenth century; however, it was the Protestant Reformation of 1560 that brought monastic life to an end, although the island continued to serve in the defence of the country right up to World War II.

Aberdour

Returning to the main route takes you into the fishing village of Aberdour, dominated by its castle.

ABERDOUR CASTLE

Aberdour Castle was once the oldest standing masonry castle in Scotland (recently, the accolade was transferred to Castle Sween, Argyll). It includes the remains of a twelfth-century two-storey hall house, which was then heightened and converted into a more typical Scottish tower house in the fifteenth century. Over a period of 500 years, the castle was owned by three noble families: the Douglases, Mortimers and Randolphs. Succeeding generations of Douglases gradually added further ranges of impressive stone buildings, which ultimately replaced the family rooms in the tower house, and are perhaps the main attraction.

ST FILLAN'S CHURCH

Situated in a graveyard at the end of a narrow path just outside the walled gardens of Aberdour Castle, St Fillan's Church dates back to the early twelfth century. It was granted to Inchcolm Abbey at its foundation in 1123. Originally a narrow rectangle consisting of a nave and chancel, the church has been altered several times over its lifetime. It was abandoned in 1790 because the Countess of Morton did not like the populace of Aberdour coming to worship so close to Aberdour Castle, so a new church was built on the High Street (now Church Hall). After falling into a ruinous condition, the church was restored 1925–26.

ST FILLAN'S WELL

Nearby, St Fillan's Well, also known as the Pilgrims' Well, was renowned for its eye-healing qualities. It was situated to the south-east corner of the churchyard, but now lies in a private garden and is covered and drained.

HOSPITAL OF ST MARTHA

In 1474 land to the north of St Fillan's Church was granted for the construction of a hospice, known as the Hospital of St Martha, to accommodate the large numbers of pilgrims coming to visit the well. As this project was not completed, in 1486 the earl gave the lands to sisters of the Third Order of St Francis. The erection of the nunnery was completed by 1487, and the manse and rights of the hospital were extinguished. The sisters finally leased their house and land to the then Earl of Morton in 1560. The Old Manse is situated on the site of the nunnery. Comprising a T-shaped building of two storeys, the north wing is sixteenth or seventeenth century in date.

Burntisland

The route then continues along the Fife Coastal Path around bays and along woodland tracts to the busy town of Burntisland.

ST COLUMBA'S CHURCH

Burntisland's first church was built at Kirkton on lands gifted by David I in the twelfth century. It was consecrated in 1234. The town became so well established that a new church known as St Columba's was constructed in 1592. This was the first new parish church built in Scotland after the Reformation, and is thus an early example of Protestant planning. It is a unique shape to Scotland: square with a central tower upheld on pillars, and lined with galleries. The church also contains one of the country's finest collections of seventeenth- and early eighteenth-century woodwork and paintings.

The church is sometimes known as the 'Kirk of the Bible', as the General Assembly of the Church of Scotland met here in 1601 when James VI approved a new English translation of the Bible. In time this was published as the King James Bible, or the authorized version.

ROSSEND CASTLE

In 1119 Rossend Castle was built on a rocky bluff overlooking the harbour, where it was ideally placed to help defend such a strategically important site. The castle comprises a large T-plan tower house dating from 1554. The west wing incorporates the remains of a thirteenth-century structure at ground-floor level. It has been suggested that the earlier surviving remains at Rossend represent an ecclesiastical building, possibly associated with a secular residence.

The land around Burntisland was amongst the property endowed by David I to the Abbots of Dunfermline in around 1130. In 1382 the abbey extended the castle and it became known as Abbot's Hall, as it was then home to the Abbot of Dunfermline. The Reformation led to a change of ownership, and in the 1560s the size of the castle was again increased. It is not clear whether this was before or after a visit by Mary, Queen of Scots when en route to St Andrews in 1563. During her stay she discovered the French courtier and poet, Pierre de Chastelard, hiding in her bedchamber. He was hauled off to St Andrews and beheaded at the Mercat Cross.

Kinghorn

Leaving Burntisland along a short strip of main road, the Way returns to a quiet section of the Fife Coastal Path, passing Pettycur and on to Kinghorn, once the prosperous residence of the kings of Scotland.

On 19 March 1286, Alexander III was returning on horseback to be with his wife, Yolande de Dreux, at Kinghorn Castle after meeting his council in Edinburgh. Journeying along the cliff road above Pettycur in dark and terrible weather, his horse stumbled and pitched him to his death over the cliffs. All trace of Alexander's Kinghorn Castle had disappeared by the end of the 1700s.

The remains of the Old Kirk in Kinghorn are in a graveyard on raised ground above the shore, to the east of the current parish church. Built in the thirteenth century, the Old Kirk was partially incorporated into the current church building when this was constructed in 1774. The present pebbledash parish church sits in a graveyard on raised ground above the shore and is known as 'The Kirk by the Sea'.

Bass Rock from the coast. DAVID ROSS

BASS ROCK

The path then skirts along the coast. Across the water, the extinct volcanoes of the Bass Rock (and its imposing castle), where North Berwick Law, a hill on the mainland, are also visible. The island is certainly worth a boat trip out, as it includes a freshwater well right at the top of the island, where today the foghorn is situated. Also, halfway up Bass Rock stands the ruin of the sixteenth-century St Baldred's Chapel, which is sited on the cell or cave in which this Scottish saint lived and then died in 606CE.

Kirkcaldy

The Way then continues to Kirkcaldy, once the linoleum capital of Scotland. Known as the 'Lang Toun' because of its traditional shape, in the seventeenth century it had one of the longest high streets in the country; initially just under a mile, it would eventually stretch to 4 miles (6.4km).

Leaving Kirkcaldy and passing the old linoleum factory, the Way descends abruptly to the beach, with the fifteenth-century Ravenscraig Castle towering above.

RAVENSCRAIG PARK

Ravenscraig Park, located in the east of the town, connects to the Fife Coastal Path and is home to ancient Ravenscraig Castle. In March 1460 James II acquired the estate of Ravenscraig for his queen, Mary of Gueldres. After the king's death a short time later, his widow asked her master mason, Henry Merlioun (who also designed the Queen's Holy Trinity Collegiate Church in Edinburgh), to continue with the construction. The building work was sufficiently advanced by 1461 to allow the Queen's steward and other servants to stay there for twenty-five days, but it is not certain whether Mary ever lived there before her death in 1463.

In 1470 her son, James III, granted the castle to William Sinclair, Earl of Caithness, in compensation for his resigning the earldom of Orkney and lordship of Shetland to the Crown. The Sinclairs completed the building and held it thereafter.

Pathhead

The Way then follows the signposted Fife Coastal Path through former fishing and coalmining villages, and past ancient buildings and memorials, to Lundin Links and Leven. The route first skirts the village of Pathhead, through which the Roman road named Dere Street runs. Originally, it linked the Roman town of Corbridge on Hadrian's Wall with the fortress at Inveresk, in today's Musselburgh.

Dysart

Next along the Way is the historic Dysart, which features many architecturally interesting sites such as the tolbooth, erected in 1576, the nineteenth-century town hall on High Street, and the remains of St Serf's Church with its imposing 72ft (22m) tower. This was built around 1500, close to the spot where it is believed St Serf lived in a cave in the 500s (and an earlier church). It was replaced by the parish church in 1802, and in 1807 a new road linking town and harbour was laid through part of the site of the old church, destroying much of the north aisle. In 1901 Dysart was visited by the noted architect and artist Charles Rennie Mackintosh, who painted a mural in the north transept of what is now St Clair's (Dysart Parish Church). Long lost from view, this was rediscovered in 2004 under later paint, and returned to prominence.

On the hillside above, the impressive Dysart House can be seen through trees. Built in 1755, the house was home to the lairds, the St Clair family. Since 1931 it has served as a closed monastery for Carmelite nuns; the garden now includes St Serf's original cave.

West Wemyss

The route then passes straight through West Wemyss, and it is worth taking time here. The village owes its origins to the Wemyss estate, based at Wemyss Castle, just to the east of the village. It is alleged that here Mary, Queen of Scots first met her husband Lord Darnley in 1565. The Wemyss family have lived in the castle ever since it was first built in the twelfth century. The striking tolbooth of early eighteenth-century date, and possibly incorporating earlier fabric, dominates the village with its tall and ornate tower. Wemyss Parish Church, built in 1890, was bought from the Church of Scotland by the Wemyss estate in 1972, on the condition that it continued to be used as a church, and they have since maintained the exterior of the building.

East Wemyss

Further along the coast is East Wemyss, once called 'Castleton' due to its proximity to MacDuff Castle. Likely dating to the end of the fourteenth century, the remains consist of a fourteenth-century tower, further fifteenth-century remains, a sixteenth-century range of buildings running southwards from the tower and terminating in a second tower, and a late sixteenth-century or early seventeenth-century outer wall.

MACDUFF CASTLE

It is believed that MacDuff Castle was the home of MacDuff, Thane of Fife, from whom the Erskines of Wemyss claim descent. Yet it was also the original home of the Wemyss family before they built Wemyss Castle. Additionally known as the 'Hall of the Wemyss' and as a 'palace', the castle is an extensive but composite mansion. The earliest part, the oblong tower, has been greatly altered and may be considered as not later than the end of the fifteenth century. The original castle likely occupied only the northern part of the site. In the early sixteenth century, the enclosing walls were rebuilt with a salient round tower.

ST MARY'S-BY-THE-SEA

The now redundant church of St Mary's-by-the-Sea at East Wemyss dates from the twelfth century, yet the present building was largely constructed in the sixteenth century, with several later phases of additions and alterations; it was closed for worship in 1976, and is now in poor condition. A later hall, now a private house, is located at the north-east corner of the site.

Buckhaven

Next along the Way is Buckhaven, once a thriving weaving village and fishing port; in 1831 it was reported as having the second largest fishing fleet in Scotland, with a total of 198 boats. In 1869 its fisherfolk bought an episcopal church in St Andrews, and transported it stone by stone to the village. Restored in the 1980s, this building was turned into a theatre on Lawrence Street.

Passing through Methil takes you straight into Leven. This area on the north side of the Firth of Forth comprises several coastal towns, villages and hamlets. The Bawbee Bridge over the River Leven links the town of Leven (on the east bank) to Methil (on the west).

After Leven, take the beach or the path to the pretty village of Lower Largo, overlooked by the double-humped Largo Law.

Lundin Links

Just before Largo, you will bypass Lundin Links: now an eighteen-hole golf course, it is an interesting site, as it features some impressive standing stones. On the second fairway of the Ladies' course there is a cluster of three stones dating from 2000BC, which forms a megalithic four-poster (one of the stones was lost around 1792). The village itself was largely built in the nineteenth century to accommodate tourists visiting Lower Largo.

Lower Largo

Go past the harbour and underneath the giant viaduct: you then pass the house commemorating the real Robinson Crusoe. Lower Largo is famous as the 1676 birthplace of Alexander Selkirk, who provided inspiration for Daniel Defoe's *Robinson Crusoe*. An amusing signpost at the harbour points to the Juan Fernández Islands, a mere 7,500 miles (12,000km) away, where Selkirk was marooned for over four years.

Earlsferry

The route then carries on to famous Largo Bay; it runs along the sands and through the dunes to Earlsferry where, before the Reformation, pilgrims heading for St Andrews landed in their thousands. Earlsferry is now seen as an extension of its neighbour Elie. The main site of architectural interest is the chapel, formerly part of Ardross Hospital, which is situated on the headland. Only the east gable and the lowest courses of the outer walls survive. The building was owned by the nuns at North Berwick and likely serviced travellers moving between the two points, especially pilgrims en route to St Andrews.

On the west end of the beach a jumble of rocks and slabs are all that remains of Earlsferry's ancient pier. The remains of the Cadger's Road can also be seen: this right of way ran from Earlsferry to the Royal Palace in Falkland, and its purpose was to shorten the time it took for fish that were caught and landed at the Earlsferry beach to be transported to the palace, a distance of 25 miles (40km) or so. Traces of the palace can still be seen on the fourth and seventeenth fairways of the golf course.

After Earlsferry the final 16 miles (26km) takes you north through quiet countryside to St Andrews. Alternatively, continue east on the spectacular Fife Coastal Path, along the section named Saint Margaret's Elbow, for about 23 miles (37km).

Kilconquhar

Striking north off the Fife Coastal Path, in the footsteps of early pilgrims heading to St Andrews, the Way continues along quiet roads and tracks until it reaches Kilconquhar. This name encompasses a parish, a village, a loch and a mansion, and is said to mean 'the cell, the burying-place, or place of worship, at the head or extremity of the freshwater lake'. However, according to tradition, the loch was only formed 260 years ago because the drain that carried the water to the sea became filled with sand by a violent wind.

Some maintain that Conquhar or Connachar was the name of the founder of the cell or church – hence, Kilconquhar. Locally it is known as Kenneuchar. The church was built between 1820 and 1821.

KILCONQUHAR CASTLE

This is also the site of Kilconquhar Castle, originally built in the late 1500s. In the 1830s the architect William Burn turned what had been a family home into a baronial mansion. The turreted castle was badly damaged by fire in 1979 and, in recent years, has been developed into the centre of a self-catering resort around the original part of the property to the south.

BALCARRES HOUSE

Balcarres House is located a mile and a half (2½km) north-west of the loch, and has been a seat of the Lindsays for 400 years. John Lindsay, the second son of the ninth Earl of Crawford, died in 1598 in his semi-fortified house of Balcarres, which he had only had built in 1595. The house has undergone two principal extensions: the first was in 1840 when General James Lindsay commissioned William Burn to design the south-west wing; the second was in 1864 when Sir Coutts Lindsay employed David Bryce to build an extensive addition to the north of the property.

CASTLE OF RIRES

The old Castle of Rires stood about a mile north-west of Balcarres House, and was built by Sir John de Wemyss at the close of the fourteenth century to replace an earlier structure. Traces can be seen as earthworks only.

Go through the village of Colinsburgh and continue upwards; you will pass by the interesting early nineteenth-century Lethallan Mill House. The route then skirts Largoward, where there is a strip of main road with a grass verge. The church, originally a chapel-of-ease, was built in 1835. The Way then continues by the mid-eighteenth-century, Michelin-starred Peat Inn (the surrounding village grew up around the inn, from which it also took its name) to the hamlet of Radernie; this was a mining village until the 1920s, whose mines once provided coal to the Royal Palace of Falkland.

Cameron

The route is signposted to Cameron reservoir and then on to Cameron itself. The present parish church – a rectangular building with a lean-to porch on the north-west corner – was built in 1808 on the site of an earlier building dating from 1645 and overlooks agricultural land, near to the reservoir. Some of the pews still display legible names of its former parishioners.

After Cameron, the Way passes through Denhead and the golf club house at Craigtoun, with a great view on to the spires of St Andrews, the long sandy beaches and the North Sea before descending along the picturesque burn and forest track of Lumbo to St Andrews.

The path leads to the junction of the Cairnsmill burn and the Lumbo burn. Turn right and follow the line of the trees until, after only a few yards, a sixteenth-century dovecot is seen. This dovecot, built of stone and with three string-courses (which prevented rats climbing up to the bird entrances), dates from the time that the Priory of St Andrews owned Cairnsmill Farm, which used to surround the dovecot but is now swallowed up by the housing development/holiday park.

Hallow Hill is also passed by on the descent into St Andrews. It was found to be a graveyard in the mid-nineteenth century and, in more recent times, excavations have discovered about 150 graves dating from the late Iron Age to the formation of Christianity.

The End of the Journey: St Andrews

The Kinness Burn now enters St Andrews and descends towards Lade Braes. St Andrews is the culmination of the journey.

LADE BRAES

The Lade Braes follows the route of a medieval mill lade and is now a popular public footpath in St Andrews. The name 'Lade Braes' derives from 'lade' or 'lead', an artificial watercourse created to lead water to where it was needed, and 'braes', meaning 'hillsides' or 'high ground next to a river'. The lade was built in the thirteenth century by the Priory of St Andrews to divert the water from the Kinness Burn to the many mills that once existed in the area. It may have been in existence before the priory was founded in 1140, since there is some evidence that a mill was extant before the priory. Gradually the lade was covered over in the nineteenth century, the water continuing to flow underground in pipes.

Also in this area was Cairns Mill, a corn (barley and/or oats) mill. Nothing remains of the mill building, which was swallowed up by the creation of the Cairnsmill Reservoir.

Law Mill, with its iconic pyramidal kiln roof and associated late nineteenth-century cottage, lies at the head of the Lade Braes. Although the current building dates to 1757, it is possible that a mill has occupied this site since the thirteenth century. The origin of the name 'Law' is believed to derive from the Anglo-Saxon word 'hlaw', meaning 'burial mound', which here is most likely a reference to the nearby Hallow Hill.

SOUTH STREET

The final section of the route then turns straight up South Street to the cathedral. Here you pass many interesting sites, including the nineteenth-century Madras School and the parish church of Holy Trinity. The Town Kirk of St Andrews was dedicated in 1234. The tower and some of the pillars of the present building date from 1412, while the rest of the building was completely rebuilt on the original ground-plan in 1909; the south porch commemorates John Knox's preaching here in the sixteenth century. The interior contains fine Arts and Crafts period furnishings.

ST MARY'S COLLEGE

The Way then passes St Mary's College and Quadrangle, home of the Faculty and School of Divinity of the University of St Andrews. The college was founded in 1539 by Archbishop James Beaton, uncle of Cardinal David Beaton, on the site of the pedagogy or St John's College, founded in 1418. St Mary's College retains many of its original sixteenth-century buildings, specifically the north and west ranges. In the quadrangle is a thorn tree said to have been planted by Mary, Queen of Scots, during one of her many visits to St Andrews. Also located in the quad is the historic King James Library founded by James VI (of Scotland; James I of England) in 1612, within which is Parliament Hall, so named as it was the meeting place for the Scots Parliament during 1645–46. The Roundel is a sixteenth-century building dedicated to doctoral students studying divinity at the university.

ST ANDREW'S CATHEDRAL

The final leg of the route passes the Victorian buildings of St Leonard's School, and travels straight to the cathedral. As noted earlier, St Andrew's Cathedral is Scotland's largest and most magnificent medieval church. It was the seat of Scotland's leading bishops (and, from 1472, archbishops), and occupies a site used for worship since the eighth century, when the relics of St Andrew, Scotland's patron saint, are said to have been brought here.

In the vicinity is the first church built on the site of the cathedral: St Rule's Church, with its 108ft (33m) western tower, built in the early twelfth century, and which acted as the first place of worship for the newly arrived Augustinian canons. Originally, the tower and adjoining choir were part of the church built in the twelfth century, but the nave, with twin western turrets, and the apse no longer stand. Legend credits St Rule (also known as St Regulus) with bringing the relics of St Andrew to the area from their original location at Patras in Greece. In fact, the large tower may have acted as a beacon for pilgrims heading for the shrine of St Andrew, although it is not clear exactly where the shrine stood.

Outside the precinct wall, on a ledge overlooking the sea, are the foundations of the Church of St Mary on the Rock (St Mary Kirkheugh), an early medieval church dating to the twelfth century. Before 1290 St Mary on the Rock had become a collegiate church and a royal chapel, and appears to have been built on, or close to, the site of an earlier

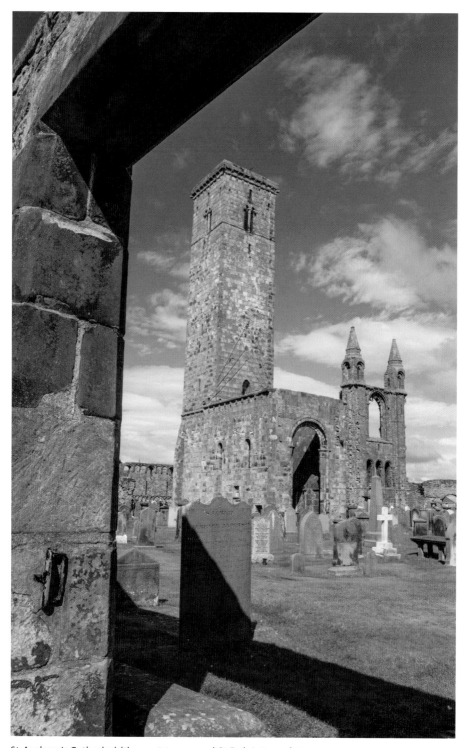

St Andrew's Cathedral (the east tower and St Rule's tower). DAVID ROSS

ninth-century Culdee church. The Culdees (from the Irish 'Ceile-De' meaning 'friend of God') were Celtic monks who refused to acknowledge the new monastic orders of the Middle Ages, and one of their most significant communities was that at St Andrews (formerly Kilrymont). When Robert, Prior of Scone, became Bishop of Kilrymont in 1123, the thirteen Culdees there opted not to become Augustinian canons but preferred instead to remain as a separate body. The Culdees of Kilrymont were given a permanent home at Kirkheugh, on a site beside the cliff edge, adjacent to the new cathedral priory yet distinctly outside its precinct wall.

The present cathedral was begun in about 1160 by Bishop Arnold. Work continued over the next 150 years, though it was interrupted most notably by a storm in 1272 which blew down the west front, and by the first War of Independence against England (1296–1328). It was eventually dedicated in 1318, in the presence of Robert I, by which date it was the largest church in Scotland. In 1559 John Knox preached a fiery sermon in Holy Trinity Parish Church, and the cathedral was 'cleansed' (destroyed) as a result, then abandoned in 1561 in favour of the parish church as the chief place of worship. Thereafter, the former headquarters of the Scottish Church were left to fall into ruin.

ST ANDREWS CASTLE

There are many sites to admire within St Andrews itself, notably the university but also the ruins of the castle, located on the coastal Royal Burgh. St Andrews Castle was the chief residence of the bishops, and later archbishops, of St Andrews. In the tenth century, the bishops of St Andrews gained overarching responsibility for the Scottish Church. Bishop Arnold (1160–2) began building a new cathedral on an unprecedented scale, while Bishop Roger (1189–1202) built the new castle as his official residence. During the Wars of Independence with England, the castle suffered significant damage, and had to be substantially rebuilt by Bishop Walter Trail (1385–1401). The increasing religious tensions in the early sixteenth century then led to further building works.

The structure of the castle included five square towers that provided residence for the bishop, his large household and guests. Ranges were built along the inside of each length of curtain wall, with further accommodation in the outer courtyards to the south and west. The castle also served as a prison, a remnant of which is the bottle dungeon, a bottle-shaped pit dug 22ft (7m) down into the rock below the Sea Tower and accessible only via the narrow neck opening through a trap door in the floor of the tower vault.

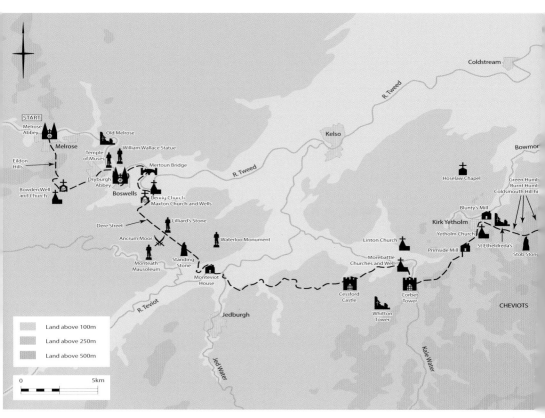

Map of St Cuthbert's Way: the west half. JIM BRIGHTMAN

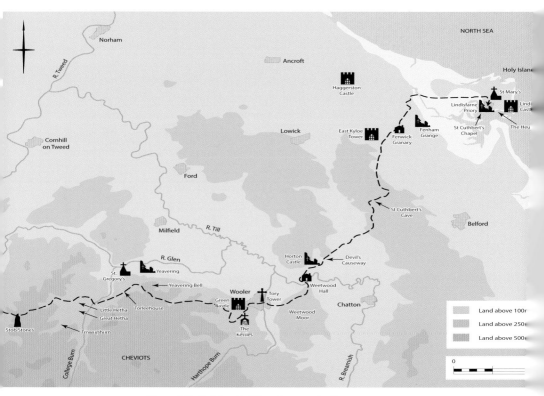

Map of St Cuthbert's Way: the east half. JIM BRIGHTMAN

CHAPTER TWO

St Cuthbert's Way

It is perhaps incorrect to begin a chapter on St Cuthbert and historical pilgrim routes by stating that this route is not of ancient origins. Nonetheless, parts of it very much are, and there are ubiquitous associative links with the saint and his ministry, and also to the history of the north of England and Scottish borders. It is perhaps more correct to say that the route was inspired by the saint, with additional sites of historical interest and natural beauty, as notes the accompanying guidebook. However, creating such an 'associative' route 'incorporating' the historic sites is not a modern practice.

Following the opening of his tomb eleven years after his death, Cuthbert's body was found to be incorrupt, and so both his body and any objects that had been in contact with the saint, before death or posthumously, were turned into relics and promoted for their miraculous properties. This led to a number of sites being identified as having a connection to the saint, and were subsequently established as sacred locations. Primarily, these consisted of the various structures adorning the landscape around Lindisfarne, but also the churches and chapels visited by the island's religious community during the journey of Cuthbert's incorrupt body between c.875 and 882CE.

Thus, the places where his body rested during the 'wanderings', and any sites associated with the saint, were in some way made holy; the stones and landscapes absorbing his sanctity for pilgrims to experience in the future. This practice was used throughout the medieval period to entice pilgrims to flock to these sites; it is not a twentieth-century construct. As such, Cuthbert's cult should be understood in terms of a series of stations on a wider pilgrimage 'route', rather than as a journey to a specific individual location.

Designed in 1995 and inaugurated in 1996 through a partnership between the Scottish BorderWalks Project and Till Valley Tourism Initiative, St Cuthbert's Way is a 62-mile (100km) heritage trail that connects the picturesque town of Melrose in the Scottish Borders, where St Cuthbert started his religious life in 650CE, to 'Holy Island' or Lindisfarne off the Northumbrian coast, his eventual resting place and the site of his original pilgrimage shrine.

The creation of the trail exemplifies the modern approach to both the medieval past and Christian religion with regard to pilgrimage. Its creators, Scottish tourist board workers Roger Smith and Ron Shaw, were directly engaged in building the physical infrastructure of the walk and deciding upon where, essentially, it should pass. To complement it, Cuthbert's gold and garnet pectoral cross was chosen as the symbolic waymarker for the route so that it was easily recognizable to all, as well as retaining links to the saint throughout.

As noted in the Introduction to this book, the official guide to the walk written by Smith and Shaw acknowledges that the route includes many sights and attractions in addition to those simply connected to the stories of St Cuthbert. This was no doubt an attempt to increase the tourism reputation of the surrounding landscape, which includes prehistoric to Victorian sites of interest. St Cuthbert's Way is thus a very successful utilization of the north of England's tourism spots.

In short, the route may be divided into the Scottish and English trails, the former beginning at Melrose and ending at Kirk Yetholm, and the latter starting from Kirk Yetholm and culminating at Lindisfarne Priory or, more correctly, St Cuthbert's Isle. The route climbs over the fringes of the Eildon Hills before following stretches of the River Tweed and the Roman Dere Street. It then passes Cessford Castle before a fine hill ridge is traversed en route to the attractive village of Kirk Yetholm. The route then skirts the northern edges of the Cheviot Hills to cross the border and descend into the old market town of Wooler. The final stretch crosses the Northumberland countryside and makes a dramatic finale across the causeway to Holy Island and its impressive castle, ruined abbey and the small island where Cuthbert once lived.

The History of St Cuthbert

St Cuthbert's Way is named after Cuthbert, the Bishop of Lindisfarne (c.634-687CE) who made many physical and spiritual journeys during his lifetime and following his death. Made a monk at Melrose in 651CE (then known as Mailros or 'bare peninsula'), throughout his life he journeyed extensively in Scotland and throughout the north of England, allegedly founding churches at St Andrews, Edinburgh, and many other locations across Northumbria.

Following his death on Inner Farne on 20 March 687, Cuthbert was buried on the island of Lindisfarne within the nave of the priory. A significant pilgrimage cult then grew up around him and his relics. In 698 the tomb was reopened, to show the incorruptibility of his body, which strengthened his saintly image by proclaiming his miraculous qualities as displayed by his triumph over mortality. As a result, his body was translated to a new shrine. This was an above-ground sarcophagus in Lindisfarne's priory church, and again immediately attracted pilgrims.

It was not until 875 that Cuthbert's body was again exhumed by the monks, who evacuated Holy Island due to its sacking by Viking raids, thus beginning a pilgrimage of their own. For seven years they 'wandered' or carried his relics to locations as far apart as Melrose, Whithorn, Ripon and then to Chester-le-Street in c.883, where they stayed for nearly a century, establishing a church in honour of Our Lady and St Cuthbert. Cuthbert's body was then finally interred at the Anglo-Saxon church at

Durham in 996.

In 1070 a wattle church was erected at Durham and the saint's body ceased its perambulations. Three years later a stone building, known as the White Church, replaced the temporary building, before being moved again to a newly constructed tomb in the Norman cathedral of Christ and the Blessed Virgin Mary, founded in 1104. His final resting place came in 1073, when he was interred in a splendid shrine behind the high altar of the newly founded Benedictine Cathedral Priory.

Together with the sites at Lindisfarne and Inner Farne, Cuthbert's tomb was a popular place of pilgrimage and devotion until the Reformation, when Catholic shrines, sacred associated places in the landscape and complementary practices were disestablished and the corresponding monuments, including Cuthbert's shrine which stood in a feretory in the east end of Durham Cathedral, were destroyed.

Evangelism took Cuthbert considerable distances during his life and in his death. As a monastic, he travelled to all around the Northumbrian and Scottish border regions. The Venerable Bede (673–735CE) notes that he visited villages and hamlets that were at a distance and remote, situated among high and craggy mountains, and inhabited by the most rustic, ignorant and savage people. There is evidence of him travelling to Coldingham, Carlisle, and he is believed to have founded churches in Scotland at Dull, St Andrews and Edinburgh. And at many of the sites where his body was rested, churches were founded in recollection that Cuthbert had lain upon their land. Norham-on-Tweed, Bedlington in Northumberland, and Crayke in North Yorkshire are among many places that were part of what came to be known as the patrimony of St Cuthbert. In fact, there are an abundance of churches dedicated to St Cuthbert in the Northumbrian area, and those of pre-Conquest date are almost ubiquitously linked to this period of wandering. Those that are later structures are often still within the patronage of Durham Cathedral.

Therefore, travel is well associated with the Cuthbertine cult, and the places he visited in life and death became indelibly associated with his memory, as they still are to this day. The paths of St Cuthbert's Way are therefore thought to have been journeyed by Cuthbert himself, and then followed by pilgrims throughout the medieval era who desired to walk in his footsteps. Bridlepaths and pathways were the primary methods, with most travelling on foot or steed. But as far as Cuthbert is concerned, while the link between Lindisfarne Priory and its daughter house, Melrose Abbey, is in no doubt (as Cuthbert and later pilgrims certainly journeyed to both monastic communities), it is fair to say that we are not entirely clear of the routes he took between the two monasteries in his lifetime. No doubt he also varied his route, as in *Historia Ecclesiastica*, Bede describes times he took a boat, and others where he walked on foot.

An Overview of the Route

After leaving Melrose a steep climb is required up into the Eildon Hills, stronghold of the Celtic Votadini, with excellent views of Dere Street, the Roman road, as it follows the line of the route. Pilgrims then turn east to Newtown St Boswells on the River

Tweed opposite Dryburgh Abbey, and follow the bank of the River Tweed for 3 miles (5km) downstream to reach the town of St Boswells, and on to Maxton. Near Maxton the trail then joins Dere Street, which it follows south-east past the site of the Battle of Ancrum Moor to Monteviot House on the banks of the River Teviot.

From Monteviot Bridge, the Way follows Dere Street for another 1km, before striking east and climbing above the village of Crailing to reach Cessford. A short stretch of roadwalking follows to Morebattle, from where the trail leads south up the valley of Kale Water. South of Morebattle, the Way climbs steeply to the ridge of Wideopen Hill, the highest point of the trail at 1,207ft (368m), before descending to the villages of Town Yetholm and Kirk Yetholm, where it meets the Pennine Way.

The border ridge is reached east of Kirk Yetholm. On the English side the trail descends through the Northumberland National Park to the village of Hethpool in the College Valley. It then climbs through the foothills of the Cheviot Hills, passing just south of the hillforts of Yeavering Bell and Humbleton Hill, to the town of Wooler.

From Wooler, the Way ascends the valley of the River Till to the twin villages of West Horton and East Horton. It then follows farmland tracks to St Cuthbert's Cave near Holburn. Near the cave it joins St Oswald's Way and the Northumberland Coast Path to head north through Fenwick to reach the coast, just east of Beal. The last section can only be walked at low tide, either by the modern road or by the historic Pilgrims' Path which takes pilgrims across the causeway – evident by the waymarker posts in the sand – to Lindisfarne (Holy Island).

Start of the Route: Melrose Abbey

Although the route claims to start at the site of Melrose Abbey, where Cuthbert became a monk, this is not in fact true. The current abbey originates from the medieval period, whereas Cuthbert lived in the seventh century. The site where the saint started his ministry was actually Old Melrose, or 'Mailros', which was founded by King Oswald and St Aidan, Bishop of Lindisfarne, along with monks from Iona, in 635CE. In 651CE St Boisil accepted Cuthbert as a novice; he was then appointed prior in 661CE. The destruction of the abbey occurred in 839CE by the order of Kenneth MacAlpin, King of the Scots.

Further links with Cuthbert were established in the ninth century, when his body was wandered around this landscape; it was eventually buried at Melrose in 875CE to protect the relics from Viking raids – thus the abbey must have been reconstructed, at least to some extent. Finally, in 1080, a chapel of Durham Cathedral was built on the site of the former abbey and dedicated to their most notable saint: Cuthbert. The chapel stood on what is now known as 'Chapelknowe' and was a place of pilgrimage until the time of the Reformation, when both site and chapel were left in ruins. David I then granted the ruins to a Cistercian community of monks in the twelfth century, who chose to re-site their new abbey 2 miles (3km) west – the current location of Melrose Abbey. The request was granted, as was retaining the name, hence the two Melrose sites.

Old Melrose is about 2½ miles (4km) east of Melrose, and not directly on the

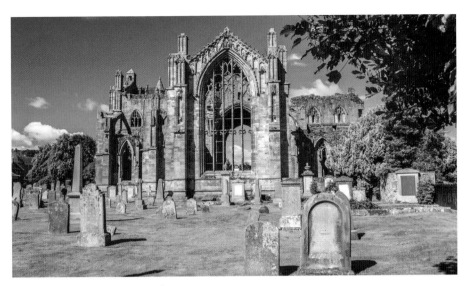

Melrose Abbey (south transept). DAVID ROSS

St Cuthbert's Way trail. Together with the chapel, the former abbey site lies on the peninsula formed by a wide eastward bend of the River Tweed cutting into Bemersyde Hill. Just to the south is the only structure to remain in the same area of the abbey: the nineteenth-century house of Old Melrose and its walled garden.

It is not surprising why the modern pilgrim route bypasses the original site in favour of the current abbey. There is little to be seen but the former site of the chapel, which is simply a mound comprising a few protruding undressed stones. Some of the dressed and simple carved stones built into the garden walls may also be from the chapel but are not readily datable. While minor excavations undertaken in the 1950s found some foundations to the south-east of the chapel mound site, along with three graves to the south-east of the house, some 100m south of the chapel, all that remains of the abbey exists along the neck of the peninsula, enclosed by a low bank – the earthworks of the monastery which form the old monastic vallum (a deep ditch or series of ditches that surrounded the site, most likely for protection).

However, the evocative nature of the landscape – the large peninsula which overlooks and is surrounded by the river – is still, to this day, a relatively isolated place evoking the intention of a site close to God and peaceful for ascetic life. It is a significant Cuthbertine site for pilgrims wishing to follow in the footsteps of the saint, and so I urge you not to overlook it. The landscape is still inherently sacred as it retains the memories of where Cuthbert began his monastic life. It is very secluded but not cut off for visitors to see, while the cliff below provides an element of protection – so it is clear why it was originally chosen as a religious site, especially as Dere Street is only a mile away and therefore well placed for receiving visiting guests, which the community so often did.

While this site was largely closed during the original years of the founding of St Cuthbert's Way, open only on special occasions, provisions are slowly being made to enable visitors to the site, with clear signage around what is to be known as the 'Monks' Trail'.

The current Cistercian abbey, founded via invitation of David I in 1136 by monks of Rievaulx in North Yorkshire, was also a pilgrimage centre in its own right throughout the medieval period, largely as a result of its second abbot, Waltheof, who died in 1159 and was venerated as a saint. It quickly became one of the wealthiest religious institutions in Scotland. However, during the later centuries of border warfare, the abbey was destroyed. The majority of this destruction occurred in 1385, but it was rebuilt until it was badly damaged again in 1544, just prior to the Reformation. The ruins of the cloister, lay choir, dormitories, kitchen, dayroom, latrine, refectory and chapter house are, however, still discernible. One further interesting story regarding the abbey is its alleged possession of Scotland's War of Independence leader, Robert the Bruce's heart. In 1996 a lead casket was discovered in the chapter house and is thought to be of the medieval monarch's body.

It is said that High Cross Avenue, near Galashiels, was named after a great cross where pilgrims, travelling from the west, got their first glimpse of the medieval abbey. This was probably not the only cross that would have symbolized the pilgrim route; no doubt one stood outside the abbey itself, and we know that in 1422 there was another outside the south gate, recognizing its origins as the market square. These crosses symbolized assembly points and places of significance for travellers.

The Eildon Hills

The Eildon Hills are a triple peak and one of the most recognized Scottish Border landmarks. The Way takes you over the saddle between the North and Mid Hills, and from here you can see back to Melrose and the abbey, or forward to the Cheviots: a landscape comprising a palimpsest of myths and legends that still, to this day, continue.

The sacred hill fort, or symbolic assembly point, of Eildon Hill North has been occupied since the late Bronze Age; it was then used as a signal station by the Romans, before being reoccupied during the Romano-British period.

The Northern Peak was completely surrounded by three concentric ramparts that are over a mile long. These encircle the remains of some 296 hut platforms excavated from the solid bedrock to provide flat foundations for wooden roundhouses. Undoubtedly an important focal point for the native population, it has been estimated that over 2,000 people may have lived within this exposed hill fort: a substantial settlement for this period in Britain.

The hill's strategic importance was clearly also understood by the Roman army, as the fort of Trimontium (named after the triple peaks) was established under General Agricola just below the hillside in c.80CE.

According to tradition Eildon Hill is also the location where the thirteenth-century Scottish laird and poet, Thomas of Erceldoune (Thomas the Rhymer), met the Fairy Queen, as recounted first in a fourteenth-century romance, and later an eighteenth-century ballad. He met and kissed her at the Eildon Tree and was forced into the fairy kingdom under the Eildon Hills for seven years. It is also the hill where King Arthur and his warriors allegedly sleep, awaiting the time to defend their country.

The third peak stretches towards Bowden; nearby there is an expanse of heather known as 'the devil's spadeful'. The hills are associated with the legendary thirteenth-century wizard, based on the mathematician, scholar and scientist, Michael Scotus, who, according to a traditional tale of 1822 recounted by James Hogg, split what was a single peak into three.

Finally, Melrose Abbey was built from stone taken from the Eildon Hills.

Eildon Hills, and waymarker in foreground.
DAVID ROSS

Bowden Kirk

A former Georgian weaving town, the small village of Bowden lies to the south of the Eildons with wide open views over the Cheviots; its original name, 'Bothandene' means 'settlement in a valley near a stream'. Although not specifically on the Way, the parish church has existed on the site since the twelfth century – it lies only a few metres off route to the south of the village, but is certainly worth visiting.

Granted to the monks of Selkirk by the future David I in around 1119, after a few years the community moved from Bowden to Kelso and founded a new abbey. At this time, Bowden Church was a chapel under the superiority of the abbey. The current rectangular building dates partly from the fifteenth century (largely the north wall with the pointed arch leading into the organ loft), although it has been the subject of many subsequent alterations and additions, dating primarily from the seventeenth and eighteenth centuries.

The building features many elements of architectural interest. Firstly, the wooden structure against the north wall is known as the Laird's Loft: bearing the initials 'S.T.K' and 'D.G.H' for 'Sir Thomas Ker' and 'Dame Grisell Halkett', whose coat of arms is in the centre of the painted decoration, the loft provided special accommodation for the Ker family, the Lairds of Bowden, following the Reformation. The loft was originally in front of the transept arch, and behind it was a retiring room for the family to use between services on a Sunday. Below is the burial aisle of the Kers of Cavers-Carre. The loft is still in use as the family pew of the Riddell-Carre family, direct descendants of the Kers.

The church is also highly unusual in that its current rectangular plan is largely the result of its four external staircases, which reach eight doors. One external stair and door gave access to the Roxburghe Loft, another gives access to the west gallery, another to the loft, and others to the vaults, which are still in use.

The stained glass is particularly beautiful, notably the window known as the Priests' Door, situated at a former entrance facing the main entrance. It should also be noted that on 9 December 1888, Lady Grisell Baillie, whom we will again come across in the next section of the route, was ordained at Bowden Kirk as the first deaconess of the Church of Scotland.

BOWDEN WELL

A further small site of interest at Bowden is the octagonal structure or 'pant' enclosing the village well, under the large tree adjacent to the old school. While its later date implies that it is not related to pilgrims passing through the village, it is the only surviving public water fountain of three shown on early maps. It was likely used as an assembly point, where villagers met and exchanged news while queuing for water each day. It may also have been used by antiquarian travellers of the area, perhaps even those attempting to follow the approximate medieval Way.

Technically not a well but a cistern, with a tank that originally held around 600 gallons (2,700ltr) of water fed from a natural spring in the nearby Eildon Hills, it is constructed of squared and snecked rubble with contrasting red sandstone ashlar dressings, and has a polygonal ball-finialled slated roof and cobbled surround. A relief on one of the stones reads 'ERECTED 1861'; it also features two boarded timber doors (a large and a small one), and two stone troughs (a semicircular and a rectangular one) situated along the bottom for access to the stop valve.

Newtown St Boswells

There is little to see of note at Newtown St Boswells, particularly in comparison to its 'ancient' neighbour, but it is not as modern as one might first think. Cartographic evidence for its existence can be found over the past 400 years, since a 'new farm' mentioned in the charter book of Dryburgh Abbey from 1150 may indeed be a reference to the same place. Yet it is largely the product of the nineteenth century coming of the railways to the borders – Newtown was formerly a very important junction, which closed in the 1960s.

Other buildings of note include the Scottish Borders Council offices, which won an architectural competition in the 1960s and which dominate the village due to their cathedral-like scale, and the 1888 Baillie Hall – now two properties, it was once used as a church hall, school and meeting room. Constructed in 1854 in memory of Major the Honourable Robert Baillie, an elder of Bowden Church, by his wife, Lady Grisell, the hall also overlooks the valley of the Bowden Burn, and the stream that cuts through the village. It has been suggested that Newtown was once a very busy town, as many mills were situated along the burn.

Dryburgh Abbey

Although not specifically along the Way, Dryburgh Abbey lies to the north of the town; it is a mere five minutes' walk from the main route, and is a 'must see' diversion. The current abbey is built on the site of an original chapel dedicated to St Modan, an early missionary of the Falkirk and Stirling areas and the Abbot of Dryburgh around 522CE, though this is disputed. It is said he ended his life as a hermit in Dunbarton – the church at Rosneath is dedicated to him; another suggestion is that Modan may well be 'Adan' with an 'm' prefix meaning 'Mo-Aedan' or 'my Aidan'.

This Premonstratensian (or White Canon) foundation dates to 1150, with the monks supposedly coming here from Alnwick on the invitation of Hugh de Morville, the Constable of Scotland and Lord of Lauderdale, and Beatrice de Beauchamp. Located in a secluded bend of the River Tweed, the abbey site is particularly tranquil. Though

Cloister door, Dryburgh Abbey. ANSELM GRIBBIN

The Chapter House, Dryburgh Abbey. ANSELM GRIBBIN

Dryburgh became the premier house in Scotland of the Premonstratensian order, it never quite reached the heights of wealth and influence achieved by its neighbours at Kelso, Jedburgh and Melrose. Like Melrose, Dryburgh was burned to the ground by Edward II of England in 1322 after he and his army camped there on their way home following a fruitless invasion of Scotland and heard the abbey's bells ringing in the distance. The abbey was destroyed once again by Richard II as he swept through the Borders in punishment for Scottish raids on the north of England; however, it was the Reformation that effectively ended Dryburgh Abbey's days and, by 1584, just two brethren remained.

Much of Dryburgh has survived the frequent depredations on its structure. The church is a fine relic of Gothic architecture, particularly the pink sandstone transepts flanking the presbytery. The highlights are the thirteenth-century chapter house, which still features its barrel-vaulted roof, arched sedilia along the eastern wall and, most interestingly, traces of surviving painted wall plaster between the stone arcading as well as the ruined rose window of the refectory. Other features of interest include the warming house and dormitory in the east range, and St Modan's Chapel located adjacent to the south transept of the church.

In the eighteenth century, the abbey, now in a ruinous state, attracted the attention of David Erskine, 11th Earl of Buchan. In 1780 Buchan became the chief founder of the Society of Antiquaries of Scotland, and purchased Dryburgh House in order to transform it into a charming landscape, in which the ancient abbey figured prominently. When he died in 1829, he was laid to rest in its sacristy. And although the monastery's church, dedicated to the Virgin Mary, lay in almost total ruin, Buchan's close friend, Sir Walter Scott, antiquarian and novelist, was buried in the north transept (which he called 'St Mary's Aisle') in 1832. A third great Scot, Field-Marshal Earl Haig, was interred beside Scott in 1928.

SCOTT'S OUTLOOK AND THE TEMPLE OF MUSES

Continuing on the theme of links to Sir Walter Scott and interesting diversions, this area around Dryburgh was one of his favourite walks. Nearby it is worth making a detour to see the 1814 statue of William Wallace located at Scott's Outlook, a scenic vantage point that looks out over the Tweed Valley and Old Melrose to the Eildon Hills.

It is also worth making a final detour to the nearby footbridge, which is set in a landscape of particular beauty and note. Sited on Bass Hill, the nearby folly is known as the Temple of Muses: it is a circular columned gazebo of classical design topped by a bust of James Thomson, the Ednam poet of 'The Seasons' and author of the words for 'Rule Britannia'. Yet this monument is not the original, because in 1817, the 11th Earl of Buchan erected the temple in the form of a Greek pavilion, as a tribute to James Thomson. It originally contained a statue of Apollo, the Greek God of music and poetry, but this has long vanished. The neo-classical pavilion, however, with the bust of Thomson on the pinnacle, remained; the modern statue in the centre is by Siobhan O'Hehir, a local artist.

St Boswells

St Boswells takes its name from St Boisil, the seventh-century prior of Melrose, and Cuthbert's mentor. It prides itself on having the largest village green in Scotland, the site of the old St Boswell's Gypsy Fair! The original village stood over at Benrig, on the flat 'haugh', which is the area between the riverbank and higher ground. The site was prone to flooding, which may explain why the villagers eventually moved to the higher ground at Lessudden (the place of Aidan) and the present site of the village. Lessudden village, as it was then known, consisted of one long street, now Main Street, and a narrow back-road which ran along Braeheads, on the high banks of the river. The Church of St Mary here was established in the twelfth century during the reign of David I. Over time the worshippers moved to the 'auld kirk' erected at Benrig near St Boisil's Chapel, which stood until 1952 when it was finally demolished.

BENRIG

The temptation here would be to stop and visit the village church at St Boswells, but actually the current building only dates to 1836, and only became the primary church in 1952 when the former institution over at Benrig ceased use. Benrig Church actually lies about a mile downstream beyond Mertoun Bridge (the old toll-house and Mertoun Mill add to the composition here): an impressive five-span, mid-nineteenth-cenury red sandstone structure sited just north-east of the village, but along the Way nonetheless. All that can be seen today are the foundations and the burial ground, which has associations with Boisil himself, but both are well worth a visit simply for their setting and alleged Anglo-Saxon origins.

ST BOISIL'S WELLS

Whilst you are in the vicinity there are further hidden sites to see. St Boisil was known to make use of two local wells and springs for their healing powers, as was common in this period, and no doubt medieval pilgrims followed in his footsteps, making them key stopping stations along their journey. The most interesting of these are the Crystal Well and Mule Gang, which are listed structures adjacent to the Way. They represent the mid-eighteenth-century landscape design so prevalent across Britain, where utilitarian structures were combined to create more picturesque and natural vistas. The Mule Gang comprises a rusticated stone arch set in the bank, with a hydraulic ram and circular gin house (so a donkey could be used to drive the water) behind fragments of cast-iron railings. Similarly, the early nineteenth-century Crystal Well is actually a grotto made up of similar stones with the spring flowing from a pointed-arched recess into a gadrooned stone basin behind fleur-de-lys headed cast-iron railings.

Although St Cuthbert's Way does not directly pass them, there are further wells of interest that are located very close by. These springs are known as the Wellbury Well, and the Hare Well or Healing Well. They are depicted on Ordnance Survey maps but are still very difficult to definitively locate. Wellbury Well is well hidden at the bottom of the banking, but the Way runs right above it, as does Benrig Cemetery. Hare Well is even more difficult to detect, but a steady stream of water still runs out of this overgrown depression in the wood. Mention must also be made of St Boswells Burn ('burn' meaning watercourse), which crosses the small stream from Hare Well, joining the burn at right angles beside the pedestrian bridge. From here a long flight of steps takes you to the next marvel of the journey.

Maxton

This site is often overlooked by pilgrims, yet it has clear associations with St Cuthbert. The medieval church of Maxton was first recorded as 'St Cuthbert's Church of Mackistun', some 500 years after the saint's era, yet it may not be too implausible to suggest that, like St Boswells' old church, it may have been linked to and served by the Old Melrose community. Its close proximity to Benrig is perhaps too coincidental and, furthermore, in the late twelfth century, Maxton was certainly officially linked to Melrose Abbey, as the landowner allowed the monks to utilize the land for pasture and quarrying. Not only is the church therefore dedicated to the saint, but also, until the 1960s, a St Cuthbert's Well was sited at the west end of the village – although now it is completely untraceable due to road improvements.

The parish of Maxton claims to be the birthplace of Scotland's greatest theologian/philosopher, the Blessed John Duns Scotus (c.1266–1308). However, although he may indeed have had family from the area, it has now been generally accepted that he in fact came from the Berwickshire town of Duns, about 20 miles (30km) away, from which his name derives.

Dere Street and the Surrounding Landscape

In terms of architectural interest, little stands along the next section of the route. However, given equal billing with the landscape and genuinely medieval sites, should be the multitude of other attractions that are of just as much note. The route soon after Maxton follows the line of the Roman military road, Dere Street (built 79–83CE), for several miles. The road originally ran from York all the way to the Forth in Edinburgh, and although the current route does not follow the original line of the road consistently, it is not far off, and since it has survived for over 2,000 years, it would have been well-trodden by Cuthbert and pilgrims alike.

LADY LILLIARD'S STONE

There are many detours to make here, so it is best to keep the old road as a waymarker. Just to the south of the Way, a short diversion takes you to Lady Lilliard's stone. This area is particularly noted for the constant skirmishes that have taken place between the Scots and the English throughout history. Dere Street lay between the two old British kingdoms even before the Anglo-Saxon invasions. An example of this bloodshed is the Battle of Ancrum Moor (1545), from which comes the reason for the sad death of Maid Lilliard. Legend tells that Lilliard fought at the battle following the death of her lover. The monument dedicated to her talks of her courage and ultimately the horrific injuries that she suffered, which were met with jibes and laughter, though she kept on fighting. However, the legend is just that: it is pure fiction, and the name existed long before the story.

There was also a great stone known as Lilyot's Cross supposedly erected here by the monks of Melrose in the early medieval period. Tradition suggests the monument was later used as an assembly point where boundary disputes were decided between the wardens of the Scottish and English marches in the fourteenth century.

LILLIARD'S EDGE

Not far from Lilliard's Stone stands Monteath Douglas Mausoleum at Lilliard's Edge (or Lilliardsedge), at the site of the Battle of Ancrum Moor. This 1864 square, neo-Byzantine domed mausoleum, with Ionic pilasters and plinths supporting recumbent lions (lion to the left awake, lion to the right asleep), the Douglas coat of arms set into the north pediment, and a cross-finialled dome pierced with glazed stars, is both a striking piece of architecture and a prominent landmark. Set on high ground on Gersit Law, and seen from several miles away in all directions, it is very finely detailed and an excellent example of the work of Edinburgh-based architects, Peddie & Kinnear, at this time.

A further interesting stone, although much older in date, survives a little further south-east, half a mile from Harrietsfield and 130yd (120m) south-west of Dere Street. In a cultivated field is a four-sided standing stone, 4ft 4in (1.3m) high and 2ft 6in (76cm) square at the base. Likely another waymarker or assembly post, this stone also stands near an ancient fort.

Harestanes

The next point of interest is situated within and around the village of Harestanes. Monteviot House and its estate comprise most of the surrounding land through which the Way travels. The first structure seen as you enter the estate woodland is a tall tower used for shooting roe deer. A little further on is the Waterloo Monument on Peniel Heugh: by Archibald Elliot, it was completed in 1824; the viewing platform was added in 1867. It is typical of its era, and provides a 360-degree view across the Border location.

Monteviot House itself, however, is the *pièce de résistance*. It was built in the grounds of Ancrum Spital, a medieval hostel/hospitium (or 'Spital') with a nearby chapel and adjoining burial ground. A secular foundation – although its type, dedication and foundation date are all unknown – the building was burned down by Hertford's forces on 14 September 1545. There have been several allegations that it was an establishment of the Knights Templar or Hospitallers, but these are unfounded.

The current house dates from 1740, with rebuilding from 1840, and is home to a branch of the notable local Kerr family, the seat of the Earls of Ancrum and of Lothian. It is possible that Dere Street followed the line of the main drive and thus was likely an important station for both the saint and his followers over successive centuries, given its origins as a hospitium – this would suggest that it acted as a resting place for Cuthbertine pilgrims travelling on to the Northumbria coast. Nothing remains of this early structure, which lies in a thickly overgrown area of bushes and trees to the west of the house.

Leaving the estate en route to cross the River Teviot, the Way passes a large, ruinous, circular, rubble-built nineteenth-century dovecote standing on a mound on the left bank of the river, a quarter of a mile south-east of the house. While the lower part may be as old as the turn of the sixteenth and seventeenth centuries, the upper part is comparatively modern.

As noted, the Way crosses the Teviot here and heads for the Cheviot Hills. At this point it is possible to take a detour out to Hawick, where (although not part of the current Way) a medieval chapel (of ease) of St Cuthbert was sited; it was first mentioned in the twelfth-century account of Reginald of Durham, and there is an old burial ground close by at Slitrig. The chapel was alleged to have been founded *c.*687, and was ruinous in the twelfth century. Its likely location lies at Cogsmill, below the farm at Adderstoneshiels.

The Slitrig burn joins the Teviot in Hawick town centre, so travellers wishing to explore the area may come across or detour to the present church. St Cuthbert's Episcopal Church was deliberately sited as close to the original church as possible, but little, if anything, remains of the chapel. The graveyard, enclosed by an old earthen bank, is covered by mixed woodland.

Cessford

The main Way route now ventures towards the Cheviot Hills, with Cessford Castle standing in the foreground. Although nowadays Cessford itself consists of no more than a farm and associated cottages, in the past there was a more considerable settlement.

Close to Cessford Farm is the imposing L-shaped fortified tower known as Cessford Castle, which still, even in its ruinous state, dominates the surrounding landscape. Built in the mid-fifteenth century of red freestone, it acted as a stronghold of the Ker family, who were often wardens of the Middle March and responsible for keeping the local peace. No other family has owned the castle. Sir Robert Ker became Lord Roxburghe in 1600, and the castle remains in the ownership of the present Duke of Roxburghe.

The castle itself was not a particularly welcoming place, with its 12–13ft (4m) thick walls and dismal dungeon, although there is evidence of travellers staying in the castle overnight, but it was clearly built as a competent stronghold, being described by the English in 1523 as the third strongest place in Scotland.

The ruinous condition of the fabric is sufficient evidence of the vicissitudes that the castle suffered in the sixteenth century. In the year 1519, Cessford, along with other Scottish fortresses, was cast down by the English. In May 1523, the Earl of Surrey, with Lord Dacre and others, attacked the castle in the absence of its owner, with a battery of eleven cannon. Further attacks took place at the time of the 'Rough Wooing' by the Earl of Hertford in 1543 and 1545.

There are fragments of outbuildings and foundations of others, including those of a small round tower on the east side. The whole site is enclosed by the remains of an earthwork, represented at present only by a rampart of earth and stone not more than 5ft (1.5m) in height; on the outside boundary there would have been a ditch, though this is barely traceable today.

The tower has two entrances, at ground level and on the first floor, which clearly identify the two different functions of the building. The first floor of the main block is devoted to the hall, once a fine room with a vaulted ceiling. In the centre of the north side are the remains of a great fireplace, evidence that this was the solar wing of the tower – that is, the private area of the lord, as opposed to the great hall. It is situated immediately above the kitchen, indicating that it was used for entertaining by the laird and family. Below, on the lowest floors, are vaulted chambers and pits: the prison.

A nearby ash tree was said to have served as the baronial gallows.

It should be noted that the ruinous state of this structure means that it is largely unapproachable.

Morebattle

Originally, Morebattle was a lochside settlement, hence the Old English name which means 'the dwelling place by the lake'. The village was also an outpost of Lindisfarne, as in 670CE, King Oswy of Northumbria gave the monks a gift of lands there.

There have been two churches at Morebattle, the first of which was Anglo-Saxon (or at least twelfth-century) and occupies the site of the present church. This church was dedicated to St Lawrence, though nothing remains of it except for one stone, which is still visible in the south-east corner of the present church. Heughhead Farmhouse also overlies the foundations of a building said to have been the residence of the Dean of Teviotdale, the archdeaconry of which was in existence by 1237 or 1238, and by virtue of this office, the archdeacon was parson of Morebattle from some time before 1406.

The original church of 'Mereboda' is recorded as belonging to the diocese of Glasgow from about 1116. The building was burnt down in 1544, but was rebuilt. The current rectangular-shaped Church of St Lawrence dates from 1757, with extensions from 1899 and 1903.

There is also the former Morebattle United Free Church standing in Main Street. Dating from 1866, it was designed by Thomas Pilkington as a single-storey, four-bay-aisled structure. It was deconsecrated in the late twentieth century.

Furthermore, the slight remains of a well that lies just east of the churchyard is named 'Lowrie's well' also after the church's patron St Lawrence. The well was a public water supply and was also used for baptisms until the last century.

There are a few places of note in this area that merit making a detour. The ruined tower of Whitton is one: destroyed by the Earl of Surrey in 1542, and now part-covered by the buildings of Whitton Farm. Conventicles were said to have been held at Whitton, with services for people from various parts in the vicinity.

Another ruin of note is Corbet Tower, situated under Morebattle Hill, which lies less than a mile south of the village. Standing in landscaped gardens owned by the Fraser family, it was originally built in the fifteenth century by the Corbet family of Clifton; it was then destroyed by Hertford's forces under the command of Sir George Bowes in 1544. In the sixteenth century, the Ker family came into possession of the tower, and then later the Douglas family of Kelso.

Linton Church

Situated at the top of a large hummock of sand from the door of Linton Church, another detour from the main Way is the loch of Morebattle. Its proximity to Morebattle is clear from the top, and denotes the existence of the loch and marsh that existed between the two villages. Linton actually means 'the farm by the lake'.

The tympanum which has been inserted in the front of the modern porch, above the south door, is unique. On the dexter side is portrayed a bearded knight on horseback, holding the reins in his left hand, while his right hand grasps a lance thrust into the jaws of the lower of two animals occupying the sinister side. There is some doubt as to the proper interpretation of the subject represented, but it is alleged to depict the local legend of the slaying of the 'Linton Worm'. Wormiston Hill, known as Worm's Glen and about two miles north-east of Yetholm, was said to have been the haunt of the twelfth-century serpent or beast killed by the ancestor of the family of Somerville. He received the Barony of Linton as a reward, and was made the king's falconer.

Somerville was actually the Baron of Linton in 1160, and the church was built at this time, so the connection may indeed hold true.

Although of twelfth-century origin, the church was much altered in 1616, 1774 and 1813; the south porch was added in 1857, and the chancel rebuilt, and the entirety of the building substantially restored between 1911 and 1912. The plan includes a rectangular nave and chancel with a modern north vestry and south porch. The lowest stone courses of the north walls are of cubical ashlar and may therefore be regarded as Romanesque, but the masonry above, as well as the south walls and the west gable, are considerably later in date. Both nave and chancel have been reduced in height. The windows, doors and chancel arch are almost entirely modern.

Inside is the Norman font, which vanished during the Reformation but reappeared in c.1850, when it was found in a blacksmith's shop being used as a cooling trough. Thereafter it became a planter in the garden of Clifton Park, before being repaired and returned to the church.

Primside Mill

Take a route just to the east of the main Way trail and this should lead you straight past Primside Mill. In the fifteenth century, Primside belonged to the Ker family of Cessford, but sadly it suffered the same fate as many other places in the area when the Earl of Hertford visited in 1545 during the 'Rough Wooing'.

This old grain mill and seventeenth-century granary is situated on the Bowmont Water: it was home to Andrew Rutherford Blythe, great-nephew of Charles I Blythe, King of the Yetholm Gypsies, and a former church elder of Yetholm Church. Yetholm is infamous for its association with Gypsy folk, who, from at least 1605, would gather there to elect a king and queen and hold their coronation. The reason for this was that a gypsy soldier was said to have saved the life of a British officer during a battle in France; the captain owned land in the area so, to mark his gratitude, made the land and some cottages in the village available to his saviour and descendants.

Town Yetholm and Kirk Yetholm are separate villages, with St Cuthbert's Way running between them, along the banks of the Bowmont Water. The route skirts round to the east of Town Yetholm, then continues into Kirk Yetholm.

Hoselaw Chapel

Straying north-west from the main Way route, Hoselaw Chapel is sited further north, above Linton Hill. Still within the bounds of Linton parish, it overlooks Hoselaw Loch, an important wildlife reserve, and beyond to the rolling Cheviots straddling the Scottish/English border. To reach the chapel, turn left off the B6352 heading towards Yetholm – it is identified as Chapel Knowe on modern Ordnance Survey (OS) maps. Unlike Linton Church, which was independent, the chapel, dedicated to St Machute, was attached to the abbey at Kelso and first recorded in 1421. By 1560 Hoselaw Chapel was in ruins, and no sign of the original building remains; however, at the end of the nineteenth century, the minister, Dr Thomas Leishman, conducted worship in a nearby thatched cottage. After his death it was felt there could be no more fitting memorial to him than the restoration of the chapel.

In 1906 the foundation stone of the new chapel was laid. The white sandstone building, which can accommodate fifty people, consists of a nave and a semi-circular apse. The latter displays a very interesting mural by Jessie R. MacGibbons: depicting three angels bearing the scroll, it is inscribed with the phrase: 'Alleluia for the Lord God Omnipoteat reigaeta.'

Finally, the associated burial ground, now lost, is reputed to be the resting place of Scots who died at the Battle of Flodden in 1513, and were returned to the nearest consecrated ground of their homeland for burial.

Blunty's Mill

The first interesting find seen on the left as you enter Kirk Yetholm is the former blanket mill built of roughly coursed stone. Part of an L-plan group, which includes a mill manager's house and chimney at the north end, the range to the south of the mill features a lintel inscribed 'HKAB 1743' (its date), and also retains some interesting glazing patterns, each window being divided into narrow vertical strips containing small, overlapping panes of glass. The riverside gable retains its original lift hoist, whilst the opposite gable retains the bell that once summoned mill workers. The mill was a major manufacturer of blankets until well into the twentieth century.

Kirk Yetholm

The St Cuthbert's Way landscape becomes significantly more associated with the saint to whom it is dedicated after leaving Kirk Yetholm, the mid-point of the route. Many of the interesting architectural features encountered are major sites of the Anglo-Saxon kingdom, or are related to the continual memory attributed to this important era of history, which survived well into the medieval period. Furthermore, the remote and largely uninhabited landscape that follows is dotted with prehistoric monuments. The border crossing from Scotland into England is a short distance from Kirk Yetholm: in translation 'Yetholm' means 'the gate town'.

The church for the twin villages and parish of Yetholm stands on a site in use since David I's apportionment of parishes. Built by Robert Brown in 1837 to replace a small thatched structure, it is now a rectangular-plan neo-Gothic church of local whinstone and sandstone. Its medieval bell from the original building is still in use. As the nearest burial ground to Flodden, the graveyard is also believed to contain the graves of officers fallen in battle.

The Chapel of St Etheldreda

A more interesting site on the way out of Kirk Yetholm is that of the now-vanished Chapel of St Etheldreda, who was a contemporary of St Cuthbert. Look left before crossing the Halter Burn, close to Yetholm Mains at Humbleton Sike, and the site where the chapel once stood can just be made out, at the foot of the hill, where the burn crosses the English border. It was marked on the OS maps until recently.

Etheldreda was an East Anglian princess who, following the death of her first husband, was given by her father to Ecfrith, King of Northumbria. According to the Venerable Bede, as a result she took a vow of perpetual virginity. After twelve years of a celibate marriage, she managed to persuade her husband to let her join the convent at St Abbs. There she remained for some time before leaving for Ely, Cambridgeshire, where she eventually became the abbess. Her shrine now stands in Ely Cathedral.

The Stob Stones

The Stob Stones (or 'Stanes', to the Scots) are two large boulders, one standing, the other recumbent, east of the hill fort at Green Humbleton. While now firmly in Roxburghshire in Scotland, the Border boundary wall is to their east, but for a time the stones were actually on the Border line itself. One measures 4½ft (1.4m) wide at the base by 1½ft (46cm) thick and 5½ft (1.7m) high. The other now lies across its original bed, 18ft (5½m) to the south; it is 5ft (1.5m) long, 3ft (90cm) wide and 2ft (60cm) thick. Both stones are of native porphyry and are locally referred to as the 'Gypsy Stobs', from the tradition that the kings of the Yetholm gypsies were crowned here. A further suggestion is that they are boundary markers, set up on the line of the Border. If this is correct they may be of early medieval date, as their location sits on the section of the Border that the English commissioners of 1222 regarded as fixed.

Eccles Cairn, Coldsmouth Hill and Burnt/Green Humbleton

After moving through and over the border, Eccles Cairn lies just off the Way, to the north. The name 'Eccles' suggests its early Christian origins, from the word 'eglés', the term that ancient Britons and Picts used for the Latin ecclesia or church. While it is uncertain what the cairn's function was, it has been proposed as a former gathering place/assembly point, or a piece of church property.

In this area other hills are prominent, such as Coldsmouth to the north, which is capped with Bronze Age burial cairns, and to the south, or Scottish side of the border, are the two Humbleton Iron Age hill forts, the ramparts of which can clearly be seen at certain times of the day or year. It should also be noted that many of the Cheviots are crowned by late prehistoric hillforts.

Trowupburn Farm

Heading east past Eilsdon Burn, Trowupburn Farm is then reached by a detour of 2km south up the Heather Burn. This site was a grange or farmstead of Melrose Abbey in the early medieval period. The abbey's lay brothers worked all over the Cheviot Hills as sheep farmers – the abbey was one of the largest wool producers in Europe, and this is where its considerable wealth derived. Earthwork remains also exist here of a Romano-British enclosed settlement consisting of two house platforms within a circular enclosure scooped into a hillside.

The hills to the right are Little and Great Hetha – again, Iron Age hill forts sit on top of each one. Next, leave the main trail just past Hethpool Linn waterfalls – the medieval pele tower there is also worth a quick visit – and follow the river round the west side of Westhill (a further hill fort lies here). The track then bears east to Kirknewton.

Kirknewton Church

Next on the route, below the large and ancient hill fort of Yeavering Bell, lies the community of Kirknewton. This area includes the interesting Church of St Gregory, and within a mile is Yeavering, said to have been the centre of the Anglo-Saxon kingdom of Northumbria, where the palace and council chambers of King Edwin were located. It is also believed that St Paulinus came to the area in 627CE, preaching the Christian faith and baptizing the locals in the nearby River Glen.

Dedicated to Gregory the Great, the pope who sent Augustine of Canterbury to England in the sixth century to convert Anglo-Saxons, the current Anglican church has parts dating to the eleventh century, while the chancel and south transept are of fifteenth-century origin. The stone carving of the Adoration of the Magi, to the left of the left chancel arch, dates from the twelfth century. There has been speculation that the Magi are in fact wearing kilts, but as these are more attributed to nineteenth-century fashion, it is more likely they are surcoats. The walls of the roughly dressed stone chancel are intentionally very thick to withstand Border warfare – in the 1430s the Bishop of Durham licensed the vicar to say Mass in any safe place in the parish. Josephine Butler, champion of social reform for women in the Victorian era, and after whom the college at Durham University is named, is also buried here.

GEFRIN MEMORIAL

Roughly half a mile (1km) east of Kirknewton, at the foot of Yeavering Bell, you can also see the Gefrin memorial: an 8ft (2.4m) stone wall, behind which the royal palace of Ad Gefrin/Yeavering is said to have stood. The detached farm here is thought to have formed part of King Edwin's seventh century Anglian Palace when it was excavated by Brian Hope Taylor in the 1950s. This palace of the Northumbrian kings, as mentioned by Bede, was sited several metres to the north-east. Few external features

Yeavering Bell. DAVID ROSS

of any age exist within the farm building, and so it is proposed that the current building has no real connection with King Edwin. Nothing survives of the palace except a monument and an empty field.

Yeavering and the Cheviot Hills

From Old Yeavering, head south to rejoin the trail, but before continuing along the Way, a few hundred metres to the south-west is Kirknewton Tors or Torleehouse. Torleehouse was originally known as Tarleazes, meaning 'a clearing on a hill'. The round cairn south of Torleehouse is well preserved and is believed to have been a funerary monument dating to the Bronze Age. These were constructed as stone mounds, each covering a single or multiple burials. In some cases the cairn was surrounded by a ditch.

Yeavering Bell is the largest hill fort in the Cheviots, covering over 13 acres (5ha). It featured an important Iron Age royal settlement, with stone ramparts 10ft (3m) thick, and inside, around 125 huts. The large, ditched enclosure around the Bell's eastern summit is later than the hut platforms that surround it. The hill fort is usually thought to date from the latter half of the first millennium BC, although it could be earlier, such as late Bronze Age. The word 'Yeavering' comes from the Brittonic words 'gafr' and 'bryn' meaning 'goat hill' – around this area are many feral goats.

Wooler

On the way into Wooler there is also the prehistoric Kettle's Camp (hill fort) and, close by, the Pin Well, so called due to the tradition that young women would throw bent pins down the well on fair days in the hope that this would bring them good luck in finding a suitable husband. Overhanging the well is a rock called the King's Chair: legend has it that a king sat on the rock and directed a battle on the plain below.

The market town of Wooler in the Glendale district has a long history of frequent raids by marauding Scots but primarily throughout the fourteenth to sixteenth centuries, and was well known for its livestock markets, held at the Mart on Berwick Road. Little of the past is visible, since the town suffered two destructive fires in 1722 and 1862. However, St Mary's Church, built of local Doddington stone and completed in 1765 (although it has faced extensive restoration since), is one of the oldest buildings in the area; in fact, there have been churches on the site since the twelfth century, as remains were discovered on the north side of the church.

Wooler was one of the baronies into which Northumberland was divided by the Normans; it was held by the de Muschamp family, who built a castle here. This site is today known as 'Green Castle', and is found on the Way just at the south-west entrance to the town. A further fortified tower was erected on the mound at the bottom of Church Street; known locally as the 'Tory', it is identified by a large Celtic cross.

Weetwood and Doddington Moor

Leaving Wooler and the Way, a short detour may be made to the south through Weetwood Moor, which features several Bronze Age cup and ring marks (rock-carved symbols).

The Way then leads directly past the grounds of Weetwood Hall, a mid-eighteenth to early nineteenth-century house incorporating a former tower house or pele tower thought to date back to the thirteenth century. Weetwood Hall also allegedly occupies the site of a deserted medieval village.

The route then moves on to Doddington Moor, which is rich in Bronze and Iron Age settlements such as forts, camps, earthworks and a stone circle. However, there are also some extremely captivating sites that relate directly to St Cuthbert – this is the beginning of the Cuthbertine-strong portion of the route.

Horton Castle

The Way now takes you directly to West Horton, the site of an important Borders fortified house, which stood on the site of what are now outbuildings of Low Horton Farm. A licence to crenellate the building survives from 1292, but the tower itself was demolished in 1809; all that survives is a slight hollow where the course of the moat ran.

The castle was owned by many families including, notably, the Monbouchers and Harbottles, before being purchased by the Delaval family. It was last occupied by two sisters of Admiral George Delaval (owner of Seaton Delaval Hall), who died in 1723.

The road and Way route from West Horton follows the course of the Devil's Causeway for around 300 yards (275m): this is part of the old Roman Road that linked Corbridge to Tweedmouth.

St Cuthbert's Cave

The Way then passes through St Cuthbert's Cave Wood towards the cave itself, perhaps one of the most evocative sites of the entire route. The site is owned and managed by the National Trust. A clear path leads down to the large natural sandstone outcrop located within the dense wood; it is said to be where the monks of Lindisfarne stopped on their journey when fleeing the invading Danes, bearing the exhumed body of Cuthbert, in 875CE. There is little here by way of physical monuments, but the setting itself is so incredibly dramatic that it is worth spending time here.

The outcrop is supported by a pillar, while an area in front is contained within an enclosure formed by an earthen bank – this may relate to its later use as a nineteenth-century lambing pen. Nonetheless, a natural cross can be seen on one of the sandstone boulders opposite the cave's mouth, with a niche cut to the left of it, perhaps to hold a lamp or an icon. This natural formation will have added to the sense of the sacred, and attracted the spiritually minded over the last thousand or so years, and quite possibly Cuthbert himself.

Known more locally as Cuddy's Cove (Cuddy is an affectionate term for Cuthbert), the cave is reputed to be one of the places where Cuthbert tended his sheep as a child, and where he lived as a hermit in the seventh century, in-between spells on the Farne Islands and Lindisfarne.

The association with Cuthbert means that sanctity has been imbued within the cave, and given the presence of the cross, the cave's remote location, the evocative setting and the constructed niche, it seems likely that the site was a place of devotion in the medieval period. It was likely a stopping station for pilgrims so they could be physically present in a place where Cuthbert resided in both life and in death, while en route to their final destination at Lindisfarne.

After your visit to the cave, you will then experience your first sight of the final destination of Holy Island/Lindisfarne. Along the hill above St Cuthbert's Cave, between Greensheen Hill and Cockenheugh, the island can be glimpsed along with its castle, as can Bamburgh, Budle Bay and the Farne Islands, where Cuthbert lived until his death. From here, the track known as Dolly Gibson's Lonnen, an ancient green road, follows the edge of Kyloe Old Wood; in the nineteenth century the wood was owned by the Leyland family of nearby Haggerston Castle. Within the grounds of East Kyloe Farm, a single tall tower can be seen – all that remains of a fortified manor house dating from 1345. This is the lower part of a tower first mentioned in about 1450, and described in 1560 as being 'in good repair'. It is roughly rectangular in plan and has 2.5m thick stone walls.

Pilgrim's Path across The Causeway to Lindisfarne. AUTHOR

HAGGERSTON CASTLE

From here, it would certainly be possible to make a large deviation north from the route in order to visit Haggerston Castle, and the nearby village of Ancroft, between Berwick-upon-Tweed and Lindisfarne, which also features several sites of both historic and architectural interest. By the eighteenth century, Haggerston Castle had been extended into a large residence, but it was abandoned in 1930, and now only a tall tower remains. The grounds have since been turned into a holiday park.

Islandshire

Returning to the Way, when following the green road, you will enter the ancient district of Islandshire. Originally, this district comprised Lindisfarne/Holy Island, plus five parishes on the mainland, and part of the County Palatine of Durham, until 1844 when it was amalgamated into Northumberland. This was essentially the coastal area that sustained the needs of the monks of Lindisfarne, which is why both Dolly Gibson's Lonnen and the track from Fenwick Granary to the coast, known as Fisher's Back Row, are believed to be of ancient origin, supposedly used by the monks to passage peat.

Fenwick/The Causeway

The Way next takes you across the A1 and through Fenwick, where the granary buildings and dovecot are of interest, although currently dilapidated. A short detour to the east would take you to the former site of Fenham monastic grange, owned by Lindisfarne

Priory, which survives as an earthwork. The site lies on sloping ground leading down to the coast, and has clear views across the sea to Holy Island. The monument includes the remains of the manor house that was surrounded by a moat and retaining wall, in addition to a series of enclosures where service and agricultural buildings once stood. Part of the mill race and a few structural remains of the medieval Fenham Mill (also thought to have been owned by the Holy Island monks) also survive.

From here you make your way to perhaps the most spiritual and evocative part of the journey, where you can literally trace the steps of pilgrims past: the causeway road to Holy Island.

The Causeway may be crossed safely at times of low tide (*see* Appendix) and is the shortest route to the island, crossing the bridge over South Low and over the sands to the village. This route is called the Pilgrims Path, as it has been the route followed by pilgrims to the island since Cuthbert's death. It is marked the entire way across the causeway by a line of timber poles from the bridge to Chare Ends, which is the entrance to the village. The causeway road goes straight towards and across the nature reserve known as the Snook, and enters the village of Lindisfarne from the north.

This cannot be classed as the route's end point or final station, however, because on the island there are many historic pilgrimage sites to visit.

The End of the Journey: Holy Island/Lindisfarne

Although the shrine/tomb of St Cuthbert is no longer extant, the sanctity of the locations in which he lived, died and was first interred are ingrained within the land and structures of this island. Nonetheless, today it is largely a 'tourist trap'. In the nineteenth century, fishing, two quarries and a lime kiln comprised the major industries. The remains of the lime industry can be found along the north of the island, while a network of associated tramways established between the quarries, kilns and jetties lies on the west.

Lindisfarne, or Holy Island as it is known, is claimed to be 'the holiest place in all of England', and is certainly one of the most famous Christian sites in Western Europe. Indeed, St Aidan founded his monastery here in 635CE, and thus the Christian message was established and sent out into the pagan north.

The atmosphere on the island is perhaps enough for most visitors today – it simply has a most holy feeling, so isolated, peaceful and entrenched with history; there is a real sense of engagement with the Anglo-Saxon world itself, rather than just a connection with St Cuthbert. This is furthered by the fact that the glorious illuminated Lindisfarne Gospels were created here around 700CE.

Today, visitors flock to the current twelfth-century Lindisfarne Priory to see the original resting place of St Cuthbert, built on the site of the seventh-century church where his tomb/shrine once stood. However, following the Viking raids in the ninth century, his body was moved from the island. While there was an expectation that a cult would involve relics in order to be considered authentic, at Lindisfarne these appear

Lindisfarne Priory. AUTHOR

St Cuthbert's Cross. AUTHOR

to have been architectural and spatial in nature. The cult here centred around the original resting place of the saint within the priory church, and its complement of dependent sacred sites embodied in the various retreats once used by him.

Between *c.*1122 and 1150 a new church was erected on Lindisfarne, a project organized by a Durham monk named Ædward, to provide a suitably elaborate setting for the original burial place of St Cuthbert, and also another focus for the cult in the hope of attracting pilgrims north. Once Cuthbert's coffin was removed, a cenotaph was erected in memory of the sanctified spot in the nave.

ST CUTHBERT'S ISLE

Before moving to Inner Farne, Cuthbert retreated to an island some 600ft (180m) south-west of Holy Island, later to be used by Cuthbert's successor, Ædberht, as a retreat. The island can be reached

St Cuthbert's Isle. AUTHOR

by walking around the priory, and up on to the grass mound of land situated to its rear known as the Heugh. Identified now by a small wooden cross, the small island's surviving remains include a T-shaped chapel consisting of a room divided into two compartments, creating a possible cell and oratory, and a north-west circular mound associated with Cuthbert's original circular cell. The chapel foundations appear to be primarily medieval in date, not contemporary to Cuthbert's lifetime, but it is likely they were rebuilt/restored for the purposes of medieval pilgrimage, as a 'tourist attraction' for pilgrims to visit and observe where the saint had lived and worshipped – which is still the case to this very day.

Along the section of land known as the Heugh lies a series of small ruins. Of these, the most notable are the rectangular foundations of what is thought to have been a watchtower –

The Heugh, watchtower. AUTHOR

although it is difficult to ascertain the original function of the building as the Heugh contains many structures and earthworks, including, on the eastern end, further ruins also commonly referred to as a watchtower. This speculation derives from an account by Bede, which makes reference to a similar structure from which the Lindisfarne monks watched across the sea for news of Cuthbert's death on Inner Farne. A vivid view of Farne can be obtained from the 'watchtower' here, raising the possibility that this is the same building recounted by Bede. The structure is also known as the Chapel of the Lamp and is thought to be the site of an early form of lighthouse dating from the fourteenth century, operated originally by the priors. Several of the other structures on the Heugh may have been small chapels – thus the entire series may have served as stations, shrines or stages comparable to the pilgrimage rituals of Irish monastic complexes (i.e. a 'created' route attraction).

ST MARY'S PARISH CHURCH

In the southwest corner of the village, next to the priory, is a further site of interest. The Grade I Listed St Mary's Church, though mainly twelfth/thirteenth century, was built on the site of the original monastery founded by Aidan in 635CE, and indeed parts of the structure date back to the seventh century. Interesting architectural details include the thirteenth-century south door; the north arcade that features round piers and capitals of c.1200, along with three round arches with banded pink and white voussoirs; the remains of the Saxon chancel arch visible above the south arcade; a trefoiled piscina in the south aisle; and, finally, a large medieval grave cover set in the chancel's north wall.

Outside the church, the socket of a large stone cross stands towards the east. This is known as the 'Petting Stone', as tradition has it that any bride who jumps over it and is helped by a fisherman on either side, is sure of a happy marriage.

LINDISFARNE CASTLE

Built largely during the reign of Henry VIII, Lindisfarne Castle is a small fort of sandstone and whinstone, situated on an outcrop of rock known as Beblowe Craig. In 1549 a gun platform was constructed on the craig, replaced by a fort in the 1560s. This replaced an earlier lookout tower, probably one of the bulwarks built to defend the island in 1542. Following the Act of Union in 1603, the risk of attack from Scotland was removed, but in its place there was a perceived threat from Dutch privateers on the east coast. To help combat this, a fort was constructed in 1671 on the Heugh. The new fort complemented Beblowe fort in the defence of the harbour.

Occupying a dramatic position, the castle comprises an irregular polygonal plan on three levels of former batteries. Following a significant period of decay, in 1902 it was converted into a house through an intensive restorative programme undertaken by Sir Edwin Lutyens for Edward Hudson, founder of *Country Life* magazine. While the exterior was preserved, Lutyens transformed the interior into a stately retreat. The castle is now owned by the National Trust.

St Mary's Parish Church, Lindisfarne. AUTHOR

Lindisfarne Castle. AUTHOR

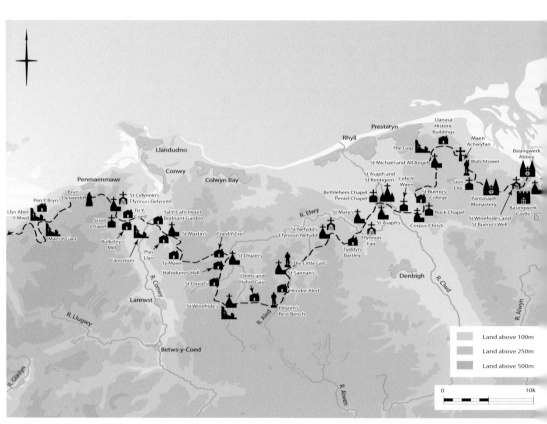

Map of North Wales Pilgrim's Way: the north-east half. JIM BRIGHTMAN

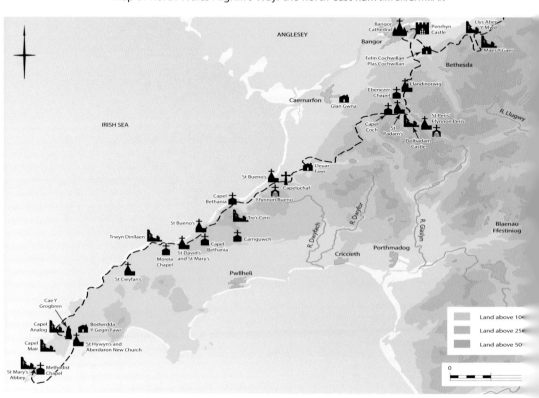

Map of North Wales Pilgrim's Way: the south-west half. JIM BRIGHTMAN

CHAPTER THREE

The North Wales Pilgrim's Way
(Holywell to Bardsey Island)

Inspired by a pilgrimage to Santiago de Compostela in Spain, this re-established route was designed and inaugurated in 2011 by Cadw's Heritage Tourism Project; it was partially funded by the European Regional Development Fund through the Welsh government.

The Pilgrim's Way runs for 130 miles (209km) from Basingwerk Abbey near Holywell on the River Dee, to the remote Bardsey Island which lies at the tip of the Llyn Peninsula, the resting place of 20,000 saints, and where St Cadfan began building a monastery in the sixth century. It follows sites predominantly connected with St Winefride, one of only two Welsh saints recognized by Rome, and who, according to legend, was beheaded and then brought back to life by St Beuno. The trail starts at the ruins of Basingwerk Abbey, Holywell, passing St Winefride's Well – the shrine of St Winefride around which Holywell was founded – and across to Ynys Enlli (Bardsey Island). Largely western in its approach, it passes through many medieval villages with churches as well as trailside icons, ancient stones, hill forts and, at St Asaph, a cathedral.

Its reinstatement as a national route arose from its alleged links with the Romans and pilgrims over the centuries. Pilgrims have certainly visited the four primary sacred sites of North Wales, three of which had established associations with the Welsh saints, Beuno and Winefride: Bardsey Island, Clynnog Fawr, Gwytherin and Holywell.

Bardsey Island was an important place of pilgrimage, given that it was known as the 'island of 20,000 saints'. In fact, the Pope even declared that three pilgrimages to Bardsey were considered the equivalent, in salvational terms, of a single journey to Rome, which is why it is sometimes referred to as the 'Rome of Britain'. It would appear that several routes allowed medieval pilgrims to visit the remote island. The name 'Porth Meudwy' (the site of the current crossing to Bardsey) suggests strongly that this was where medieval boats sailed across, and 'Bodermid' ('ermid' meaning 'hermit') associated with several farms near the cliff top confirm this link. But the shortest route was from the mainland to the island. Directly opposite Bardsey Sound (or 'Swnt Enlli', the stretch of water between the tip of the Llyn peninsular and the island) from Ffynnon Fair is Bae'r Nany, where experienced boatmen say the currents allow a crossing of the Swnt at any time of the day, using the coves. It is therefore very likely that pilgrims crossed to Enlli from Ogof y Gath, the inlet sheltering Ffynnon Fair.

The start of the route is just as noteworthy. Situated on the North Wales coast in the Greenfield Valley, close to Chester and the Cistercian Basingwerk Priory, Winefride's Well at Holywell is of national, if not international, importance. The only shrine in Britain to survive the Reformation, largely due to the fact that it attracted a fairly uninterrupted stream of pilgrims from its founding in the late seventh century, and thus the offerings were so valuable that even the chapel was not destroyed by Henry VIII, but rather leased out. Since the late Victorian era it has provided the town with the epithet of 'The Lourdes of Wales', its name deriving from an anglicized version of the original Welsh name 'Trêffynnon' ('Town of the Well').

While certainly possessing links with past pilgrimage, the route acts as a celebration of the heritage of the Celtic saints it embodies, as much as it conveys the history of the area.

The History of the Welsh Saints

Often referred to as the 'land of the saints', similar to the south-west, sanctity is embedded within the Welsh landscape, which is rife with various traditions of local saint cults. Similar to Cornwall, the majority of these saints had their roots firmly embedded in the communities in which they lived out their lives, though here there were two exceptions: St David and St Winefride.

This route begins at the site dedicated to St Winefride (this is the anglicized version of the Latin 'Wenefreda', the Welsh being 'Gwenfrewy'). In life she was very much a local saint, yet her area of venerated locality is significantly larger than those of her compatriots. She was a seventh-century Welsh noblewoman who was martyred following her refusal of the advances of a suitor, the king's son, Caradog; he decapitated Winefride and her head rolled downhill, and where it came to rest a spring erupted out of the ground. The site became known as St Winefride's Well, and gained notoriety for its healing properties after Winefride's head was miraculously rejoined to her body by her uncle, St Beuno (or St Mungo, in Scottish dedications).

Winefride lived for another fifteen years, moving to Gwytherin to become a nun of the abbey of which her aunt was abbess. There she remained until her death in 660CE. Her cult became authenticated following accounts of miraculous tales of healing after pilgrims had prayed to the saint or taken the waters of the well – both Holywell and Gwytherin became popular places of pilgrimage.

Throughout its history, and despite its local origins, Winefride's shrine was often visited by royalty. By the early fifteenth century it had gained so much attention across the Marchlands that her feast day became a major pilgrimage event throughout the rest of the isle, so much so that Margaret Beaufort, the mother of the then monarch, Henry VII, commissioned the upgrading of the well-house, at great expense, into the elaborate Perpendicular Gothic structure still extant today.

Aside from the well complex deriving from her miraculous 'recapitation', the most significant sites associated with Winefride are the cathedral seal of St Asaph, and her shrine at Shrewsbury Abbey – one of the pilgrims cured of an illness at her well was a monk from Shrewsbury, hence her relics were taken there. The shrine was destroyed during the Reformation. Thus, while for this book St Winefride's holy well site will be referred to as her shrine, her relics were not in fact kept there (although allegedly her finger bone still is).

As mentioned above, the actual well has its origins as a (natural) spring, which erupted as a result of Winefride's decapitation and subsequent healing, and so was seen as a holy place instilled with sanctity as the site where her head landed. Visible beneath the water is an additional feature of reverence: the stone upon which St Beuno is said to have stood whilst saying farewell to St Winefride. To the east is a large statue of St Winefride, an image-shrine for the pilgrims' venerations and their votive offerings of candles and prayers.

The most significant building within the complex of St Winefride's Well is the vaulted well-house and bathing pool where these events supposedly took place. Also of note are the remains of the fifteenth-century St Winefride's Chapel, which sits above the well-house; the eighteenth-century St James' Church, which is a rebuilding of the seventh-century church founded by St Beuno and originally dedicated to St Winefride; and a mile to the north, the Cistercian Basingwerk Abbey, which possessed a historical link to the well complex, as it served as a hospitium or guest house for journeying pilgrims, which was staffed by the monks who maintained the well and used it to power their mill.

Basingwerk Castle also owes some of its prevalence and survival to Winefride's cult. Firstly, Henry II rebuilt the castle during his visit to St Winefride's Well in 1157, though following arrest by Dafydd ap Owain, Prince of Gwynedd, the castle was recaptured and burnt. It was rebuilt by Ranulf III, Earl of Chester, to protect the pilgrims arriving at the well, and it continued in this role until it was made redundant by the construction of a stone castle at Flint by Edward I. A well-site dedicated to St Beuno, now overgrown, lies up the side of the valley adjacent to the road leading down to Winefride's Well.

Yet it was not only the sites associated with St Winefride that were celebrated and venerated along this Way. Once again, as in Cornwall, north-east Wales had a range of pilgrim destinations. Winefride's familial connections with St Beuno were also revered, including, as noted above, his well-site at Holywell, while the land portion of the route passes St Beuno's Church in Clynnog Fawr on the Llyn Peninsula and was therefore a key stopping place for pilgrims heading for Bardsey Island.

St Asaph, one of the first stations along the Pilgrim's Way, was also seen as a site of significance: the cathedral contained St Asaph's relics, and the area has notable links with sites associated with St Winefride, as the diocese of St Asaph encompassed a large portion of north-eastern Wales, including Holywell. Established by St Kentigern in the sixth century, the diocese contained many primary shrines, but St Winefride's Well remained its most celebrated cult centre up to and following the Reformation. St Asaph lies to the west of Holywell in the hundred area of Rhuddlan, and although it never saw the same number of pilgrims as Holywell, it was equally as renowned for its cathedral, which is the smallest in Britain. Furthermore, the town was the established ecclesiastical hub of Denbighshire, and the cathedral was the focus of the Church in north-east Wales throughout the medieval period.

As such, pilgrimages between St Asaph and Holywell were not uncommon in the medieval period. The archdeacon and chronicler, Gerald of Wales, describes his journeys to the sites, while the Welsh route network was featured in the itinerary of Edward I's travels. The 'Deva-Varae' Roman Road leads broadly from St Asaph to the Greenfield Valley where St Winifride's Well lies and so it is likely that the road allowed many travellers to pass through the region with some ease and on towards the Dee Estuary and Chester. St Asaph's name is also found throughout Denbighshire and neighbouring Flintshire, at places such as Llanasa ('Asa's Church'), Pantasa ('Asa's Hollow'), Ffynnon Asa ('Asa's Well') and Onen Asa ('Asa's Ash-tree'), indicating his cult was venerated throughout north-east Wales.

An Overview of the Route

This route is characterized by its length and, in certain areas, by its relative remoteness, often stretching across large swathes of open countryside with few sites of interest. The content of this chapter therefore varies slightly from the others, as it includes more detailed directions of the route itself, in addition to descriptions of the key sites encountered along the Way.

This long-distance path starts at Basingwerk Abbey and heads to St Winefride's Well in Holywell; it then ascends the hill upon which St Beuno performed his miracle. Pantasaph Monastery is next, and from here begins a series of walks across the countryside, including a hill said to include a Roman Pharos. The mysterious stone cross of Maen Achwyfan ends this part of the journey and begins the next, which heads to the twin villages of Berthengham and Trelogan. From here, the route heads to Llanasa and the Church of Saints Asaph & Cyndeyrn; it then runs through a series of tracks and lanes before ascending to the summit of The Gop.

From the summit, descend into the village of Trelawnyd and St Michael's Church. Follow the lane past the church then cross the bridge and take the track on your left. The Church of Corpus Christi in the village of Tremeirchion begins this section of the route. A particularly historical portion of the route follows the Clwydian Way here, terminating at the Cathedral of St Asaph. Continue into the village of Llannefydd, where farm tracks and fields begin the next section into the community of Rhyd yr Arian.

The route is once again on the Clwydian Way and in Conwy county; continue to the village of Llansannan and its church. The village of Gwytherin is the end of the next section, and the beginning of a possible two routes. The primary path followed by historical pilgrims would no doubt be the one that runs through the valley of Pennant, past the abbey where St Winefride spent her final years, and finishing at Pandy Tudur. The path then goes on to Hafodunos Hall.

This section is particularly attractive: after the second pilgrim sculpture, the route descends through a picturesque wooded gorge, and heads into the village of Llangernyw. It then meanders to the village of Eglwysbach, and continues to Rowen and its chapel there. The woods here take you along an ancient 'coffin path', which leads eventually to the little church at Llangelynin. It then joins the Wales Coast Path and continues on to the complex of stone circles above the town of Penmaenmawr. After visiting the stone circles, return to the Wales Coast Path to go down to Llanfairfechan. Continue ahead on the waymarked North Wales path to the entrance to Nant y Coed Nature Reserve.

The path eventually reaches a large stone at the Roman road and then the forest at Abergwyngregyn, with the village about a kilometre down the road. It passes several waterfalls, and then climbs until it arrives at a seat with wide views over Ynys Mon, the Great Orme and beyond to the north-west of England. Bangor City Centre and its cathedral ends the next part of the route. This part of the path goes over Bangor mountain, then continues through a series of villages including Tregarth, Deiniolen and Llanberis, and then on to Waunfawr. Penygroes to Clynnog Fawr is the next section, then on to Clynnog Fawr Church. Leaving the village, the Way passes Ffynnon Beuno – or St Beuno's Well – and continues to Trefor, 4 miles (6km) ahead.

Follow the coastal path waymarkers from the village towards two possible routes: the inland coast route leads you down, past Ffynnon Sanctaidd, to Pystyll and St Beuno's Church, while the coastal path winds its way down towards the beach – from there it leads across to St Beuno's Church (at Pystyll), which comes into sight as you descend. This is now the Wales Coast Path with new waymark posts.

There are also two possible routes from the next village, Nefyn. The longer, more challenging route takes you along the beach to Porth Dinllaen and around the headland: you can walk the entire coastal edge via the Wales Coast Path to Abergeirch. The shorter route follows the Wales Coast Path but plunges down to Abergeirch.

The route then follows another magnificent coastal path for a good 3 miles (5km) to Ty-hen; from here there is a footpath to the village of Tudweiliog. You can then either walk along the Wales Coast Path around the tip of the Llŷn Peninsula, with excellent views over to Bardsey Island, until you reach Aberdaron, or take the direct route to Aberdaron. Following the coast path, you should be able to see Ynys Enlli/Bardsey Island with its lighthouse and the thirteenth-century Augustinian Abbey of St Mary's.

The ferry for Ynys Enlli (Bardsey Island) leaves from Porth Meudwy, which is 1.2 miles (1.8km) from Aberdaron by the coast path, or 1.7 miles (2.7km) by road.

Start of the Route: Basingwerk Abbey

The route begins at Basingwerk Abbey. Substantial remains can be seen of the Cistercian abbey, which was founded in *c*.1131–32 by Ranulf II, Earl of Chester, as a daughterhouse of Savigny Abbey in western Normandy. In 1147, however, the Savigniac Order merged with the Cistercians, and in 1157 Basingwerk was affiliated

Basingwerk Abbey. MARTIN LOCKER

with Buildwas in Shropshire, also a former Savigniac house. Much of the plan at Basingwerk follows the standard Cistercian layout, which reinforced and incorporated the two communities it housed, i.e. lay servants and monastics.

During the thirteenth-century Welsh wars, Basingwerk's sympathies lay with the English; in fact, the abbey provided a chaplain for Flint Castle. It was dissolved in 1536, and the remains passed to the Mostyns of Talacre (Welsh baronets). Only a little of the twelfth-century walling survives, around the cloister and in the east range. Much of the fabric visible today dates from the early thirteenth century, when the buildings were refurbished and extended. These included the church, with its two south side chapels in each transept, the sacristy to its south and, beyond this, the chapter house with its vaulted eastward extension, which still survives. There are also the novices' lodgings or monks' day room, and a warming house that was added to the end of the range in the fifteenth century. On the south side of the cloister the impressive frater or dining-hall dates from the thirteenth century.

Greenfield Valley

Next, leave the abbey by walking towards the old village school, and then left up Greenfield Valley. Historically, the valley was a busy place, employing hundreds of people in both its copper factories and mills. Within the valley is Heritage Park, a 1.5 mile (2.5km) long park that follows the course of the Holywell Stream between the town and the estuary of the River Dee; the most steeply-graded conventional standard-gauge railway in the UK once ran through the park. Here, in addition to St

St Winefride's Well. MARTIN CRAMPIN

Winefride's Holy Well and Basingwerk Abbey, lie the remains of a number of historic mill buildings. More recently, cottages, farmhouses and even the Victorian school have been moved here stone by stone from other locations, and carefully reconstructed and furnished to appear as they might have looked in the past.

ST WINEFRIDE HALT

You then reach the site of the former St Winefride Halt. This small station was built for the benefit of visitors to the holy well and workers at the nearby mills. A few remnants of the station are still visible.

ST WINEFRIDE'S WELL

Take the footpath out of the valley to the main road and to St Winefride's Well. With its holy well and chapel dating to the early sixteenth century, the site was actually a place of pilgrimage from at least 1115. The buildings extant today were commissioned by Lady Margaret Beaufort in the first years of the sixteenth century as a two-storey structure in thanksgiving for the victory of her son Henry Tudor (VII) over Richard III at the Battle of Bosworth.

The spring rises in a well chamber within the lower open crypt, and flows out into the large exterior bathing pool. Above the crypt is St Winefride's Chapel. The buildings are not of the typical Welsh style as they are constructed of dressed sandstone and in the English Perpendicular. The chapel is also battlemented with intricate corbels with fine carvings of animals. Finally, the Victorian former custodian's house has been converted to a museum of the Holywell pilgrimage.

Church of St James, Holywell. MARTIN CRAMPIN

CHURCH OF ST JAMES

Next to the chapel is the Church of St James, which was much restored in the eighteenth century. It may be situated on the site of the original seventh-century church of St Beuno; there is evidence of a church at Holywell before the Norman Conquest. The church was dedicated to St Winifred for many centuries, but after extensive rebuilding in 1769, it was re-dedicated to St James the Apostle. The tower is thought to be fourteenth century – its windows are Perpendicular in style. The aisles and galleries were added in 1769–70; there was further restoration in 1884–5, when a semi-circular apse was added. There is a late thirteenth-century (headless) effigy of a priest, and seventeenth- and eighteenth-century monuments. The churchyard is shared with St Winefride's Chapel, and overlooks the site of the Holy Well.

BASINGWERK CASTLE

Bryn y Castell, or Basingwerk Castle, is a motte consisting of a mutilated mound, less than 6ft (1.8m) high, located at the north end of a steep-sided promontory directly above the church. This could be the site of Treffynnon Castle, reportedly built by the Earl of Chester in 1210. The adjacent house of the same name was constructed in 1704. Suggestions are that it was either built by the Normans in the eleventh or early twelfth century within an earlier Saxon fortress, or it originated as a frontier stronghold and was destroyed at some point prior to 1155, during the reign of King Stephen.

Pantasaph Monastery, Holywell. MARTIN CRAMPIN

St Beuno's Well

After visiting St Winefride's Well, take the track opposite. The hill to the left is the site where St Beuno performed his miracle; there was a well dedicated to him here. St Beuno's Well formerly consisted of a pool of water, partially enclosed by a stone wall; now there is little more than a large, irregular hollow.

The Way is then largely dominated by open countryside, passing the edge of a disused quarry and on to Pantasaph Monastery.

Pantasaph Monastery

Pantasaph is a Roman Catholic complex of buildings, comprising the Church of St David's and the Franciscan friary. On the hill behind are landscaped stations of the Cross, laid out in the mid to late nineteenth century, in the form of a zig-zag path up through the wooded hillside with fourteen stations in alcoves. From the top of the hill is a view of the Irish Sea.

Pantasaph is first recorded in 1536, when it was referred to as 'Pant Assay'; at this time it was possessed by the Cistercian Abbey of Basingwerk (founded *c*.1131). In 1240 Prince Dafydd ap Llywelyn granted both the church at Holywell, and the well-shrine of St Winefride, to the abbey. The monks likely named the area after St Asaph, the local patron. However, by 1537, the abbey had been dissolved, and the last abbot, Nicholas Pennant, made it his business to distribute the abbey lands among his relations. Thus, the lands of Pantasaph remained in the Pennant family for 309 years until 1846, when the sole heiress conveyed them by marriage to Rudolph, later the 8th Earl of Denbigh.

The Church of St David was dedicated to St David, with St Asaph as a secondary patron, and was opened on 13 October 1852.

The first community of Franciscan Capuchin fathers arrived soon after at Denbigh House, Pantasaph, adjacent to the friary. Between 1858 and 1865, the construction of the friary took place, although some work continued for years afterwards. By 1866, Pantasaph constituted a novitiate, a mother house for the Capuchin Franciscan Order in Great Britain.

Sïon Lloc

Further along the route, a short detour to the west takes you to a small Welsh Methodist chapel called Sïon Lloc, which holds an annual plygain – a traditional Welsh service of music and worship that takes place early on Christmas morning. The chapel was built as a Wesleyan place of worship in 1829, then rebuilt sixty years later. 'Lloc' is the Welsh word for a livestock enclosure.

Coed y Garreg

The Way then heads uphill and into the woods known as Coed y Garreg. Coed y Garreg watchtower is located on the highest point of the woods and is well worth a visit, simply for the views.

One suggestion is that this round stone structure was a Roman lighthouse built to help ships navigating the River Dee Estuary. Another is that it is a seventeenth-century watchtower, built to give warning of pirate raids – the latter seems much more likely. An inscription on a stone set into the tower reads 'This pharos was restored by Llewelyn Baron Mostyn in commemoration of the 60th year of the glorious reign of Victoria queen and empress June 20th 1897'.

Maen Achwyfan

The route then passes Maen Achwyfan Cross, at the junction of three roads at the turning from Whitford to Trelogan, halfway between Whitford and Sarn. The stone slab-cross probably dates from 1000CE and is said to be the tallest wheel-headed cross in Wales, standing 12ft (3.7m) high, with Celtic and Viking carvings on its shaft. It is also called 'The Stone of Lamentation' because penances were carried out at the cross in the Middle Ages. This procedure would have concluded with the weeping and 'act of contrition' performed by pilgrims making their way between St Winefride's Well and St David's.

According to one legend, St Cwyfan, a local seventh-century Celtic saint, preached on this site and set up the cross – hence the name, Maen Achwyfan. Another legend has it that Queen Boudica fought her last battle against the Romans close by in the fields called 'Cydio ar Leni' or 'the fields of the seizing legions'. During the Middle Ages, the monks of Basingwerk Abbey preached at the cross, and also set up a chapel for pilgrims just to the south at Whitford.

Follow the route along, passing private woodland and old mine shafts on the right. At the junction continue ahead through two gates and then across two fields with stiles. Here, you can see a view of Point of Ayr lighthouse, built in 1776, though inactive since 1883. It stands on Talacre Beach, at the entrance to the River Dee Estuary. The route then enters the twin villages of Berthengam and Trelogan.

Llanasa

Next along the Way is the very sacred and historic village of Llanasa. Named after St Asaph, the village is known to have existed since at least *c*.600CE and was originally called Llanasaph, meaning the 'Church of Saint Asaph'. The tomb and relics of St Asaph were enshrined here before they were moved to the larger St Asaph Cathedral some time before 1281.

First indications of a church here are from the seventh century; however, the current Church of Saints Asaph & Cyndeyrn dates from the fifteenth century. 'Cyndeyrn' is Welsh for 'Kentigern', so the church is named after the bishop of Glasgow and his student, Asaph. It was later the burial place of Gruffydd Fychan (the father of Owain Glyndŵr).

Other historical buildings here include the coach house, dated to 1636, and now a residential dwelling; a public house – The Red Lion, *c*.1600; converted barns and a granary; and Gyrn Castle – early nineteenth century, incorporating features from the late seventeenth and eighteenth centuries. To the west of the village is Golden Grove, (now a luxury bed and breakfast establishment), a sixteenth-century Elizabethan manor house set in a 1,000-acre (400ha) estate. Built in about 1580 by Sir Edward Morgan, and renovated during the reign of Queen Anne, it was then passed down through the Morgan family – several of whom were sheriffs of Flintshire – until 1877, when it was sold to industrial chemist Henry Davis Pochin.

The Gop

The route then travels through the countryside and up to the summit of the Gop, or the Gop Cairn. The Gop is a neolithic mound and the largest prehistoric monument in Wales. The mound lies on top of Gop Hill (823ft/251m), a natural limestone outcrop, in the side of which are the Gop Caves. Excavations have uncovered no burial chambers or other underground works, which may indicate that the hill was used as a lookout or hill fort; there is evidence of a considerable amount of stone on the top of the hill. Its prominent position allowed a beacon to be placed there in the seventeenth century.

The Gop Caves were discovered in 1886–7, and extend some way into the limestone of Gop Hill. There is evidence of hyaena activity during the last Ice Age, and there was also a square enclosure, enclosed by rubble, which contained the remains of at least fourteen humans, dating from throughout the Neolithic period.

Trelawnyd

From the summit of the Gop, walk down to the village of Trelawnyd, one of Flintshire's ancient parishes. The village was renamed 'Newmarket' in 1710 by John Wynne of Y Gop, who obtained a faculty from the Bishop's Registry. Wynne had by then redeveloped much of the village, established several industries, a weekly market and an annual fair, in an attempt to turn Newmarket into the area's market town. The plan failed, as nearby Rhyl developed and served this function instead. The village was officially renamed Trelawnyd in 1954, meaning 'Town full of wheat' in Welsh.

St Michael and All Angels Church is small, only 55ft (16.8m) long and 19ft (5.8m) wide, yet a church was first recorded here in 1291. The present church was built in 1724 and heavily restored in the nineteenth century. It contains a late medieval roof and part of a sepulchral slab, but little other early fabric. The porch doorway has survived from the Georgian building. A vestry was added in 1917.

The church occupies a sub-rectangular churchyard, which is notable for a fourteenth-century cross and rare eighteenth-century hooded tomb. The cross, which is likely to date from the late twelfth century, stands 11ft 7in (3.5m) high, with an octagonal capital featuring four niches. Two of these still contain figures. On the eastern side is St John, the beloved disciple, and the Blessed Virgin Mary watching at the cross. The western face depicts the crucifixion – a crown of thorns encircles the head of Christ. It is probable that the cross predates any church building, and that itinerant priests would have taken services in its shadow.

Next, the route follows the Clwydian Way – it continues through the countryside for quite a distance, passing the Snowdonian campsite and then the hill, Coed Jenny-Morgan. It crosses the modern bridge over the A55, and then runs alongside the road and across the fields towards Bryngwyn Bach airfield.

Tremeirchion

The route joins part of the Offa's Dyke Path and then enters the village of Tremeirchion.

ST BEUNO'S COLLEGE

St Beuno's College in Tremeirchion may be visited by prior arrangement. It was built in 1848 as a 'theologate' (or seminary) on the lines of a small Oxbridge University college, as a place of study for Jesuits. Up until this time prospective Jesuit priests studied at Stonyhurst College, Lancashire, and for a short time abroad, but the increasing numbers put a strain on the old buildings. In 1846, the then provincial of the Jesuits in Britain, Friar Randal Lythgoe, when visiting the Jesuit parish in Holywell, travelled to see some farmland near Tremeirchion owned by the Society of Jesus, and immediately decided that it should be the site for his new theologate. The architect engaged for the building work was Joseph Aloysius Hansom, the creator of the hansom cab. But within twenty years of being built, the college was too small, and extra rooms were added in the attic, while a new north wing was built to the left of the tower.

In 1862 the college was presented with a medieval cross from Corpus Christi, Tremeirchion. The Rood of Grace stood for 140 years on a plinth at the entrance to St Beuno's before being restored and then transported back to Tremeirchion churchyard as a millennium gift. It now stands by the yew under which it was found buried in the mid-nineteenth century.

'ROCK CHAPEL'

In 1866 a folly known as the 'Rock Chapel' was built on a wooded hill 550yd (500m) to the south of St Beuno's College. It was designed by a Jesuit student, Ignatius Scoles, who had followed in his father's footsteps and trained as an architect before joining the Jesuits to become a priest. It comprises an Early English single-cell chapel of local axe-dressed coursed limestone masonry with a small steeple at the west end.

The chapel is alternatively known as St Mary's, or Our Lady of Sorrows. It is erroneously named as St Michael's Chapel on OS maps, but the dedication to the Virgin is beyond question. The bishop's letter of approval makes it clear that the chapel was seen as reparation for the loss of many medieval Lady shrines in the area.

THE CHURCH OF CORPUS CHRISTI

Next, turn right to what is reputedly the only medieval church in Britain dedicated to Corpus Christi. It has been suggested that its original dedication was to the Holy Trinity, with a possible rededication in the sixteenth century as the original site of a cell founded in the sixth century by one of St Beuno's followers. St Beuno's Well, or Ffynnon Beuno, is located about 550yd (500m) from the site, but there is little substantive evidence to indicate an early medieval foundation. The Ffynnon Beuno bone caves, in the hills above the well, bear testament to the length of time the area has been inhabited, as significant finds of animal bones and prehistoric tools have been made here.

Dating mainly from the fourteenth and fifteenth centuries, the Church of Corpus Christi still retains many early features. Among the oldest, forming a seat in the porch, is the interlaced thirteenth-century cross slab to Hunyd, wife of Carwed. The elaborately-carved head of the medieval churchyard cross was sold in 1862 and ended up in the neighbouring St Beuno's College, but it has since been returned and reinstalled in the churchyard.

Medieval cross in the churchyard of the
Church of Corpus Christi, Tremeirchion.
DAVID ROSS

The south windows display a mosaic of late-medieval stained glass, including a haloed head of St Ann. A south window near the pulpit has unusual seventeenth-century portraits (from the old vicarage) of James I, Charles I and John Williams, a North Walian who became Bishop of Lincoln and Archbishop of York, and then fought alternately for both king and parliament during the Civil War. Perhaps most impressive is the great canopied fourteenth-century tomb by the altar, of the priest Dafydd ap Hywel ap Madog, known as Dafydd Ddu Athro o Hiraddug – 'Black David, the Teacher of Hiraddug'. Famous as a bard, writer and a soothsaying prophet, he was also the vicar of Tremeirchion.

Brynbella, a privately owned, eighteen-century neo-classical villa, stands below the village, behind a long stone wall beside the B5429.

Waen

The route then heads to the village of Waen. Cefn-y-Waen Chapel was built in 1838 on the site of a former school, but later rebuilt in 1868 in the Romanesque revival style. The attached vestry/schoolroom, at right angles to the rear, is said to have been converted from the 1838 chapel in about 1896/8, but its appearance is now all late nineteenth century.

After passing the eighteenth-century Farmer Arms pub, follow the footpath across open fields with a view of St Asaph Cathedral tower, and then across the steel footbridge over the River Clwyd. Follow the Clwydian Way once more, to the disused railway track, and turn up to the cathedral.

St Asaph

St Asaph dates back to the sixth century when a community was founded by the Scottish saint Kentigern, who left his disciple Asaph in charge when he returned to Scotland. Its Welsh name is Llanelwy.

The cathedral is the home of the William Morgan Bible (1588 – the first full Welsh translation of the Bible). The legend of the founding of the church and monastery between the years *c*.560 and *c*.573CE is to be found in *The Life of St Kentigern*, written by Jocelyn, a monk of Furness Abbey, in about 1180.

St Kentigern built his church here in 560CE. When he returned to Strathclyde in 573CE, he left Asaph as his successor; then following his death in the seventh century, posthumous miracle-working stories began. Since that time the cathedral has been dedicated to St Asaph, and the diocese also bears his name.

The site of the current late thirteenth-century red and purple sandstone cathedral, prominently located on top of a hill above the medieval High Street, lies on the original timber monastic complex founded by St Kentigern. By 1281, the relics of St Asaph were moved from Llanasa (a small parish in the north of Flintshire) to the newly-built stone cathedral, with a large amount of the money required to finance the cathedral's rebuilding gained through pilgrim offerings and indulgences. The chief object of their devotion must have been the Shrine of St Asaph, and the reliquary in which the copy of the Gospel of the Evengalthen was housed.

The present building was constructed between 1284 and 1392, and the cathedral is reputed to be the smallest in Great Britain. The nave arcades, the crossing and the upper parts of the west front were built afresh, and a new west doorway was inserted. The aisle walls were partially rebuilt and refenestrated. The transepts, which were the last works to be rebuilt, were added between 1315 and 1320.

In addition to the cathedral, there are several other historic churches in St Asaph: the parish church of St Asaph and St Kentigern, placed prominently at the bottom of the High Street and dating principally from the fifteenth century with a double nave in characteristic Welsh style and an impressive hammer-beam roof adorned with angels in the older south aisle; the nineteenth-century Methodist Peniel Chapel across the river; and the nineteenth-century Bethlehem Chapel (Welsh Presbyterian) in Bronwylfa Square.

Cefn Meiriadog

When you leave St Asaph, walk through the town and over the bridge; take the first road on your left, and follow this for 1.4 miles (2.2km). Go right where the road forks, and you will shortly reach the imposing St Mary's Church at Cefn Meiriadog (just Cefn on some maps). The new parish of Cefn was created on 7 February 1865, and comprised the two townships of Wigfair and Meiriadog (both in Denbighshire), which until then had been in the parish of St Asaph in Flintshire.

Cefn Meiriadog is situated on the left bank of the River Elwy. Nearby is a fine spring, called Y Ffynnon Fair (*see* below). 'Cefn' in Welsh means 'the side of a hill', while St Meiriadog was a fifth-century saint. The foundation stone of St Mary's was laid in 1863, and the church was consecrated by Bishop Short of St Asaph on 3 September 1864. Almost all the stonework was quarried and worked on the site.

Cefn Caves are nearby, where human remains dating back 250,000 years have been discovered. Visitors to the site have included Charles Darwin, in 1831.

St Mary's Well (Y Ffynnon Fair)

Nearby is a must-see detour. Hidden away in a wooded area near Cefn Meiriadog is St Mary's Well (Y Ffynnon Fair) and its associated chapel (now in ruins), once a much-visited Roman Catholic centre of pilgrimage. The site is of interest because of its ornate well basin, considered to be very similar in design and age to the well-chamber at St Winefride's Well, Holywell, and was also renowned for its healing properties. The well and chapel are located on private land beneath trees, close to the River Elwy in the hamlet of Wigfair (Wigfair translates as 'Mary's Retreat'), Cefn Meiriadog parish, a mile or so to the north-west of Trefnant. It is difficult to reach, but from the A525, make for the bridge over Afon Elwy, then go left into the lane. Go across the fields and into the valley just to the north of the river to reach the well site in Chapel Wood.

The well chapel (Capel Ffynnon) was first built in the thirteenth century, though the octagonal, star-shaped well basin and attached cistern (bath) were added in 1500; the rest of the building consists of a chancel (of a later date), and a north and south transept, while the holy well stands at the far western side of the chapel. Adjoining the well are the ruins of a cruciform chapel, in the Decorated and later English styles.

Originally this was a chapel-of-ease to St Asaph, and was served by one of the vicars to that church. Following the Reformation, the well began to fall into disrepair, although it remained in use by the landowning family. Records dating from the 1640s make reference to clandestine marriages being conducted here – it was described as the Gretna Green of North Wales.

WIGFAIR HALL

Wigfair Hall is worth a short detour after St Mary's Church as it lies just to the east. Standing in an elevated position above the River Elwy near the village of Wigfair, the Hall was built by Chester architect John Douglas on the site of an older house between 1882 and 1884. Its large tower was originally a water tower for the house, used to generate electricity. The equipment for this purpose, including the tanks, pipework and generator, although no longer in use, is still present.

Other notable dwellings in the area include Bryn y Pin (built around the watch tower of a Welsh Prince), Plas Newydd, Plas yn Cefn and Dolbelydr (sixteenth century), and also a few longhouses.

The River Elwy, the banks of which are finely wooded, is crossed here at Bont Newydd. The Way then runs out towards the seventeenth-century farm at Tyddyn Bartley, past the wood and on to the lane at Ty'n y Bedw, and continues through the countryside for several miles. A few hundred metres after Fferm Bryn Isa (off to your right), the route turns left – or you can continue into the village of Llannefydd by staying on the lane.

Llannefydd

The village is named after St Nefydd. Tradition has it that the church was founded by Nefydd in the fifth century, and it was mentioned in the Lincoln Taxation of 1291. It is now dedicated to St Nefydd and St Mary the Virgin. The church is double-naved and of Perpendicular design; the northern nave is perhaps the earlier of the two. The south porch has a cyclopean inner doorway reconstructed in the early eighteenth century. There is a double western bellcote on the south nave, renewed in the 1859 restoration. The raised churchyard is polygonal in shape, and contains the base and shaft of a medieval cross.

Ffynnon Nefydd, considered a holy well, is a spring less than 330yd (300m) to the north of the church. Even as early as 1912 it was considered 'neglected', and appears to have attracted little attention since. There is little visible trace of it, although it allegedly once took the form of a bath enclosed by a wall and had been built by the vicar in 1604.

Leave the village and follow the path around the steep north-facing slope. Keep up on the hillside and head towards Hafodty Farm. The route heads over the fields, over a stream, and passes the front of the farm at Cae'r Groes. Go down to cross the footbridge over the River Afon Aled with the stream on your left, and then continue over the two bridges into the community of Rhyd yr Arian – here there are legends relating to King Arthur's Round Table. Leaving here, the Way now follows the Clwydian Way again, up through the wood and down to cross the river once more, and then on into the village of Llansannan.

Llansannan

The village landmark of Llansannan is the bronze statue of the 'Little Girl' that commemorates five notable figures from the area. The work of William Goscombe John, the statue was officially unveiled in 1899, shortly after the death of local politician T. E. Ellis, whose brainchild it had been.

The parish church's dedication to St Sannan has led some to suggest that Sannan founded a religious establishment here in the sixth century. Sannan was an Irish monk who travelled widely and may have befriended Dewi (David), patron saint of Wales, and St Winefride's father. It is said he was buried near her in Gwytherin after his death in Ireland. The name of the village denotes the walled enclosure (llan) of Sannan.

The church is listed in a tax record of 1254; a document from 1682 then refers to a rood loft in the church, but the building seen today is the result of later modifications, especially those of 1778 and 1878–79. It features a double nave, a chancel and a bellcote rising from between the gables of the naves. The pulpit dates from the seventeenth century, and was moved here from St Luke's Church in Liverpool in 1894. There is also a chest dated 1683, known as 'Cist yr Eglwys' (the church chest).

From the church, walk past the pub and the sculpture, and take the lane called Ffordd Gogor. As you leave the village, you are again on the Clwydian Way. Cross over the bridge, and walk with the river on your right. The path then enters a woodland. Walk along the riverside to the former mill; after this, the track crosses the countryside for some distance until eventually it becomes a path. The path re-crosses the river – follow it to the vernacular-built cottage, Hendre Aled. The route then continues out into the fields and uphill, to the farm at Cleiriach.

Pilgrim's Rest Bench

Above Cleiriach the view really opens out. This is Hiraethog, the heart of north-east Wales. The route then bends to the left at the Pilgrim's Rest Bench – this magnificent viewpoint is crowned by Simon O'Rourke's chainsaw sculpture of the pilgrim sitting on his bench.

Hafod-gau

Follow the path until you reach the derelict buildings at Hafod-gau, situated in a slight dip and surrounded by conifers. These holdings are not necessarily of medieval origin. During the mid-twentieth century, population figures plummeted from an all-time high in the late nineteenth and early twentieth century to possibly the lowest level for many centuries – the isolated dwellings here are tangible reminders of this change.

After the buildings, walk uphill until you reach a stile, and cross over to the lane.

Llethr

The route then continues to the farm at Llethr. It is likely that the old house here is seventeenth-century, but ceased to be a dwelling when the new house was built in the late eighteenth or early nineteenth century. The farm building is later, added at the uphill end and therefore probably after its use as a dwelling. Both were converted to cowhouses, and continued as such into the twentieth century.

The Way next enters the village of Gwytherin.

Gwytherin

This is an extremely significant location on this pilgrim route. Legend has it that Winefride became abbess of a convent in the remote village of Gwytherin, where she died and was buried in the churchyard – until 1137, when a monk from Shrewsbury was cured of an illness after bathing in her well; they then exhumed her bones and took her to their cathedral.

A chapel was built over her open grave in a small field near the church called Penbryn Capel, and people came on pilgrimages to sleep in the grave and be cured. A low, rounded knoll, south of the churchyard, is the site of the small chapel of St Winifred, demolished in the early eighteenth century after an elderly lady used the chapel as a cottage and dug up the graveyard. According to local folklore, she came to a sticky end. The cottage was then demolished and the local rector used the stone for a stable. All that is left of Winefride's former burial site is a field to the south side of the churchyard and the present church, built on the foundations of the old convent.

The present church dedicated to St Winefride was built in 1869, but is believed to have originated in the mid-600s CE, when it was established by Prince Eleri, who then went on to set up a double monastery in the village. He was the abbot to the monks, and his cousin's daughter, St Gwenfrewy/i (Winefride) was the abbess to the nuns. The now redundant church has been transformed into the Gwenfrewi Project, a centre for arts and music dedicated to St Winefride. In the churchyard are three ancient yew trees that are perhaps 2,500 to 3,000 years old – typical of a former sacred gathering place. There is also a row of four ancient standing stones approximately one metre high and aligned roughly east to west. A close look at the first stone reveals carvings and what appears to be a 'W'.

Finally, Gwytherin is the setting for much of the novel, *A Morbid Taste for Bones*, first published in 1977 by Ellis Peters. It was the first book in a series of twenty to introduce the fictional Brother Cadfael, the real Prior Robert Pennant, and the rest of the monks at Shrewsbury Abbey in the twelfth century (and a personal favourite!)

There are two alternative routes from here, but the primary path followed by historic pilgrims takes the valley of Pennant to Pandy Tudur.

THE ROUTE TO THE ABBEY

In addition to the field near Penbryn Chapel, a further location has been reputed in this remote valley as the abbey site in which Winefride was abbess and died, though little, if anything, remains. To visit the site take the road past the Lion Inn in Gwytherin and up into the valley. Ignore the road going uphill, and go downhill to reach another road going off to the right. This is the access road to Taipellaf. Follow this past the farm and buildings. The putative site of the abbey is marked by a large stone mound on your left. Continue up this track through gates to the lane and turn right. Take the path on the left through a gate, and follow through two more gates directly ahead on to rough countryside. Eventually you join a fence on your left – follow this to a stile. Go over it, head for the track ahead, and follow this to the road at Ty-uchaf-i'r-ffordd. This section is not waymarked with Pilgrim's Way markers.

Pandy Tudur

After this diversion to Pennant, return to Gwytherin and follow the main trail north-west for several kilometres to the village of Pandy Tudur. St David's Church, now converted to a house, is situated about a quarter of a mile away to the north-east of the village. Built in 1867, the church has a north-west tower and had a vestry to the south-east (now demolished).

Hafodunos Hall

The path now follows on some way towards the entrance to Hafodunos Hall. Hafodunos is said to be named after a legend associated with St Winefride, in which her body rested there for one night, en route from Holywell to Gwytherin churchyard.

A manor house was built at Hafodunos in 1674, and remained in the Lloyd family until 1830, replacing the monastic foundation. The original E-shaped house was demolished, and the new building was designed by Sir Gilbert Scott (designer of St Pancras station) between 1861 and 1866 for Henry Robertson Sandbach – this and the lodge (*see* below) are Scott's only executed domestic buildings in Wales. It is built of red brick in the neo-Gothic style with a diaper flushwork design and extensive stone dressings to windows and doors, and utilized Victorian technology, such as central heating and fresh running water. After leaving the hands of the Sandbach family in 1933, Hafodunos had a variety of uses, including a girl's school, an accountancy college and a nursing home. A period of neglect ensued from 1993 onwards, but a major restoration project is now ongoing.

This section of the route is particularly attractive. After the second pilgrim sculpture alongside the Pilgrim's Way – a pilgrim carved into a tree and pointing out the route – it descends through a picturesque wooded gorge. At the Hafodunos Hall Lodge, turn right into the village of Llangernyw. The lodge itself is a single-storey Gothic Revival gatehouse, T-shaped in plan, also designed by Sir George Gilbert Scott.

Llangernyw

This village is most renowned for the 4,000-year-old yew tree which stands in the grounds of St Digain's Church in the centre of the village. The yew tree took root some time in the Bronze Age, and is still a thriving and healthy tree.

St Digain's Church is thought to be no earlier than the thirteenth century, but is of an early medieval foundation. Yet, it contains little of pre-nineteenth-century architectural interest besides the roof, which is likely late medieval, and an original south doorway. South of the church is a pair of standing stones, one of which has an incised cross, dating from around the seventh to ninth century; the other has a cross thought to date from the ninth to the eleventh century.

The Henry Jones museum in the village tells the story of Sir Henry Jones, one of the forefathers of the Welsh education system – it was his childhood home.

Crei

The path then passes by the infamous derelict farmhouse of Crei near Coed y Crei, now a time capsule to its previous owners, as it has simply been left to decay with all its contents left in place. The house is vernacular-built and appears to be early nineteenth century in date. There is little of interest to see along this stretch of the route, apart from the fantastic rolling countryside.

Ty Mawr

The route then runs up towards and through the farm buildings at Ty Mawr. The farmhouse is a three-unit, cruck-framed hall house, built during the sixteenth century and later. It was originally half-timbered, and consisted of an open hall of two bays between secondary rooms at each end. During the seventeenth century, the walls were rebuilt in stone, and an upper floor and porch were added. It is of architectural interest as it proves that the half-timbered house reached as far as the River Conwy in pre-Elizabethan times.

The route then largely runs deep in the countryside, passing by many historic and rather large farmsteads, as well as a disused quarry before heading into Eglwysbach.

Eglwysbach

From the bridge at the south-west extremity of the village, approximately 270yd (250m) south-east of the village school, there is a view across the meadow to Plas Llan (or Plas yn Llan), a white house with tall chimneys, accessed via an unmetalled farm track. The house is sixteenth-century, storeyed and sub-medieval of cross-passage type; inside are roof beams that bear carpenters' marks from the fifteenth century. The house was improved by Sir John Wynn of Gwydir, whose coat of arms with the date 1684 still adorn one of the fireplace overmantels. There is also an impressive oak door bolt securing the heavily studded front door. The Great Barn, to the left of the house, has sixty-three nesting holes built into one of the walls, to raise pigeons for the table.

The earliest written record of St Martin's Church here dates from 1254, when it belonged to the diocese of St Asaph. In 1284 it transferred to Aberconwy Abbey at Maenan as part of the resettlement agreement that allowed Edward I to build the walled town of Conwy on the site of Aberconwy Abbey. The church reverted to the diocese in 1540. It was then rebuilt in *c*.1782, after the previous one became dilapidated.

Afon Hiraethlyn

Flowing beneath the bridge is Afon Hiraethlyn, occasionally referred to as Erethlyn in some historic documents. From here, the river eventually reaches Bodnant Garden, where it falls in a dramatic waterfall into the Dell; the Way essentially follows its course. Firstly, however, it heads out of Eglwysbach and towards Ty Gwyn.

From here you can make a detour north to Bodnant Garden, a National Trust property near Tal-y-Cafn, situated overlooking the Conwy Valley towards the Carneddau range of mountains. The garden was founded in 1874, and developed by five generations of one family; it was gifted to the care of the National Trust in 1949. The garden spans 80 acres (32ha) of hillside, and includes formal Italianate terraces, informal shrub borders stocked with plants from around the world, and the Dell, a gorge garden with United Kingdom champion trees and a waterfall. The hall is the residence of Lord Aberconway. It was built in 1792, but unfortunately is not open to the public.

Return to the main route, which then goes on to Tal-y-cafn.

Tal-y-cafn

Tal-y-cafn (Welsh, meaning 'place opposite the ferry-boat') lies in the Conwy Valley, close to the Roman settlement of Canovium at Caerhun. The fort is a slight detour from the route, but is certainly manageable. It is situated to the south-west, over the river. The beautiful thirteenth-century Church of St Mary can also be seen here.

Tal-y-cafn was the site of a Roman river-crossing point of the River Conwy. Originally a medieval ferry, which operated from as early as 1301, it was replaced in 1897 by a steel bridge of riveted plates and angles on piers of concrete and masonry. The ferry was almost certainly used by pilgrims. The present bridge dates from 1977–8. Tal-y-Cafn is primarily known as the site of the Tal-y-Cafn Hotel, a former sixteenth-century coaching inn located on the A470 road, and adjacent to Tal-y-Cafn railway station.

Rowen

Continue over the bridge, then walk uphill and follow the path to the B5106. Go across the countryside towards the village of Rowen.

Just outside the village, Tir Y Coed is a country-house-turned-hotel built in 1896 on the edge of Snowdonia National Park. On the opposite side of the road, a small track leads to Bulkeley Mill (completed in 1684), one of the notable old mills of the village. The gardens at Oakbank and Bulkeley Mill were laid out and planted by the gardener and writer A. T. Johnson in the early to mid-twentieth century. He wrote several books about his gardening experiences there.

Now entering Rowen, from the pub walk past the chapel, which is usually open to visitors. Seion Chapel is one of only two Wesleyan Methodist chapels in Wales to be listed Grade II*. It is built in a local creamy-grey coloured stone, with red sandstone dressings to the window surrounds. The chapel was designed by the architects Shayler & Ridge, and completed in 1904 to serve an even larger congregation of new converts to Christianity. Adjacent to the chapel is a large hall, which pre-dates it by twelve years. This seems to have been the previous chapel, which was then converted to use as a hall when the chapel was constructed.

Llangelynin

Walk across the countryside again, past Llwyn Onn farm, enter the wood and then continue until you reach the ancient 'Coffin Path', which leads eventually to the little church at Llangelynin. An extremely interesting site, the building is one of the oldest churches in Wales, dedicated to the sixth-century St Celynin, who is reputed to have founded the first religious settlement on the site.

It is likely that Llangelynin Church dates back to the twelfth century; the porch is a later addition and dates to the seventeenth century. It features a 'squint' or hagioscope (an opening to enable view of the high altar) in its east wall. The door hinges and threshold are of fourteenth-century construction, although the door itself is more recent. The nave is the oldest part of the building and dates to the twelfth century, while the present chancel is probably of fourteenth-century date. The north transept, known as Capel Meibion – which translates as the 'men's chapel' – was added in the fifteenth century. Some remains of the nineteenth-century south transept may still be seen outside the building.

Removal of a coat of whitewash revealed wall paintings including the Creed, the Lord's Prayer and the Ten Commandments, written in Welsh, and a large *memento mori* in the form of a skeleton, standing upright, holding a scythe in its right hand and what appears to be a flaming torch in its left hand. The remains of the rood screen date from the fourteenth century.

A holy well is situated in the south-eastern corner of the churchyard, known as Ffynnon Gelynin or the Holy Well of St Celynin. It consists of a small, walled, oblong-shaped pool, which once possessed a roof believed to have been added in the sixteenth century. The well itself, which pre-dates the church building, was renowned in the area for its power to cure sick children.

Remains of an ancient hut circle also lie next to the church, which tradition states was where St Celynin lived. An Iron Age fort is situated on the nearby crags of Cerrig-y-ddinas.

From this little church continue out into the open countryside, with broad views over the Conwy Valley, town and castle. You will pass some interesting sheep pens at Tyddyn-grasod; continue straight on, ignoring paths on the left and right, and when you come to the brow, walk ahead towards a clump of trees within a wall. Pass these, and the route then joins the North Wales Path at a waymarker post, and then the Wales Coast Path. The North Wales Path and Wales Coast Path now follow the same route. Continue to follow the waymarked path for ¾ mile (1km) past Bryn Derwedd to the complex of stone circles, high above the town of Penmaenmawr.

Penmaenmawr

The Druid's Circle (in Welsh, Meini Hirion) is the most famous of a number of monuments to be found on the hillside above the town of Penmaenmawr. It was erected at the crossroads of Bronze Age tracks. Some say the circle dates back to 3000BC, while others date it to the Bronze Age. The Druid's Circle consists of a ring of large stones set on the inner edge of a low bank approximately 25yd (23m) in diameter. It is a classic example of an embanked stone circle.

After visiting the stone circle, return to the main path and follow it westwards to a marker post where the Wales Coast Path leaves to go down to Llanfairfechan. Now continue ahead on the waymarked North Wales Path, and follow the road down to the entrance to Nant y Coed Nature Reserve.

Continuing on the North Wales Path, carry on uphill for another distance, crossing open land; eventually you will reach a large stone, dated 262CE, at the Roman Road. Follow this ancient route to Abergwyngregyn. The village is about ¾ mile (1km) down the road, but well worth a detour.

Abergwyngregyn

Maes y Gaer is a pre-Roman defensive enclosure that rises above Pen y Bryn on the eastern side of the valley; it has far-reaching views over the Irish Sea, with the Isle of Man visible on a clear day. The Roman road from Chester (Deva) linking the forts of Canovium (later name Conovium) and Segontium crossed the river at this point. This was the seat of Llywelyn ap Gruffydd, the last native Prince of Wales, whose daughter, Gwenllian of Wales, was born here in 1282. His wife, Eleanor de Montfort, died here as a result of the birth on 19 June 1282. In June 1283, Dafydd ap Gruffydd, Llywelyn's brother, who assumed the title of Prince of Wales after Llywelyn's murder in December 1282, was captured at Bera Mountain, above the present village.

Y MŴD

Y Mŵd is an earthen mound on the valley floor in the middle of the village. The mound is circular, 22ft (6.7m) high, with a level oval top 57ft (17m) by 48ft (15m). It has been regarded as the base of a Norman castle, and was thus renamed 'Aber Castle Mound'. The word 'Mŵd' in early Welsh means 'vault' or 'chamber', and although there are traces of a ditch on the south side, no further defensive features have been identified.

LLYS ABER

There is a further large structure on the valley bottom between Y Mŵd and Pen y Bryn, which appears to be the remains of a high-status building dating from the thirteenth century, possibly contemporary with the last independent princes of Wales or with the early decades after the Conquest. There are therefore suggestions that it was a medieval royal llys – the royal court of the princes of Gwynedd. No defensive structures have been found. The floor plan has been interpreted as a medieval hall, 37ft by 26ft (11.2m by 8m) internally, with large wings at the ends. A separate enclosure may have been used for large ovens or for metalworking.

PEN Y BRYN

Pen y Bryn is a manor house dating from the Jacobean period yet with earlier lower stonework; it is situated on a promontory some 200yd (180m) to the east of Abergwyngregyn village centre. The present structure incorporates a four-storey stone tower, and roof timbers were dated by dendrochronology to 1624, when the house was refurbished. There is evidence of long use with multiple rebuildings before 1624, but there is disagreement as to the duration and nature of its medieval use. With its adjacent buildings and groundworks, it forms a double bank and ditch enclosure now known as Garth Celyn. This is also claimed to be the site of the pre-Conquest royal llys. A neolithic burial urn was discovered when a driveway was being made to the house in 1824.

Aber Falls

If you choose not to visit the village, turn left before the bridge to follow the North Wales Path and walk up the road to the car park. Just before the car park take the path on the right signed 'Waterfalls', and go over the bridge. Follow this path for 1.25 miles (2.1km) to the waterfalls. The North Wales Path goes past another waterfall and then climbs slowly round the side of the hill, to Aber Falls, where the Afon Goch plunges about 120ft (37m) over a sill of igneous rock in the foothills of the Carneddau range. Two tributaries merge, and the enlarged stream is known as Afon Rhaeadr Fawr; from the road bridge, Bont Newydd, the name becomes Afon Aber. Along the main footpath towards the falls are several small Bronze Age settlements, including an excavated roundhouse and smithy, which are fenced off. There are also several standing stones and cairns here.

You will then arrive at a seat with wide views over Ynys Mon, the Great Orme and beyond to the north-west of England. Continue along the winding main path until you pass a wooded area on your right: this is Nant Heilyn, a small oval ring cairn made of large boulders not marked on any map.

Plas Cochwillan

Continue straight across the fields. At the back of the house here make your way through bushes to the lane, and continue along it until you see a turn to Plas Cochwillan. This farmhouse was built between c.1850 and 1860 to serve the unusually large Penrhyn-estate-owned farm complex at Cochwillan. As such, it can be seen as a characteristic element in the widespread improvements carried out to its farms by the estate at this period.

Felin Cochwillan

Follow the path down until eventually you see the river, before arriving at the watermill. Felin Cochwillan is a well-preserved, late nineteenth-century large estate corn mill. Built originally as a fulling mill, it was later converted into a corn and oatmeal mill with four pairs of millstones, an oatmeal fan, grain cleaner, dressing machine and a drying kiln. The first reference to a mill on the site appears in a register of the lands of Cochwillan estate, dated 1560 – the remains of the original mill can still be seen to this day.

Turn left at the mill and follow the path across the river, coming out on to a track/lane. Go under the A55 and join the Wales Coast Path, then follow it along to the old railway track into Port Penrhyn.

Port Penrhyn

Port Penrhyn is a harbour of formerly great importance as the main port for the export of slate from Penrhyn Quarry, the largest slate quarry in the world at the end of the nineteenth century. It was built, and later expanded, by the Pennant (later Douglas-Pennant) family of nearby Penrhyn Castle.

A short detour across to the east takes you to Penrhyn Castle, originally a medieval manor house, founded by Ednyfed Fychan in 1438. Ioan ap Gruffydd was granted a licence to crenellate and he founded the stone castle, when adding a tower house. Sited at the angle of a square courtyard, it defends the gateway, chapel and great hall. Today, only the original spiral stairs can be seen, with the vaulted basement and other masonry incorporated into a dramatic nineteenth-century neo-Norman mansion, constructed by George Dawkins Pennant.

From here, follow the Wales Coast Path to Bangor City Centre and the cathedral.

Bangor

The origins of the city date back to the founding of a monastic establishment on the site of Bangor Cathedral by the Celtic saint, Deiniol, in *c*.530CE. Having been given land, probably by Maelgwn, King of Gwynedd, he enclosed it with a fence constructed by driving poles into the ground and weaving branches in between them. The native technical term for this type of fence was 'bangor'. Within this enclosure, Deiniol built his church.

The present cathedral is a more recent building and has been extensively modified over the centuries. Dean James Vincent (1862–76) commissioned Sir George Gilbert Scott for a radical restoration. Scott described his scheme as a departure from the conservative treatment he usually advocated. On his advice, it was decided to restore or partially reconstruct the choir, transepts and chapter house 'in such a style as is indicated by their few remaining fragments'.

While the building itself is not the earliest, and certainly not the largest, the bishopric of Bangor is one of the oldest in Britain. Another claim to fame is that Bangor allegedly has the longest high street, not only in Wales, but in the whole of the United Kingdom.

Friars School was founded as a free grammar school in 1557, and Bangor University was founded in 1884. There are a handful of other chapels and religious institutions dotted throughout Bangor, largely dating from the nineteenth century.

Leaving the cathedral, continue along the High Street and out over Bangor Mountain – the scarp face of a hill with the city sitting below it. Though not a mountain in the true sense of the word, it is so called because of the way it rears up behind Bangor and appears mountainous, especially when viewed from the Glan Adda, High Street and Hirael areas of the city.

The route then drops down steeply to a ford and picks up the old quarry railway track; continue along the track towards Tregarth, about 2½ miles (4km) ahead, and then cross the bridge over the A4244. Follow this path to a group of buildings (the old hamlet of Pandy), then into the Woodland Trust site, and follow the path uphill to reach the top of the hill at Tynllidiart. This path/lane passes through two farms at Cae'r Gof, and through the wall on to the Common.

Go across the field, and down and across the stream until you reach a derelict farmhouse; pass this to reach open land again. Continue over the hillside and down to the road at Ffridd Uchaf, then on to the main road and into Deiniolen High Street.

Deiniolen

The most interesting sites in Deiniolen are the churches. Llandinorwig Church was built in 1857, with money donated by the Assheton-Smith family; an interesting fact is that its windows comprise designs from nearly all revival styles. Ebenezer Chapel was built in 1823, its name taken from the village's original name of Ebeneser, while Cefn y Waen Capel was built by local quarrymen in 1838; before this the village people held their services either in local farmhouses or in the open air.

Follow the Way to the houses at Maes Eilian, then into the wood of Padarn Country Park, and on to the Slate Museum, and Llanberis.

Llanberis

Llanberis is situated on the southern bank of the lake, Llyn Padarn, and at the foot of Snowdon, the highest mountain in Wales. It takes its name from St Peris, an early Welsh saint. The village originally grew up around the slate-quarrying industry, but since the demise of the quarries in the 1930s, it is essentially a tourism spot only.

Dolbadarn Castle (keep). DAVID ROSS

DOLBADARN CASTLE

The ruins of Dolbadarn Castle stand above the village. The thirteenth-century fortress was built by Llywelyn the Great, and was important both militarily and as a symbol of Llywelyn's power and authority. It features a large stone keep, perhaps the finest surviving example of a Welsh round tower. In 1284, Dolbadarn was taken by Edward I, who removed some of its timbers to build his new castle at Caernarfon. The castle was then used as a manor house for some years, until it fell into ruin in the Georgian era. In the eighteenth and nineteenth centuries it was a popular destination for painters (including J.M.W. Turner) interested in Sublime and Picturesque landscapes.

THE CHURCH OF ST PERIS

St Peris, to whom the church is dedicated, is said to have settled and died in the valley. Close to the church is the holy well or sacred spring known as Ffynnon y Sant, from which Peris is supposed to have drunk each day. There are many legends associated with the old well, and it is said that crowds flocked here to secure relief from their illnesses.

The earliest part of the church dates from the fourteenth century, the transepts from the fifteenth or sixteenth century, and it was extended eastwards and the chancel rebuilt in the early seventeenth century. Its surviving medieval fabric includes the former fifteenth- or early sixteenth-century rood screen, and the fifteenth-century arch-braced roof. However, in common with many old Welsh churches, it was considerably restored by Henry Kennedy in 1848, including the rebuilding of the upper part of the west wall.

THE CHURCH OF ST PADARN

The foundation stone of the high-Victorian, Early English revival-style church of St Padarn was laid in 1884, and the building was dedicated on 24 June 1885. The church was completed with the addition of the Lady Chapel in 1914–15 in a complementary style by Harold Hughes. The late-medieval font comes from the old church at Nant Peris (for a time it was in the rectory garden). The original church for the area was St Peris' Church, but this is some 2½ miles (4km) to the south-east of Llanberis. As the town's population grew in tandem with slate quarrying, a place of worship was needed closer to the bulk of the population. Initially, worship took place at a 'club house' in the town, then for fifteen years the congregation met at the Church House, until the new church was opened.

CAPEL COCH

Situated on very slightly-rising ground on the south side of Ffordd Capel-Coch, the chapel occupies a prominent position in the street. It was a Calvinistic Methodist chapel founded in the slate-quarrying village in 1777. Various religious revivals, and the expansion of the quarrying industry locally, led to the expansion of Capel Coch's congregation and the building itself. The chapel was rebuilt in 1802 and 1846, with the present building dating from 1893. The attached Sunday School was built in 1909.

After passing the chapel, head uphill. Follow this road out into the open country, passing some disused quarries, and then to the right of a forest and along to the nature park – which is open to the public – of Bryn Pistyll at Waunfawr.

Waunfawr

At Waunfawr, located on the north side of Ffordd Waenfawr, is Glan Gwna Hall – this is a good few kilometres from the route, however, sited close to Caeathro. You could make this a longer detour and then head on to Caernarfon on the coast before returning back to the main route.

Erected in 1893 to define the land belonging to Glan Gwna Hall, the Elizabethan Gothic revival-style hall stands in the 200 acre (80ha) Glan Gwna estate, within the community of Waunfawr on the banks of the River Seiont; much of the estate is now occupied by Glan Gwna Holiday Park. In 1893, the estate was bought by the wealthy slate quarry owner, John Ernest Greaves, who also owned Bron Eifion near Criccieth. He knocked down the old hall and built the present one on the same site.

Follow the Way towards Rhosgadfan across the moorland until a junction of paths, marked by an extremely large stone, then by the disused Moel Tryfan slate quarry. There are good views of the Nantlle ridge and the lake below. Follow the path past another disused and flooded quarry to the crossroads at Y Fron.

Y Fron

Y Fron, also known locally as Cesarea, after the nearby chapel, is a country village on the south-west side of Moel Tryfan, overlooking the Nantlle Valley, and Trum Y Ddysgl and Craig Cwm Silyn. Capel y Fron was a substantial halo-arch chapel of the later nineteenth century, but was demolished in 2009 to make way for housing developments. Capel Bwlch-Llyn, however, still stands; it is of the neo-Romanesque style with a gable-entry, built in 1907.

Cilgwyn

Continue along the track to the settlement of Cilgwyn. This is one of the earliest slate quarries in Great Britain, in production since the twelfth century. Edward I was reputed to have stayed in a house roofed by Cilgwyn slates, during the Welsh wars of independence.

At the road junction there is an interesting modern wayside shrine dedicated to Our Lady of Mount Carmel; it was founded by the Orthodox Church.

Continue down towards the old quarry/landfill; as you reach the wall, you will see a tunnel through it on your right: go through this, and continue down through various kissing gates. When you reach a roundabout with trees in the middle, take the left fork and continue down the lane to another kissing gate on your left.

Entering Talysarn, follow the route to a stream; take the riverside path with the Afon Llyfni on your left, and continue into Penygroes.

Lleuar Fawr

Follow the Way across country, passing several farms, until you arrive at Lleuar Fawr. The present building lies to the south of the site of the original house, which was occupied by William Glynne until his death in 1609; there is a monument to Glynne in Clynnog Church. In 1660 the house passed by marriage to the Parliamentarian commander, Colonel George Twistleton, who rebuilt the property. This building was later destroyed by fire, but a stone doorcase with his coat of arms, dated 1675, survived to be incorporated into the present farmhouse, built by the Glynllifon estate in the early mid-nineteenth century.

The Way passes Capel Uchaf (a medieval wheeled Celtic cross with a circle enclosing the upper section about 8in (20cm) in diameter is inscribed on a stone on the north side of the road), and then down to the village of Clynnog Fawr.

Clynnog

The main feature of the village is the parish church, dedicated to St Beuno. The site is said to be that of a Celtic monastery founded by Beuno in the early seventh century. Clynnog means 'the place of the holly trees'. It developed into an important foundation, with some Welsh law manuscripts stating that the Abbot of Clynnog was entitled to a seat at the court of the king of Gwynedd.

The church is recorded as being burnt in 978CE by the Vikings, and again later by the Normans. By the end of the fifteenth century it was a collegiate church, one of only six in Wales. The church was an important stopping place for pilgrims heading for Bardsey Island, and contains Cyff Beuno, an ancient wooden chest hollowed out of a single piece of ash used to keep alms donated by pilgrims. Also kept in the adjoining sixteenth-century chapel (said to occupy the site of Beuno's original chapel and monastery) is Maen Beuno or 'Beuno's Stone', an inscribed stone cross that features markings reputed to be those of Beuno's fingers.

Beuno's remains were buried in a tomb at Clynnog Fawr, and later moved to the present church. The oldest part of the church is believed to be the eastern crossing, dating from the 1480s. The nave was extended westwards in c.1500, when the choir stalls in the chancel were also added. The western tower and two-storey vestry are from the early sixteenth century. The building was restored in the mid-nineteenth century, but the work was not particularly intrusive to the medieval fabric.

In the churchyard there is a sundial dated between the late tenth and early twelfth century. Also, Ffynnon Bueno (St Bueno's Well) lies by the old roadside about 200 yards (180m) to the west of the church – it is one of the finest surviving wells dedicated to the saint in Wales – and its waters have long been reputed to possess curative properties for numerous ailments.

Trefor

Leave the village by following the old road (now a cycleway) past Ffynnon Beuno, and continue along the A499 to the hamlet of Gyrn Goch, and then into the village of Trefor.

CAPEL BETHANIA

From the village, pass over a bridge and by Capel Bethania (Bethania Baptist Chapel was built in 1896 in the Lombardic/Italian style with a gable entry) to Bwlch yr Eifl. Yr Eifl is a range of three tall hills that dominate the skyline above Trefor, and this is often supposed to be the source of the English name, The Rivals, but this is merely an anglicised form of Yr Eifl. Pass the quarry workings and follow this track down to Nant Gwrtheyrn.

Tre'r Ceiri, the second highest of the hills, has one of the best examples of a Neolithic settlement on its summit in Europe. Views from the summits on a clear day extend to Ireland, the whole of Cardigan Bay, Anglesey, Snowdonia and the northern mountains of England.

Nant Gwrtheyrn

The route bypasses Nant Gwrtheyrn, but it lies overlooking the coast, not far from the main route, and is worth a visit. It is a Welsh language and heritage centre named after the valley where it is located, Nant Gwrtheyrn ('Vortigern's Creek'), which lies in isolation by the sea at the foot of Yr Eifl. The centre is built within the structures of the former quarrying village of Porth y Nant, which was abandoned midway through World War II after quarrying ceased.

Head towards Llithfaen and past it, so the bay of Porth Dinllaen can be seen about 4 miles (6km) ahead.

Carnguwch

Here, a short detour east may be made to St Beuno's Church at Carnguwch and its associated holy well shelter, close to the foot of the mountain, around the far side from Tre'r Ceiri. It is best reached by a lane to the left, signposted to the church just as you reach Llithfaen. Established since at least the thirteenth century, the church was substantially rebuilt in the nineteenth century (the east window dates from the fifteenth or sixteenth century), but soon after abandoned as the population moved away from the surrounding farming communities towards expanding Llithfaen, and new churches were built there. The holy well, Ffynnon Sanctaidd, is known to lie close by the church. There is suggestion that a vessel of the well water and a brush were kept by the church's door and used to sprinkle water on members of the congregation.

Pistyll

Returning to the main Way, the path leads you down to Pistyll and St Beuno's Church. In the sixth century, this spot was a place of solitude for Beuno (Pistyll meaning 'fountain'). It was later a hospice for medieval pilgrims travelling to Bardsey. The church largely dates from the twelfth and fifteenth centuries, including a squint, a carved Catholic front, and a wall painting. The walls are of rhyolite rubble, and the interior features a fifteenth-century, five-bay arch-braced roof. Until the early twentieth century, the roof was thatched – holes for the ropes that secured it are still visible. Also, an interesting tradition still takes place here: the floor is covered with rushes and fragrant herbs at Christmas, Easter and harvest.

Although the route skirts the main village of Pistyll, it is worth making a short detour through it to visit Capel Bethania. Founded in 1875, the chapel was the Calvinistic Methodists' chapel associated with the controversial evangelist Tom Nefyn Williams (commonly referred to as Tom Nefyn), who was raised at nearby Bodeilas.

St Beuno's Church, Pistyll. MARTIN CRAMPIN

After visiting the church, continue along to pass the site of the now-demolished Plas Pistyll Hotel. Built as a farm and improved in the mid-nineteenth century, it formed an outlying part of the Vaynol estate, having formerly been a holding of Bodvel. The farm was sold in 1898 to the Goddard family, who constructed a large guesthouse on land that had formed part of the farm. This hotel was sold again in 1949, and became derelict; it was demolished in the twenty-first century.

Follow the Wales Coast Path across fields and then round the side of a hill, through the disused quarry to St Mary's Church and into Nefyn.

Nefyn

The name 'Nefyn' is thought to derive from the Irish/Gaelic name Nevin, or Cnaimhín. The Romans recorded a tribe occupying the peninsula called the 'Gangani', who are also recorded as a tribe in Ireland. 'Nevin' generally translates as 'Little Saint', and Nefyn is another form of Nyfain, an early Welsh female saint. The town was the place of a jousting tournament held by Edward I in 1284 to celebrate his victory over the Welsh, emphasizing its importance at that time as a trading town. In 1355, it became a free borough, and remained an important centre of commerce.

ST MARY'S CHURCH

St Mary's Church was built c.1825–7, on the site of a former church whose registers date from 1694. A church was established here in the fifth century by Nefyn ar Nefain, daughter of Brychan Brycheiniog of Garth Madryn. The name was recorded as

Llanfair-yn-Nefyn in the twelfth century, when the church was held by Augustinian Canons of Haughmond Abbey. In the thirteenth century, a priory was attached to the church. It was then entirely rebuilt in the nineteenth century. It would have been an important stopping point for pilgrimages to Ynys Enlli (Bardsey Island). No longer a place of worship, it now contains a museum dedicated to the maritime history of Nefyn.

From the centre of Nefyn pass St David's Church (built in 1904), on to Lon Y Traeth, and on to the footpath (Wales Coast Path/Pilgrim's Way). This follows the cliff top to Penrhyn Nefyn (seen ahead), and continues to Morfa Nefyn, where you descend steps to the slipway and the beach.

Morfa Nefyn

Make a detour into the main village to visit Moreia Methodist Chapel; it was built in 1825, rebuilt in 1853 and again in 1882. The present chapel is of the neo-classical style of the gable-entry type, to the design of architect Owen Morris Roberts of Portmadog.

You then pass Trwyn Dinllaen Iron Age hill fort on the headland to the west, which archaeologists have dated to c.100BC, Morfa Nefyn's earliest known settlers. A walk along the headland today shows little evidence of their existence, as the Iron Age fort is obscured by the modern Nefyn golf course.

Tudweiliog

The route now crosses the golf club, plunging down to the pipeline at Abergeirch, before following a magnificent coastal path for a good 3 miles (5km) to Ty-hen. From here there is a footpath to the village of Tudweiliog, if you would like to take a detour.

St Cwyfan's Church, designed by Sir Gilbert Scott, was built in 1849 of local stone on the site of an earlier medieval structure. It consists of a divided nave and chancel. The church was originally founded by St Cwyfan, a seventh-century saint who was the son of Brwynen Hewn, and served as a landmark to mariners sailing to and from Liverpool. The fourteenth-century font from the original church was removed and now sits in the grounds of Cefnamwlch estate, as do further medieval stone corbels which can be seen in a wall near the gatehouse.

Continue to follow the coastal path directly to the beach. The path keeps to the coast via Porth Colmon all the way to Whistling Sands – so called because the sand squeaks under your feet (the Welsh name 'Porth Oer' means 'Cold Port'). Then follow the coastal path around the tip of the Llŷn Peninsula where there are excellent views over to Ynys Enlli/Bardsey Island, before passing through Anelog.

ANELOG

Two stones were found at Capel Anelog, a site on the eastern slope of Mynydd Anelog, a few miles north of Aberdaron; it may have been the original monastery of the community that was later established on Bardsey and Aberdaron. Both stones date from the early sixth century and record the graves of priests who were possibly members of a small religious community here. One is inscribed VERACIUS / PBR / HIC / IACIT, or: 'Veracius the priest lies here'. The letters PBR are an abbreviation for PRESBYTER, shortened by contraction. The other stone reads SENACUS / PSBR / HIC IACIT / CVM MULTITV/D(I)NEM / FRATRVM / PRESB(IT)E[R], or: 'Senacus the priest lies here with the multitude of the brethren, Priest'.

The site locally identified as that of the chapel from which the inscribed stones were taken to Cefnamwlch lies just east of the modern road near Gors, at about 200ft (60m) above OD ('ordnance datum' – altitude). All that remains is the robber-trench from which the foundations have been removed, outlining the east end of a rectangular building about 12ft (3.5m)wide. Traces of other buildings occur about 50yd (45m) to the north.

A direct route to Aberdaron then completes the final leg of the mainland journey.

Aberdaron

Sometimes referred to as the 'Land's End of Wales' (Welsh: Pendraw'r Byd), Aberdaron had a monastic community linked to that on Bardsey. The fine twelfth-century west door, and the extension of the church in the early sixteenth century, are evidence of the wealth the pilgrims brought. In the eighteenth and nineteenth centuries it developed as a shipbuilding centre and port. The mining and quarrying industries became major employers, and limestone, lead, jasper and manganese were exported. The ruins of an old pier can be seen, running out to sea at Porth Simdde, the local name for the west end of Aberdaron Beach.

ST HYWYN'S CHURCH

Known as the 'Cathedral of Llyn', the church of St Hywyn is in a striking location at the edge of the beach, at the end of the Llŷn Peninsula – the last staging post before crossing to Ynys Enlli (Bardsey Island). Thousands of pilgrims over the centuries have offered their prayers in this small church.

One of the most interesting architectural features of St Hywyn's is the Norman west door. The church is also home to the Anelog stones, the pair of sixth-century gravestones mentioned above, which are displayed against the north-east wall.

There has been a place of Christian worship at the edge of the sea at Aberdaron since the fifth century. At first, a simple wooden structure sheltered both Hywyn and his prayer cell from where the Gospel was preached. In 1137, Gruffydd ap Cynan, King of Gwynedd, began erecting stone churches to replace the wooden buildings in the most important parishes, and so the oldest portion of St Hywyn's dates from this time. It became a sanctuary church where, on the stone chair called the 'chair of peace', disputes could be settled, and no fugitive could be ejected for forty days and nights. There was also a 'clas' here, an institution of the Celtic church similar to a monastery but without allegiance to any monastic order. In 1624, St John's College, Cambridge, became the patron of the parish, and remained so for almost 300 years.

As noted, some of the church's fabric dates from the twelfth century, but the church was enlarged in 1417. Records show that it was still closely connected with St Mary's Abbey on Bardsey. By the late eighteenth century, the church building had fallen into a poor state of repair. Restoration was carried out in the nineteenth century, and there was a further refurbishment in 1906, when the churchyard was increased in size. In the 1990s, new sea defences were installed to prevent the church being undermined.

ABERDARON NEW CHURCH

It was recorded by Hyde-Hall in 1809–11 that part of the church of St Hywyn, was, like many churches in Llŷn, in a seriously dilapidated condition, but that a school was being held in a part of it. The sea was eroding the cemetery and endangering the building, so it was decided to build a new church on land belonging to Bodernabwy, in the upper part of the village. This was a completely different building, built in a neo-Romanesque style, of which many people were critical. It was opened in 1841 but was not popular, and the parishioners soon returned to the church of St Hywyn after it was repaired in 1868. The new church continued in use until the 1940s, but thereafter has only been used for burial services. It remains an unusual survival of a church interior of the early part of the Gothic Revival, and was presumably also dedicated to St Hywyn.

Y GEGIN FAWR

Y Gegin Fawr (English: 'The Big Kitchen') was built in the thirteenth century as a communal kitchen where pilgrims could claim a meal on their way to Bardsey Island. Aberdaron was the last place on the route for rest and refreshment, and pilgrims often had to wait weeks in the village for a chance to cross the treacherous waters of Bardsey Sound (Welsh: 'Swnt Enlli'). The current two-storey, rubble-built building likely dates to the seventeenth century; it was said to have been restored in the twentieth century by Sir Clough Williams-Ellis.

CAE Y GROGBREN

Next to the car park is a field known as Cae y Grogbren (English: 'Gallows Field'), near which is a large red rock. In the Middle Ages, the abbot from the monastery on Bardsey Island visited the rock to dispense justice to local criminals; if found guilty, they were hanged and thrown into Pwll Ddiwaelod (English: 'The Bottomless Pool'). The pool is a kettle lake, formed at the end of the Ice Age, when blocks of ice were trapped underground and melted to form round, deep pools.

Bardsey Island from the coast. DAVID ROSS

BODWRDDA

Here, it is possible to make a slight detour, but an interesting one nonetheless (perhaps while waiting to cross over to Bardsey), to Bodwrdda, an early sixteenth-century stone-built gentry house situated approximately a mile from the village of Aberdaron. The building originally had a fulling mill adjacent to it, and a bakehouse; two large brick-built wings were added later, giving an imposing three-storey façade containing seventeenth-century windows. It was extended in the early seventeenth century, dated 1621, and the use of brick in wings of this date is exceptional in the region.

The End of the Journey: Bardsey Island

The ferry for Ynys Enlli (Bardsey Island), with its lighthouse and the thirteenth-century Augustinian Abbey of St Mary's, leaves from Porth Meudwy, which is 1.2 miles (1.8km) from Aberdaron by the coast path, or 1.7 miles (2.7km) by road. The dangerous stretch of water you cross to the island – Bardsey Sound/the Swnt – is allegedly where 'Gwennan', King Arthur's ship, was sunk. Caswennan was then the name for the Swnt.

Bardsey Island, 9 miles (14.5km) off the mainland, was inhabited as early as the Neolithic era, and traces of hut circles and rectangular structures remain primarily on a small sheltered terrace on the mountain, or in groups at Penrhyn Gogor at the northern end of the island. The latter are thought to be agricultural buildings dating from the Middle Ages.

THE ABBEY

During the fifth century the island became a refuge for persecuted Christians, and a small Celtic monastery existed at that time. St Cadfan arrived from Brittany in 516CE and, under his guidance, St Mary's Abbey was built. For centuries the island was important as 'the holy place of burial for all the bravest and best in the land'. In the medieval period, three pilgrimages to Bardsey Island were considered to be of equivalent benefit to the soul as a single journey to Rome.

In 1188 the abbey was still a Celtic institution, but by 1212 it had been reconstituted by the Augustinians, a rich order, who rebuilt the abbey as a result. The tower located within the present burial ground is the only part of its structure remaining above ground, and is the most prominent historic monument on the island. The two-stage tower is 19ft (5.8m) square internally, with 3.6ft (1.1m) wide walls, and stands up to 26ft (8m) high. The exact extent of all the buildings associated with the abbey is unknown, but it is likely that the site supported a sizeable community of monks. Little remains except a few loose pieces of dressed stone.

TY NEWYDD

Near the site of the present track it is also possible to see ruins of former farmhouses. One of these, Ty Newydd, was investigated by Christopher Arnold in 1995, and it was found that the house had been built on the site of several graves. A silver penny dated to the 1070s was found in the mouth of one of the skeletons unearthed during the excavation.

THE CHAPEL

In the shelter of the mountain at the north end of the island, not far from the abbey, is the site of a simple neo-Gothic Calvinistic Methodist chapel; it was built in 1875, when the farmhouses nearby were renovated. It is said that the inhabitants chose to have a chapel rather than a new harbour, a choice presented by their landowner, Lord Newborough. Inside the chapel is a carved stone, bearing an inscription and dating from the ninth century.

The island was first described as the burial place of 20,000 saints in the *Book of Llandaff* (written between 1120 and 1140); there is a Celtic cross in the cemetery to commemorate this. The description is really an exaggeration, but the island has been remarkably attractive to pilgrims from many different places over the centuries; many of them wanted to spend the final days of their lives on Enlli and be buried there – numerous burials have been found in the vicinity of the abbey.

THE SCHOOL

The school building, which was once the island chapel, stands above the track near Cristin (home of Bardsey Lodge and the Bird Observatory); it was built in the late eighteenth or early nineteenth century. Regularly used as a school until the last employed teacher left in 1953, it is now a meeting place.

THE LIGHTHOUSE

Bardsey lighthouse stands on the southerly tip of the island and guides vessels passing through St George's Channel and the Irish Sea. Application for a light here was first made in 1816 by Lt Thomas Evans RN, but several other applications made in 1820 finally resulted in the building of the tower by Trinity House (the official lighthouse authority) in 1821. It is said to be the only square tower lighthouse maintained by Trinity House.

Y STORWS

Frequently referred to as the Boathouse, the Storws is often the first building – apart from the lighthouse – that you see from the landing place at Y Cafn. A long, low stone building with a lichen-covered roof, it was built a few years before the lighthouse. The sheltered bench stretching the length of the building is a favourite place to sit.

Capel Mair

Finally, before or after a visit to Aberdaron, a detour to the chapel of Capel Mair is a real 'must'. St Mary's Chapel stood on the flat land between Mynydd Mawr and Mynydd Gwyddel, on the very outcrop above Pen Y Cil of the Llŷn Peninsula. It was a refuge and place of prayer for pilgrms, while the well there was a source of water and, no doubt, healing; it was the last in a string of pilgrimage chapels to Bardsey. It is now totally ruinous/earthworks but its foundations and enclosure can still be recognized. The church was also used by sailors and fisher families to pray for their safety before sailing out into the dangerous channel, as well as for keeping bodies waiting to be taken to Bardsey for burial. It initially comprised a rectangular building about 40 by 22ft (12 by 7m) in an enclosure of about 40sq yd (33sq m), the area bounded by a field system indicating medieval cultivation.

Ffynnon Fair is the associated well. A natural spring, the water collects in a small, rock-lined pool in the cliff side, and then falls to the rocky shore below, but is inaccessible at high tide.

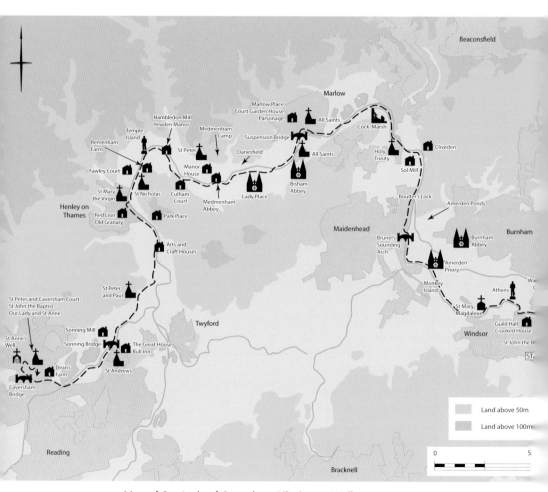

Map of Our Lady of Caversham Pilgrimage Walk. JIM BRIGHTMAN

CHAPTER FOUR

Our Lady of Caversham Pilgrimage Walk

A further route said to have been populated throughout the medieval period by royals and nobles alike, the 36-mile (58km) walk follows the River Thames from Windsor to Caversham, which, now near Reading, was formerly in Oxfordshire. The route culminates at the re-established Shrine of Our Lady in the chapel adjacent to the Church of Our Lady and St Anne, but many of the stations along the way, including a holy well, are also linked to the Virgin Mary. However, this is very much a modern re-creation and interpretation of a medieval pilgrimage route and shrine site. Today, visitors are taken through the labyrinth of historic streets to the shrine chapel to see the carved oak statue – but this is not what medieval pilgrims would have seen, nor was the current site the original location of the shrine.

The History of Our Lady of Caversham

The image shrine of Our Lady of Caversham stood across the River Thames, to the north of the town of Reading. A popular place of pilgrimage throughout the medieval period, the cult featured a handful of associated sites, including the Chapel of St Anne, which stood on the bridge, and her well, the waters of which were believed to have healing properties.

While it appears the shrine was primarily visited for the benefits of physical healing, there is no clear surviving story of its inception, and therefore we have no certain indication of its antiquity. According to a later tradition incorporated into the cartulary of Nutley Abbey – the Augustinian priory in Buckinghamshire by which the shrine was cared for by one of its canons, who resided at Caversham as its warden since 1162 – the Norman chapel by the River Thames was already in existence as early as 1106. In this year Robert, Duke of Normandy, eldest son of William the Conqueror, is said to have presented to the shrine a relic of Christ's Passion – namely the spearhead that pierced Christ's side – which he had brought back from the first Crusade. While the relic was one of the main draws, the cult centred round a wooden jewel-encrusted crowned statue of the Virgin, but the chapel also contained a piece of the rope with which Judas hung himself, and the knives that killed King Edward the Martyr (and Henry VI).

It is possible that the chapel was built by one of the guilds dedicated to Our Lady, as they often constructed chapels beside river crossings – the shrine at Caversham was located beside such a crossing of the Thames. Returning to the abbey, its main involvement, in addition to its pastoral role, was in aiding the building of the first bridge over the river, with a chapel to the Holy Spirit on the Reading side and another dedicated to St Anne on the Caversham side. There was also a holy well known as St Anne's Well (still extant) at the top of Priest Hill, Caversham.

So completely were the traces of the shrine obliterated during the Reformation that, by the eighteenth century, the memory of the exact location of the shrine itself was consigned to history. The destruction of the statue by Thomas Cromwell's emissary, Dr John London, took place on 17 September 1538, when he claimed to have '... pulled down the Image of Our Lady at Caversham, whereunto was great pilgrimage... I have also pulled down the place she stood in with all other ceremonies, as lights, shrouds, crutches and images of wax hanging about the chapel and have defaced the same thoroughly as eschewing of any further resort thither.'

The statue was sent to Cromwell in London and burned. The original shrine chapel site is thus still unclear, save for a plaque located on the opposite side of the current 1926 bridge commemorating the founding of the Chapel of St Anne in 1231, which survived until 1550. In fact, further success of its elimination can be confirmed by the words of John Leland, antiquarian, chaplain and librarian to Henry VIII. Passing by not long after the shrine's removal, Leland commented upon the structure of Caversham Bridge and the Chapel of St Anne which it bore, yet failed entirely to mention the proximity of the former shrine, which was once thought to rival that at Walsingham in Norfolk. And while there was certainly never a proper priory at Caversham, there may, at least for a time, have been a cell that was accorded that courtesy title. If so, then the memory of the site may have been preserved in the building which appears with that name on a nineteenth-century Ordnance Survey map, about a quarter of a mile north-east of the north end of the bridge. Such a location would be consistent with the majority of evidence to have survived.

Additional evidence suggests that the Chapel of Our Lady of Caversham may have stood within the grounds of St Peter's Church, which dates from *c*.1162, or possibly earlier. Its original location is generally thought to have been built on the site of the Old Rectory, now Caversham Court. It survived an almost total rebuilding programme by A.W.N. Pugin in 1840 under the patronage of the great brewing Simonds family, but the house only lasted about a hundred more years, and is now a public park. A final suggested site is Deans Farm, as a field next to the farm was known as 'Capull (ie. Chapel) alias Rayley' in 1633.

Subsequently, the current shrine chapel is not the original site, and was actually a creation of the parish priest, Father Haskew, who began the cult's revival in 1897, the year following the foundation of the parish of Our Lady and St Anne. However, Father Haskew, who wrote the first account of the shrine in the modern era, mistook the shrine chapel for the Chapel of St Anne on Caversham Bridge, which was actually a stopping station for pilgrims visiting from the south. When the new Caversham Bridge was built in the 1920s, stone from the foundations of the original medieval bridge chapel was reused to create a restored shrine.

During this period, a marble statue of Our Lady and Child was presented to the church to encourage/stimulate devotion at the site, and now acts as the main focus of the cult here. It currently resides in the cenacle (an upper room, named after the site of the Last Supper). Following this, the shrine was made more magnificent in 1958 by Father William O'Malley, who built a stone chapel and brought in a 500-year old oak statue of the Lady and Child. Exterior to the chapel, a small window and stone kneeling platform exists, through which the statue may be viewed for pilgrims to venerate. In 1996, following a parish pilgrimage to Rome, Pope John Paul II blessed the gold and silver crown for the statue.

Although it has been claimed as a popular site of pilgrimage, by the time that Dr London arrived in 1538, the Caversham shrine had a predominantly local significance only. Few benefactions were given in the fifteenth and sixteenth centuries, although pilgrims did continue to visit. Most notably, by the fifteenth century, the statue had been plated in silver, and in 1439, Isabella Beauchamp, Countess of Warwick, left 20lb (9kg) of gold to be made into a jewel-encrusted crown for it. Yet apart from Henry III's interest in the thirteenth century – he provided the canons of Nutley serving at Caversham with two oak trees for the building of a boat to ferry pilgrims across the river to the shrine, as well as a 4lb (1.8kg) wax candle in 1239, 1,500 tapers in 1241, and a chasuble of red velvet in 1246 – no subsequent monarch showed any comparable interest. Catherine of Aragon, who was an unrelenting pilgrim, visited only once, in 1532, and is not known to have made any benefaction at all.

Our Lady of Caversham was clearly a shrine of some significance during its brief heyday in the thirteenth century, and largely because of visits by the king, the Marshal Earls of Pembroke and the de Clare Earls of Hertford, but its appeal appears to have declined in the fourteenth century; like many such manifestations of the faith of the medieval church, it prospered when great men and women showed interest, yet languished at other times.

An Overview of the Route

The route essentially follows the River Thames and the Thames Path National Trail, beginning at Windsor and finishing at Caversham. Starting at Windsor High Street, beneath the castle walls, the route follows Thames Street to the River Thames, where it runs along the south bank of the river to the A355 and then over to the north bank, which is then followed all the way to Bray Lock, some 6 miles (10km) away.

Keep to the right of the river to Maidenhead; here, cross over to the left, and follow the river to near Cliveden. Then walk inland until you reach Cookham, and rejoin the Thames Path. Just beyond Holy Trinity Church, turn left along the Thames Path, keeping the river to your right. Walk beside Cock Marsh for well over half a mile to the railway bridge, where you cross the river. Then follow a fenced path to Bourne End and on to the marina (Enid Blyton lived here in the 1920s, as did crime writer, Edgar Wallace). The river curves left here, and flows on to Spade Oak Meadow. A few miles from Bourne End, the river bears right and passes underneath the A404 to reach the outskirts of Marlow. Passing the dock at Marlow, you reach All Saints Church, with the suspension bridge to your left. The route is now in the county of Buckinghamshire.

Leaving Marlow, the route runs through Higginson Park; soon after, to the left, is Bisham church and abbey. After passing Hurley Lock a short way beyond, the village of Medmenham is passed on the opposite side of the bank.

Continue along the river crossing three footbridges, then after half a mile, bear left, leaving the river and up to a farm drive. Here, pass beneath Culham Court and then, a short distance ahead, Hambleden Lock. The Upper Thames Rowing Club at Henley-on-Thames is the culmination of the next section, with Temple Island, Fawley Court and Remenham and its church prior to that. Continue by the river, but then leave it to walk past Thameside Court, passing The White House and Rivermead House before entering Lower Shiplake.

The river is again followed from here until a footbridge near the A155, which takes you to the road bridge in Sonning. Continue now by the river to Sonning Lock; soon after the Reading Blue Coat School Boat Club you will approach Reading, with a wide meadow on the left. Passing the start of the Kennet and Avon Canal, continue to Caversham Lock, and then on to Reading Bridge. Pass under the bridge, and continue by the river to Caversham Bridge.

Leave the river here; cross over the bridge, and follow St Peter's Road to St Peter's Church and the former Caversham Court. After visiting both, retrace the route back to St Anne's Road: at the top is Priests Hill with St Anne's Holy Well. Descend Priests Hill and, at the bottom, continue to the main road to reach St Anne's Church, to visit Our Lady of Caversham's shrine.

Start of the Route: Windsor

The Way commences in the historical and, more importantly, royal town of Windsor, where Windsor Castle is the architectural favourite; in fact, a book all of its own would be needed just to recount its architectural history. However, there are many other significant buildings, including the Market Cross House, the Guildhall and St John the Baptist Church.

WINDSOR CASTLE

The castle is the oldest and largest inhabited castle in the world, and the official residence of Her Majesty the Queen. It has been used by succeeding monarchs since the time of Henry I, and is the longest continuously occupied fortress in Europe.

The original motte and bailey castle was built in the eleventh century. Following the Norman invasion by William the Conqueror it was constructed to protect Norman dominance around the outskirts of London, and to oversee a strategically important part of the River Thames. Gradually replacing stone fortifications, Henry III built a luxurious royal palace within the castle, and Edward III went further, rebuilding

Windsor Castle. STEVE DUNN

the palace to produce an even grander set of buildings. Edward's core design lasted through the Tudor period, during which Henry VIII and Elizabeth I made increasing use of the castle as a royal court.

During the Restoration era, Charles II rebuilt much of Windsor Castle with extravagant baroque interiors. After a period of neglect during the eighteenth century, George III and George IV renovated and rebuilt Charles II's palace at colossal expense, producing the current design of the state apartments, full of rococo, gothic and baroque furnishings. Victoria also made minor changes to the castle, which became the centre for royal entertainment for much of her reign.

THE CROOKED HOUSE/THE MARKET CROSS HOUSE

This building has been an integral part of Windsorian life for more than 400 years. Throughout this time, the area at the top of the town adjacent to the castle and parish church would have also served the market place, as established by the Normans.

Until 1592, on market days, local farmers met at the town's original market cross, built by John Sadler in 1380, where local produce could be bought and sold; Queen Victoria's statue is currently located here. In 1592, the original Crooked House of Windsor, known historically as Market Cross House, was built, north of the site of the present Guildhall. Then, in 1687, the council ordered this first Market Cross House to be demolished in order to build the neighbouring Guildhall. A land dispute ensued, and the council was ordered to rebuild Market Cross House and to construct the Guildhall no larger than its present size.

The Crooked House/the Market Cross House, Windsor. STEVE DUNN

Originally a butcher's shop, over the centuries the building has housed many types of businesses, including a jewellers, a brewery, an antique and a gift shop. It was then a tearoom for over thirty years. Its famous tilt is due to the use of unseasoned green oak and structural changes over the years. There is also a legend that a secret passage existed between the hall and the castle to allow Charles II to meet his mistress, Nell Gwyn, in secret, and later, so that groceries could be brought to the castle kitchens.

THE GUILDHALL

Strictly speaking, Windsor's Guildhall should be known as the town hall, because it was never the meeting place of the town's guilds. The meeting place, or 'guild hall', would have been the 'Three Tuns' next door, which dates from around 1518.

The Guildhall, Windsor. STEVE DUNN

The town hall as we know it today was commenced in 1687. It was designed by Sir Thomas Fitz, surveyor to the Cinque Ports, though Sir Thomas died before the work was finished; it was completed by Sir Christopher Wren, and was ready for occupation on 17 October 1689. The design of the building allowed for a corn market beneath the meeting chamber above.

The four Portland stone pillars in the centre of the corn market are interesting and a wonderful example of Wren's talent as they do not actually support the ceiling. Legend has it that the council were concerned that the unsupported floor of the chamber might collapse, but Wren, to prove a point, left the additional columns just short of the ceiling.

ST JOHN THE BAPTIST

St John the Baptist is the parish church of Windsor, and is the product of two very different schemes. It is on the site of the earlier twelfth-century church, which consisted of a nave, chancel and aisles, each under a separate gable and flush with one another at the east end. The condition of the building led to a proposal in 1818 to rebuild, and the work was carried out in fine ashlar between 1820 and 1822 by the little-known architect, Charles Hollis, yet under the direction of Jeffry Wyatt, who had undertaken a considerable amount of work on Windsor Castle. Major restoration work, as well as the building of a chancel, was then carried out between 1869 and 1873, using small, grey ashlar stone blocks with Bath stone dressings.

The church has a large number of wall monuments, many of which were re-sited from the old church, and date back to the early seventeenth century. The east end features a series of mosaic panels beneath the windows by Antonio Salviati. In the centre, these form a reredos depicting the Agnus Dei and Pelican in her Piety. Some finely carved railings are the work of Grinling Gibbons, and were previously in a chapel at Windsor Castle. Beside the chancel are two royal thrones, while in the gallery above the west door, is a large painting of 'The Last Supper' by Franz de Cleyn (1588–1658), the German court painter to James I. It was restored in 2003. The royal pew is situated on the south side of the sanctuary.

St John the Baptist Church, Windsor.
STEVE DUNN

Boveney

St Mary Magdalene Church in Boveney is now cared for by the Friends of Friendless Churches. The earliest part of the building dates from around the twelfth century, but it stands on a site which has been a place of worship since before the Roman conquest. The building is constructed of chalk and flint-coursed rubble (known as galletting) with ashlar dressings, and features a weather-boarded tower and wonderful eighteenth and nineteenth-century vernacular interior. It acted as a chapel-of-ease for St Peter's Church, Burnham. An attempt to make it into a separate parish in 1737 failed because sufficient endowment could not be raised. Originally, it served the bargemen or 'bargees' of the nearby quay, but this is long lost.

The Athens Stone

Approximately 440 yards (400m) past Boveney Lock, the route meets up with the gravel Thames Path, a National Trail opened in 1996. After about 330 yards (300m), on the right-hand side of the path, you will come across the 'Bathing Place of Athens'.

Swimming in the River Thames was once a commonplace activity, and Eton College constructed four bathing places in the area. The memorial stone at the site of the Athens bathing area is dedicated to an ex-member of Eton College, John Baker, who, having bathed at this spot as a child, died in a flying accident in 1917. The other side notes the 'BATHING REGULATIONS AT ATHENS' from the School Rules of the River, 1921:

> *Fifth Form Nants in First Hundred and Upper and Middle Divisions may*
> *bathe at Athens. No bathing at Athens on Sundays after 8.30 a.m.*
> *At Athens, boys who are undressed must either get at once into the*
> *water or get behind screens when boats containing ladies come in sight.*
> *Boys when bathing are not allowed to land on the Windsor Bank or to*
> *swim out to launches and barges or to hang onto, or interfere with,*
> *boats of any kind. Any boy breaking this rule will be severely punished.*

Moving on, the next section of the route is known for its rife historic landscape.

Monkey Island

There are several theories surrounding the island's name. One is that Monkey Island is derived from Andieu de Clermont's paintings in the nearby Monkey Room (see below); however, it is more likely that it evolved from the original name 'Monks' Eyot', after the monks who first used the island. 'Eyot', like 'eyte' and 'ayt', is an Old English word for 'island'.

The island has been in use since at least the twelfth century. Monks resided at Merton Priory at Amerden Bank, a moated site on Bray Lock on the Buckinghamshire bank of the river, until the Dissolution of the Monasteries in the sixteenth century, and they used the island during their fishing activities. According to some accounts, they leased the island from the Whiteknights estate, which now includes the site of Reading University.

At some point in the fourteenth century, the island passed into the hands of the canonesses of Burnham Abbey, situated a mile to the north. There are various records of the island dating from that time, using various names including Bournhames Eyte and Burnham Ayt.

The Englefield family then acquired Monkey Island in 1606. Oddly enough, it was the Great Fire of London in 1666 that saw the making of the island, when stone was shipped downstream to help rebuild the capital. Returning from London, the barges carried rubble, which they offloaded on to several islands in the Thames. This provided Monkey Island with a solid base, raising its level above the river and thus eliminating the risk of serious flooding.

Perhaps most important in the history of the island was its purchase by Charles Spencer, the 3rd Duke of Marlborough. He bought it from Sir Francis Englefield in 1723 after attending meetings of the notorious Kit-Kat Club at nearby Down Place. The club, which formed in the early 1700s, had a sociable façade, but there were in fact covert objectives concerned with supporting the House of Hanover.

The Duke erected the first two buildings on the island to indulge his angling hobby. The Palladian fishing lodge and the fishing temple, as they were then described, are still part of the hotel and are now known as the Pavilion and the Temple (which features a suite decorated with high relief plasterwork in the Wedgwood style) respectively. Reflecting the craftsmanship of the time, the Duke had the Pavilion built out of wood blocks cut to look like stone. Inside the Pavilion the most intriguing feature is the suite of delightful Singerie paintings in the Monkey Room, which depict monkeys engaged in rather human-like activities such as shooting, fishing and smoking; these were painted by the French artist, Andieu de Clermont, some time before 1738.

By 1840 the Pavilion had become a riverside inn, welcoming guests via a ferry that docked on the island's south bank. By the time Mrs Plummer was running the hotel from the late 1800s to 1910, the island had already become a fashionable spot, thanks in part to Edward VII and Queen Alexandra taking tea on the lawns.

The twentieth century brought extensive additions and refurbishment. In 1963, the dining area was increased with the addition of the River Room: a large, glass-walled building that jutted out over the Thames. A famous hotel not far from the village is the Monkey Island Hotel, named after the islet in the Thames on which it stands.

'Amerden Priory'

It would appear that 'Amerden Priory' never actually existed as a priory *per se*, but it has been identified as a possible grange of Merton Priory, and is surrounded by earthworks suggestive of a moat – but it is questionable whether Merton Priory ever had a grange there, since there is no documentary evidence of it.

Today, there is a caravan and camping park on the site, as well as a late sixteenth- or early seventeenth-century timber-framed building with colour-washed brick nogging, and a further building designated as 'The Other House'.

Burnham Abbey

In the fourteenth century, Monkey Island became the property of nearby Burnham Abbey, one of the best-surviving medieval religious houses in Buckinghamshire, and it is worth making a short detour north-east of Amerden Priory to visit it. A house of Augustinian canonesses was founded in 1266 by Richard, Earl of Cornwall, brother of Henry III, and closed during the Dissolution. The abbey was built around a cloister garth, with a frater, church, guest house and kitchen, and two-storey quarters for the nuns. The infirmary was a separate building connected by a passage to the east range. In the sixteenth century, the church was demolished and a private house fashioned from many of the remaining buildings. In due course it became a farm, though the buildings gradually fell into disrepair.

The remains of the abbey were bought by Lawrence Bissley in 1913, who restored many of the buildings and converted the original chapter house into a chapel. In 1916, a community of Anglican Augustinian nuns moved back to the site and, even to this day, the sisters of the 'Society of Precious Blood' reside there.

AMERDEN PONDS OR GROVE

Further west, a short detour also takes you to Amerden Ponds, or Grove. The two lakes and outdoor swimming pool belonged to a now-demolished nineteenth-century country house, the estate of Sir Henry Valentine Rae Reid (a London wine merchant). The house was built before 1895; it burned down in 1998, and new town houses were built on the site in 2005.

Returning to the main route, while it skirts the fringes of Bray, the village itself is not only picturesque but contains many interesting historic properties, including the former Bray Film Studios, and St Michael's Church.

Bray (on the other side of the river)

Made famous in the popular ballad, the parish is widely known due to the turncoat ways of the Vicar of Bray.

Built in 1293, St Michael's Church was allegedly erected here to replace a Saxon church at Water Oakley. It was partly rebuilt c.1500 and extensively restored between 1857 and 1882 by Thomas Henry Wyatt. It has a number of sculptures which may have come from the earlier church, including a dog (or a horse?) built into the outer wall of the Chantry Chapel of Our Lady, and a damaged Sheela na Gig (a pre-Christian fertility symbol, often found in Ireland, showing a female figure proudly displaying

St Michael's Church, Bray. STEVE DUNN

her nether regions); there is also the superb 1378 memorial brass of Sir John Foxley, the Constable of Southampton Castle, and his two wives. One of the local cottages has a tunnel which is supposed to lead to the church and served as an escape route for clergymen (i.e. like a priest hole).

Underneath the central portion of the nave is said to be buried Bray's most famous resident: Simon Alleyn, the so-called 'Singing Vicar'. This famous Vicar of Bray had a well-known ballad written about him in which he promised to stick to the principle that, no matter what religious denomination he was forced to adopt, he would always remain 'the Vicar of Bray, Sir'. The poem is suggestive of a man living through the troubled years of the late seventeenth century, but the story is known to be much older and likely refers to the even more turbulent times of the Reformation. Hence, Alleyn, who was vicar from 1523 to 1565, is thought to be the man in question.

The Jesus Hospital at Bray is a red-brick group of almshouses founded in 1609 by William Goddard (whose full-size effigy stands over the entrance) with the purpose of caring for thirty-four of the aged poor of Bray and six of the Worshipful Company of Fishmongers, to which Goddard belonged. Jesus Hospital is now run by the Donnington Hospital Trust, having been transferred from the Fishmongers Company in 2010.

Brunel's Sounding Arch

Built in 1838, the two arches of Maidenhead Railway Bridge are the widest and flattest in the world. Each span is 128ft (about 39m), with a rise of only 24ft (about 7m). It is testimony to the genius of Isambard Kingdom Brunel that not only was a bridge with such flat arches actually built, but it still continues to carry the Great Western Railway main line from Paddington Station.

Boulters Lock. STEVE DUNN

Cliveden House. STEVE DUNN

Boulters Lock

A lock was first built here by the Thames Navigation Commission in 1772. The lock is on the western side of the river between the main Maidenhead to Cookham road (the A4094) and Ray Mill Island.

The earliest reference to a flash lock is in the late sixteenth century, although a mill is known to have existed here in the fourteenth century. The first lock was built in the late eighteenth century, but by 1825, the City of London Corporation complained of its condition and recommended it be rebuilt on the Berkshire side of the river. The lock was a popular place to visit on the Sunday after Royal Ascot.

Boulters Lock was formerly called Ray Mill Lock, after the adjacent flour mill owned by the Ray family. The mill became Boulters Inn in 1950 (now a restaurant). The word 'bolter' is an old English word for 'miller', hence the name Boulters Lock. In 1909, the Thames Conservancy purchased Ray Mill Island to provide for expansion of the lock, and it was rebuilt in 1912.

Cliveden Tower and House (on the other side of the river)

Just over a mile away, the clock tower of Cliveden House can be seen peering over the high valley sides; it is now a luxury hotel but is cared for by the National Trust. Designed by Sir Charles Barry in 1851 to replace a house previously destroyed by fire, the present house of Cliveden is located at Taplow, and is a blend of the English Palladian revival style and the Roman Cinquecento. The exterior of the house is rendered in Roman cement, with terracotta additions such as balusters, capitals, keystones and finials.

Set above the River Thames, the site has been home to an earl, three countesses, two dukes, a Prince of Wales and the Viscounts Astor – it is the third house to occupy this site. As the home of Waldorf and Nancy Astor, the house was the meeting place of the 'Cliveden Set' of the 1920s and 1930s, a group of political intellectuals. During the 1970s, it was occupied by Stanford University of California, which used it as an overseas campus.

In the grounds is the 100ft (30m) clock tower: it was added in 1861 and is the work of the architect Henry Clutton. As a functioning water tower it still provides water for the house today. The tower is topped with a modern reproduction of Augustin Dumont's nineteenth-century winged male figure Le Génie de la Liberté (the Spirit of Liberty).

Also, the garden features the famous Great Parterre, laid out by John Fleming in 1855. It was also the setting for the 1965 Beatles' movie *Help*.

Sol Mill

Leaving here you pass Sol Mill, the former home of Led Zeppelin guitarist Jimmy Page, as well as Chris Rea. This six-bedroom, sixteenth-century waterside mansion is

Cliveden Tower. STEVE DUNN

in the village of Cookham, Berkshire. It was also once a recording studio, and played host to The Rolling Stones, Fleetwood Mac and The Pet Shop Boys. The house is now a yoga retreat.

Cookham

It is most likely that the present village of Cookham developed around an eighth-century Anglo-Saxon monastery situated in the parish; the site of a power struggle between the Kingdoms of Mercia and Wessex. The Anglo-Saxon kings also had a royal palace here, where the Witan (King's Council) met in 997CE. The latter likely stood in Little Berry Field, while the former may have centred around the nearby Holy Trinity Parish Church, which does show signs of Anglo-Saxon work in the fabric of the chancel; it became a Saxon minster in later years.

The present part-chalk, part-flint church with chalk diapering dates mostly from the thirteenth century, but the Lady Chapel is the earliest identifiable part, dated to 1182. It was built on the site of a hermitage that adjoined the old Norman building. An anchoress lived here through the generosity of Henry II, who may have been trying to expiate himself for the murder of St Thomas Becket at Canterbury Cathedral in 1170. An image shrine of the Madonna and Child is sited in one of the trefoil recesses. Further alteration work was carried out in the early fourteenth century, the west tower was added in c.1500, and the entire building was restored in 1860.

Cookham Bridge. STEVE DUNN

The churchyard is the setting for Sir Stanley Spencer's 1924–7 famous painting 'The Resurrection', in which Christ is enthroned in the church porch, cradling three babies, with God the Father standing behind. Spencer himself appears near the centre, naked, leaning against a gravestone; his fiancée, Hilda, lies sleeping in a bed of ivy. At the top left, risen souls are transported to Heaven in the pleasure steamers that then sailed the Thames. Spencer referred to Cookham as 'a village in Heaven'.

A former resident of Cookham was Kenneth Grahame, author of *The Wind in the Willows*. He lived at 'The Mount' in Cookham Dean. It is thought this is where he penned the book, and it is certainly accepted that the river scenes between Cookham and Henley inspired the work, along with Winter Hill above it.

In the Middle Ages, most of Cookham was owned by Cirencester Abbey, and the timber-framed Churchgate House was the abbot's apparent residence when he was visiting the town. The Tarry Stone, still to be seen on the boundary wall of the Dower House, marked the extent of the monastic lands.

Leaving Cookham you pass the ancient landscape of Cock Marsh, now owned by the National Trust.

Cock Marsh

Several prehistoric burial mounds were excavated at Cock Marsh in the nineteenth century and several cremated bodies were found, together with parts of a shield and a possible Anglo-Saxon knife. It is thought likely that the barrows were constructed in the early Bronze Age, with secondary Anglo-Saxon use. In 2007, a resistivity survey was carried out by Chiltern Archaeology, which confirmed the existence of four barrows and another feature.

Marlow

Marlow is recorded in Domesday Book as 'Merlaue'. It owed its importance to its location on the River Thames, where the road from Reading to High Wycombe crosses the river, and had its own market by 1227 – hence, it is also referred to as Chipping Marlow – although this lapsed before 1600.

While Marlow initially looks like a modern town, further investigation shows that there are fine period buildings (mainly Georgian) in the High Street and West Street.

In the eleventh century, Marlow was ringed by monastic foundations, and the remains of the oldest building, a twelfth-century chapel and crypt, still exist at Widmer Farm (although this is quite far to the north of the main route and now a private residence). In St Peter Street is The Old Parsonage and Deanery, which formed part of the finest fourteenth-century house in Buckinghamshire.

The suspension bridge was built between 1829 and 1832, and just along the river is the eighteenth-century Court Garden House. Finally, Mary Shelley wrote *Frankenstein* in a cottage in the town in 1818.

All Saints Church, Marlow. STEVE DUNN

MARLOW PLACE

Not far from the route, the red-brick Baroque house, Marlow Place was built for George II when he was Prince of Wales. It dates from 1720, and later formed part of the Royal Military College before it moved to Sandhurst.

The junior wing of the Royal Military College was once based here, at Remnantz, a large house built in the early eighteenth century; it served as the junior department of the college from 1801 until 1812. The weathervane on the building features a man firing a cannon and may date from that period. The building is now owned by the Bosley family.

ALL SAINTS CHURCH

The parish church at Marlow was erected in 1835 on the site of a twelfth-century building. Though there was a church in Marlow as early as 1070, the present neo-Per-pendicular building of All Saints is a Victorian creation, built after the spire of the old church collapsed in 1831; it is now prominently sited beside the Thames, next to Marlow's noted suspension bridge. The old building was demolished, and a new church was constructed of Bath stone, topped by a spire. John Oldrid Scott (1841–1913), a younger son of Sir George Gilbert Scott, later restored the church.

Bisham

As you leave Marlow you pass Bisham church, then the abbey on the opposite bank.

ALL SAINTS CHURCH

The oldest part of the current part-chalk, part-flint building with stone dressings is the twelfth-century tower. The parapet, battlements and brick quoins were added in the fifteenth century, while the tower contains three bells dating back to 1840.

In the Elizabethan era, Lady Hoby of neighbouring Bisham Abbey was responsible for the building of the Hoby Chapel to house the magnificent tombs of two knights: her husband, Sir Thomas, and his half-brother, Sir Philip. The chapel also contains the impressive canopied tomb of Lady Hoby herself, and the sons and daughters of her two marriages, all kneeling but for one infant lying at her knees. Lady Hoby was the aunt of Sir Francis Bacon, and was a learned and formidable dame.

The chapel also contains an obelisk known as the 'swan' monument: at its base are four swans, and it is surmounted by a flaming heart. It commemorates Margaret, the wife of Sir Edward Hoby.

The church was significantly restored in the neo-Decorated style by Benjamin Ferrey in 1849, and a north aisle and chancel extended eastwards in 1877. Further alterations were made in 1856 when the south aisle was rebuilt and the south gallery erected. This gallery contained the pew of the Williams family who lived at Temple House (now demolished), where they were visited by the future King Edward VII who worshipped in the church on those occasions.

Bisham Abbey. STEVE DUNN

BISHAM ABBEY

Bisham Abbey is a manor house and today home to one of the National Sports Centres managed on behalf of Sport England. The name is taken from the monastery that once stood alongside the manor house. The abbey church, previously known as Bisham Priory, was the traditional resting place of many of the Earls of Salisbury, who inhabited the manor house.

The manor house was built around 1260 as a preceptory for the Knights Templar. The Templar knights were recognized by their white mantle with a red cross, and were famed for fighting in the Crusades in the Holy Land. When the Templars were suppressed in 1307, Edward II took over the manorial rights of the abbey and granted them to various relatives. The building was then altered and extended.

It became an Augustinian priory in 1337, then, in 1537, a Benedictine abbey. This was dissolved in 1540, and Henry VIII left it to his fourth wife, Anne of Cleves, as part of her divorce settlement. Anne later swapped the house with Sir Philip Hoby for Westhorpe in Suffolk, and the Hoby family rebuilt it and lived there until 1768; they were regularly visited by Elizabeth I.

In 1310, the building was used as a place of confinement for Queen Elizabeth of Scots, her husband, Robert the Bruce, her stepdaughter, Princess Marjorie and her sister-in-law, Lady Christine Carrick, following their capture on the Isle of Rathlin during the wars of the Scottish succession.

Hurley Lock

At Hurley Lock there are the remains of a priory. In 1086 Geoffrey de Mandeville founded a Benedictine priory as a cell of Westminster Abbey in memory of his first wife; this survived until Henry VIII's reforms in 1536. After the Dissolution, in 1545 the monastic estate passed into the hands of John Lovelace, and subsequently, he and his successors became lords of the manor. The Lovelaces built a mansion called 'Ladye Place' on the site of the ruined priory. The first, Sir Richard Lovelace, went on an expedition with Sir Francis Drake, and apparently the fine Elizabethan mansion was built in 1600 with the proceeds from his legalized piracy.

Lady Place was considered one of the great mansions in the town, but it fell into disrepair and was demolished in 1837; it stood adjoining the present parish church, originally the priory.

The long narrow nave of the Norman priory church survives, and is used as Hurley parish church. To the north, the range of buildings containing the frater or monastic dining hall are incorporated into a private house. To the west of the church is the probable monastic circular dovecote and a nearby larger barn, both dating from the early fourteenth century. The former hostelry or guesthouse is incorporated into the Olde Bell Inn, one of the oldest inns still working in Britain.

From here there are two possible routes. Firstly, a short detour across the river from Hurley will take you to the village of Medmenham. This routes takes you straight past two enclosures of possibly late prehistoric provenance: one surrounds what is now Danesfield Hotel (this neo-Tudor building dates from the turn of the twentieth century), and the other is Medmenham Camp, on the high ground to the north of the village. The second route follows the Thames Path along the south bank, ending up at Culham Court.

Medmenham Camp is the first of two Iron Age hill forts. Danesfield Camp, also known as Danes Ditches, is located slightly further along the road to the east, near to the village of Hurley.

Medmenham

The village of Medmenham is situated in the south of the parish at the foot of a wooded hill, and contains several buildings of seventeenth-century origin, including the Dog and Badger Inn and the post office. The name 'Medmenham' possibly derives from the Old English for 'middle-sized homestead'; an alternative explanation is that it came from the Anglo-Saxon leader, Meda, whose followers were known as 'Medings', hence Medin'ham, Medham, or Medmenham.

The village has some early timber-framed brick and flint cottages; there are also some estate workers' cottages built at the beginning of the twentieth century from local chalk rock. A fifteenth-century manor house stands on the west of Ferry Lane. Extensively restored in 1903 by Sir Reginald Blomfield, the whitewashed roughcast building with half timbering was possibly the house mentioned in the will of Geoffrey Pole (grandfather of Cardinal Reginald Pole) in 1479.

THE CHURCH OF ST PETER AND PAUL

The Church of St Peter and Paul was originally under the patronage of Hugh de Bolebec (1100–1165), who also endowed Woburn Abbey and founded Medmenham Abbey.

The current church dates from the twelfth century, with the tower and chancel from c.1480, while the western tower is also fifteenth century; all were much restored in the Victorian era. However, the first church on this site was established c.650 by Birinus, the first bishop of Dorchester. His image is depicted in the south window of the chancel. The nave walls, built of chalk blocks and flint rubble, have been underpinned with modern brickwork and are supported by two external buttresses.

MEDMENHAM ABBEY

A Cistercian abbey was founded in Medmenham in the twelfth century under the ownership of Woburn Abbey. Then, in 1547, at the Dissolution of the Monasteries, the abbey was seized and given to the Moore family, and afterwards sold privately to the Duffields.

This former mansion, now two houses, lies on the site of, and possibly incorporates masonry from, the Cistercian Abbey of St Mary. The ruined folly tower and 'cloister' arcade were added in 1595 for Sir Francis Duffield. In 1755 the west wing was added for Sir Francis Dashwood and the Medmenham Club, then, much later, in 1898 the remainder was extensively restored by Romaine Walker.

Virtually nothing of antiquary survives apart from fragments of the old conventual chapel that remains at the rear of the house. The ruinous Abbey House was rented by Sir Francis Dashwood, afterwards Lord Le Despenser, and was so skilfully restored for him by Italian artists that it subsequently became difficult to distinguish the old work from the new.

In the mid-eighteenth century, Dashwood founded a famous brotherhood, 'The Knights of St Francis of Wycombe', with the motto of Love and Friendship, the dress consisting of a gown and turban of crimson and blue satin, with the device in silver. This profligate society has been confused with the famous Hell-Fire Club founded by Philip, Duke of Wharton, early in the reign of George I, and has also been erroneously styled the 'Franciscans' or 'Monks of Medmenham' – yet even Historic England's Listed Building description for the abbey states it was the setting for meetings of the notorious Medmenham Club or Order of St Francis of Wycombe, later known as the Hell-Fire Club! Allegedly the abbey became too notorious even for the Hell-Fire members, and Dashwood moved his club to the caves of West Wycombe that he had dug out for this very purpose. Today, the abbey is a private residence and is unfortunately not open to the public.

Culham Court

In the medieval period, the estate was held by the Bishops of Winchester, and no doubt run on their behalf by an episcopal steward. In 1552, it became part of the Neville estates, and later, those of the Lovelaces of Ladye Place in Hurley. The original house suffered a fire in the eighteenth century, so the owner, Robert Mitchell, had Sir William Chambers erect a new building. This large country house was built in 1771, of red brick with Portland stone dressings and set in a landscaped park overlooking the River Thames. Inside, there is a fine vaulted entrance hall with an Ionic-columned screen, a stone staircase with elegant ironwork railings, and neo-Classical plastered reception rooms, one with a lady holding a scythe on the overmantel. George III with the Queen and princesses visited the house in 1804.

Hambleden Lock

Hambleden Lock has a long weir on the Berkshire bank between Aston and Remenham; it was built by the Thames Navigation Commission in 1773. In 1869, Hambleden Lock featured in Charles Dickens' short ghost story, *The Phantom of Regatta Island*. The first Oxford and Cambridge University boat race was also rowed between Hambleden Lock and Henley Bridge in 1829.

MILL END

There are walkways over the great weir from the lock to the small village of Mill End, located on the north side of the river. Here is situated the picturesque Hambleden Mill, and nearby is the site of a Roman villa. The mill at Hambleden is mentioned in Domesday Book, which implies there was also a weir here then – but the current white shiplap-boarded mill building, now housing, derives from the eighteenth century. In 1777, a small brick house was built, and Caleb Gould became keeper of the lock. He was an eccentric, who baked bread for bargemen, ate a dish of onion porridge every night, wore a long coat with many buttons, and walked daily to Hambleden, marking a cross on the ground at the place he reached. He was in post for fifty-nine years, and was succeeded by his son. The mill buildings feature in Jerome K. Jerome's novel, *Three Men in a Boat*.

The largest historic home here is the many-gabled house (now converted into four dwellings), Yewden Manor. The earliest part is probably late sixteenth to early seventeenth century, but the house was remodelled and extended in the late nineteenth century.

Anne Petrie, daughter of the famous Egyptian archaeologist, Flinders Petrie, lived in Mill End; she is buried in Hambleden churchyard.

Temple Island

Temple Island is on the reach above Hambleden Lock, between the Buckinghamshire and Berkshire banks, and is part of Remenham in Berkshire. The main significance of the island is that it lies at the start of the course for the Henley Royal Regatta.

There is an elegant ornamental temple (a folly) on the island, designed by the eighteenth-century English architect, James Wyatt, and constructed in 1771. It was designed as a fishing lodge for Fawley Court, a nearby historic house that Wyatt also remodelled in the 1770s. The wall paintings in the principal room are thought to be the earliest surviving example of the Etruscan style in Great Britain, pre-dating more famous examples such as the Etruscan dressing room at Osterley Park in Middlesex by Robert Adam.

In December 1987, the Royal Regatta was able to purchase a 999-year lease of the island and temple, and following this, the stewards of the regatta undertook restoration works to both island and temple. The Victorian balcony, which had decayed, was replaced; the wall paintings, which had deteriorated and had been badly over-painted, were repaired; and a statue of a nymph, in keeping with the style and age of the temple, was placed under the cupola.

Fawley Court

Further down, on the opposite side of the river, stands Fawley Court. There is evidence to suggest the site has been occupied since Domesday, although the current building is most likely to have begun in 1616, when James Whitelocke purchased Fawley Court. There is some evidence that the house was extended under his parliamentarian son, Sir Bulstrode Whitelocke, but after a disastrous sacking in 1642 during the Civil War, it was left in a state of disrepair.

Between 1682 and 1688, merchant William Freeman purchased Fawley Court to be his country seat, and created a dwelling in the new style. The architect of the house is reputed to be Sir Christopher Wren, although this has been disputed. Some of the earthworks for the old house may have been incorporated into the new house at Fawley, but above ground it is very much of the Baroque style, being a large symmetrical square brick and stone house, two storeys in height, with a basement and an attic.

William of Orange (later William III) stayed at the house on his way to London and the Glorious Revolution during the year of its completion. John Cooke Freeman, also a merchant, inherited the estate, and from the 1720s onwards began to make changes to the house and grounds until his death in 1752. These included the Gothic folly in the gardens, and he is also responsible for the Freeman family mausoleum at Fawley church.

Upon John Cooke Freeman's death, the house passed to his son, Sambrooke (Sammy) Freeman, who employed Capability Brown to landscape Fawley's extensive grounds, and engaged James Wyatt to remodel and decorate some of the rooms and to create the temple-style lodge on what became known as Temple Island.

Fawley Court was eventually sold, in 1853, to Scottish banker and railway industrialist, Edward Mackenzie, who purchased it for his retirement; he made significant changes to various aspects of the house, and added the north-east wing in 1884. It was then requisitioned for use by the Special Operations Executive (SOE) during World War II. Upon their departure, the house at Fawley was left in a poor state of repair and so in 1953, the property was purchased by the Congregation of the Marian

Fathers and used as a school for Polish boys. A fire in 1976 caused considerable damage in some parts of the house. In the same year, Prince Stanisław Albrecht Radziwiłł (husband of Lee Bouvier-Radziwill, younger sister of Jacqueline Kennedy Onassis) was interred in the modern church he had funded within the grounds.

In 1986, the school closed, and in 2008, the Marian Fathers placed the Fawley estate on the market when it was purchased by its current owner. It is reputed to have been Kenneth Grahame's inspiration for Toad Hall in his 1908 book, *The Wind in the Willows*.

Remenham

Next along the Way is the village of Remenham. The parish covers the starting point of the Henley Royal Regatta course. The Leander Club, founded in 1818, is one of the oldest rowing clubs in the world.

Remenham village is a small collection of buildings, principally comprising St Nicholas' Church and rectory, a village hall, Remenham Farm, the site of the former manor house, and the former school. Parts of the moat of the original manor house remain. Sir Edmund Montfort owned it in the reigns of Edward IV and Richard III.

PARK PLACE

The largest mansion in Remenham is Park Place; however, this is located further to the south of Remenham Hill, and will require a detour. The first house on this site was called Strowde's or Vyne's Place, and dated to the thirteenth century. The names derive from the owners Richard de la Strode, who bought land in Aston in 1257, and Thomas Vyne, who held the land in trust in 1479. In Henry VI's reign it was owned by William Peck and became known as Peck's or Park's Place.

Lord Archibald Hamilton acquired the land in 1719 and built the first mansion on the site of the current house. He sold it to Frederick, Prince of Wales, who was the father of George III. George grew up on the estate.

In 1752, Park Place was bought by General Henry Conway. He was responsible for the layout of the grounds, building a bridge (known as Conway's Bridge or the Ragged Arch) to carry the Wargrave Road at the lower end of Happy Valley, to gain access to the River Thames, and a Grecian ruin at the upper end, both using stones from Reading Abbey. A Druid's temple was rebuilt in the grounds, having come from Jersey, where Conway had been governor. Following a fire in 1768, the house was partly rebuilt.

In 1870, the estate passed to John Noble (of 'Noble's Paints & Varnishes'). He rebuilt the house in its current form, and the estate remained in the ownership of the Noble family until 1947. Between 1947 and 1988 Park Place was run as a boarding school.

The house was used for exterior shots in the filming of the 2007 film *St Trinian's*, and it was subsequently sold for £42 million, which made it the most expensive house bought outside London. However, in 2011, it sold again, this time for £140 million, making it the most expensive house sale in the United Kingdom.

A field on the Park Place estate has a large obelisk which was originally the spire of St Bride's Church in the City of London.

ST NICHOLAS CHURCH

Built of flint with stone dressings, the parish church of St Nicholas is Norman in origin. The tower has chequer-work turrets, and in the chancel there are some Sienese wrought-iron gates. Originally, the first church was a chapelry of Hurley, and served by the monks of Hurley Priory. Starting as a fourteenth-century structure, the church was rebuilt in 1838 on the same site, and then restored between 1870 and 1872 by Ronald Plumbe. Very little remains of the ancient church, but the foundations of the apse and the chalk window near the pulpit and parts of the north wall are believed to date back to *c.*1320; also, the floor tiles around the base of the pulpit are fourteenth century – a similar design can be found at Oxford Cathedral. The lych gate was built in 1868, in memory of Violet Noble, the youngest daughter of John Noble of Park Place.

Henley-on-Thames

The town of Henley has been in existence beside the River Thames since long before the Norman Conquest in 1066. St Birinus of Dorchester sent a missionary here in the seventh century, and a small church was built. Now gone, so too has the subsequent twelfth-century building.

ST MARY THE VIRGIN CHURCH

The earliest key date in this church's history is a charter of 1272 granting indulgences to those contributing to its building or repair. However, little remains of this Early English phase; the current aisled Church of St Mary's having undergone a major remodelling in about 1400. The west tower is Perpendicular in style, and the north-east chapel is dated 1460. The south aisle was rebuilt in 1789, while the second north aisle was added by Benjamin Ferrey in 1853–4, in the neo-Decorated style.

Singer Dusty Springfield (1939–1999) has a memorial in the grounds – she had been living at Harpsden, near Henley, at the time of her death.

THE RED LION

The Red Lion pub in Henley is also of interest. The Red Lion Hotel is believed to have been built in 1531 to accommodate the craftsmen and apprentices who constructed the church of St Mary. The early fourteenth-century chantry house, originally the home of the chantry priests, can be seen in the courtyard of the hotel. In 1664 it was used as a schoolroom, the Grammar School occupying the upper half, and Lady Purim's Bluecoats, the lower half. It later became part of the Red Lion Hotel for many years, before being restored to the church as a memorial to Canon Maul, a former rector of Henley who died in 1915.

Henley-on-Thames bridge. STEVE DUNN

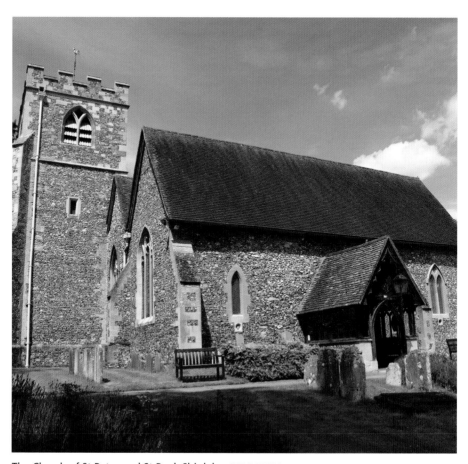

The Church of St Peter and St Paul, Shiplake. STEVE DUNN

The Way then passes The Old Granary, dated by dendrochronology to 1549 and a further wonderful example of vernacular Tudor architecture. The adjoining Barn Cottage was built at around the same time, possibly as part of the same structure. The buildings' original use most likely related to the river trade, with offices and accommodation below and a series of storage units above. While the late eighteenth century saw Barn Cottage serving as a granary, by the early twentieth century, the buildings were largely given over to storage and had become dilapidated. They were saved from demolition in 1925 by Lady Burke, who had them converted into two cottages; in recent years these have been united to make a single dwelling.

Lower Shiplake

The route then moves into the hamlet of Lower Shiplake. Several interesting properties can be seen here, including Bolney Court and The White House – the Thameside Arts and Crafts houses.

Shiplake

The Way continues past Shiplake. The Church of St Peter and St Paul dates from at least *c*.1140 and is the centre of the ecclesiastical parish of Shiplake in the diocese of Oxford. In 1869, the Gothic Revival architect, G. E. Street, rebuilt the chancel, the north aisle and parts of the south aisle, and replaced all the window traceries. The main entry to the church is through the Lady Chapel, which is the original church. There is also a thirteenth-century piscina, and stained glass originating from the abbey church of St-Bertin at Saint-Omer in France (fifteenth century). Finally, Lord Tennyson married here in 1850.

Sonning Bridge. STEVE DUNN

Sonning Eye

The Way then passes the picturesque small island known as Sonning Eye, opposite the village of Sonning, to which it is linked by the eighteenth-century brick-arched Sonning Bridge. It is a small gravel mound surrounded by the river's flood plain; roughly heart-shaped, cut through by a millrace. 'Sonning' is derived from the Viking/Anglo-Saxon chieftain Sunna, and 'Eye' means 'island' (*cf.* 'eyot').

THE MILL AT SONNING

On the islet is The Mill at Sonning, a restored eighteenth-century flour mill (which had its own fleet of barges) on an earlier medieval mill site, now converted into a dinner theatre. The millrace runs through what is now the theatre bar, and powers a small turbine that runs an 18.5kW hydroelectric generator; this supplies the National Grid.

MILL HOUSE

Set behind The Mill is Mill House, also known as Aberlash House – a beautiful Georgian mansion. Originally built in the seventeenth century, it was refronted in the eighteenth and nineteenth centuries. It was once owned by the wealthy Rich family, Lords of the Manor of Sonning, who also owned the manor house at the top of Sonning's Thames Street. Sir Thomas Rich founded Reading Blue Coat School, just south of here, in 1766 by endowing it with the income from his neighbouring farmland. In 2014, Mill House was bought by the American film star George Clooney and his new British wife, the human rights lawyer Amal Alamuddin.

Constructed of Bath stone ashlar under a tile roof with stone balustrading, the front elevation of the house is of symmetrical proportions, with a square-plan entrance of paired Doric columns.

SONNING BRIDGE

The route passes under the iconic Sonning Bridge with its ten brick arches, built in 1775 to replace an earlier wooden medieval bridge. It links Sonning with Sonning Eye, and crosses the Thames on the reach above Shiplake Lock, just short of Sonning Lock.

There is a stone marker at the centre of the bridge with the letters 'B | O', designating the counties of Berkshire and Oxfordshire on each side of the river; the vertical line indicates the boundary, which runs down the exact middle of the river. This was an ancient border, once sited between Wessex and Mercia. Rumour has it that Dick Turpin used the bridge as an escape route from Berkshire to Oxfordshire, to evade the authorities.

Sonning

Sonning village is situated on the River Thames and was described by Jerome K. Jerome in his book, *Three Men in a Boat* as 'the most fairy-like little nook on the whole river'. The parish of Sonning originally included Charvil, Woodley and Earley, and before the formation of civil parishes in 1866, was a cross-county boundary parish also containing Sonning Eye, Dunsden Green and Playhatch in Oxfordshire. It is now much smaller and triangular in shape. The ecclesiastical parish of Sonning continues to include Sonning, Charvil and Sonning Eye.

The historical name of the village is 'Sunning', derived from the Old English name 'Sunna'. Some villagers still pronounce the name of the village in this way. In the Anglo-Saxon period, the village was of considerable importance as the lesser centre of the bishopric of Ramsbury, i.e. the See of Ramsbury and Sonning. The church was a secondary cathedral, and the present structure, St Andrew's Church, contains reused Anglo-Saxon carvings. By the twelfth century Sonning had eight dependent churches, though, by the fifteenth century, four of these had become independent parishes. This is an example of the change in organization of the Anglo-Saxon Church into minsters, each with their own parochial boundaries, which was known as the minster system.

Following a substantial grant of land from the Crown, the ancient parish of Sonning gradually extended from Sonning Common (five miles to the north-west) to the heath lands of Sandhurst (some fifteen miles to the south-east).

ST ANDREW'S CHURCH

Christianity arrived in the Thames Valley in the seventh century via missionaries and St Birinus, Bishop of Dorchester-on-Thames. Soon afterwards, the first foundations of St Andrew's Parish Church were laid, likely on or near an earlier place of pagan worship. In 909CE it was transformed into one of the twin cathedrals of the diocese of Ramsbury and Sonning. The building was extensively restored in 1852, but a few fragments of sculpted Saxon stonework are built into the fabric of the present building on the site.

This church sits in an idyllic spot overlooking the Thames and the Old Mill. Originally Norman, the current flint church with stone dressings features a Perpendicular tower of cheque flint and stone with three stages and a battlemented parapet.

The church once had a south-eastern chapel dedicated to St Sarik (or Siric, Cyriacus) on the site of the present organ, which was said to contain a number of small relics from the body of this man. The fifteenth-century sculpted arch on the northern side of the chancel is thought to have come from this chapel. The Rich family of Holme Park replaced St Sarik's chapel with their own, which notably contained the 'Rich Monument', dedicated to Sir Thomas Rich who was buried in the vault below in 1667. It features weeping cherubs and vast urns, but no effigy. It has been moved to a position beneath the tower where it can be viewed through the curtained grille.

Sonning prospered as an important stopping post for travellers and pilgrims visiting the church's relics, both by road and boat. There were a number of hostelries providing lodgings, notably the Great House on the site of the original ferryman's cottage and the Bull Inn.

HOLME PARK

Just outside the village, above Sonning Lock, is the nineteenth-century manor house, Holme Park, which is home to the independent secondary school, Reading Blue Coat School. Built in the 'Holme Park' of the old palace, the current school replaced a Georgian mansion erected for the lords of the manor, which superseded the bishops and their palace.

Sonning became the seat of a sizeable 'hall' or 'palace' built on a steep incline on the Holme Park estate. The original palace of the bishops of Salisbury survived until the sixteenth century: Richard II's young bride, Queen Isabella of Valois, was kept captive here during his imprisonment and deposition, while Elizabeth I visited the building on several of her progresses – her steward, Sir Henry Neville, is commemorated via his heraldic symbol, the Bull, at the local pub. However, a short time later the palace fell into a state of disrepair, and so in 1628 Charles I raised some money for his rule without parliament by selling it to Lawrence Halstead. Twenty-six years later it was purchased by Sir Thomas Rich.

Rich was a wealthy merchant who used his ready cash to become a great patron of the Blue Coat School in Reading. He demolished the medieval palace at Sonning, and built himself a fine new mansion where his family lived for the next 150 years. When the last of his line died in 1795, Holme Park was purchased by another local landowner and Tory MP, Robert Palmer. The year following the purchase, Palmer pulled down the old house and set to work erecting a fine new building in the latest Georgian style. His family lived at the Park for just over a century, rebuilding the house again in 1881 in the Victorian neo-Gothic style that was the height of fashion. The estate eventually left private hands in 1912, when it was sold to become a preparatory school. During World

War II it was used by the Royal Veterinary College, and in 1947 appropriately became the home of the Reading Blue Coat School.

THE DEANERY

In *c*.1901 a second country house was built in the village, the Deanery. Built by Sir Edwin Lutyens for Edward Hudson, as a show house for the founder and owner of *Country Life* magazine (in addition to the castle at Lindisfarne), the gardens were then laid out by Gertrude Jekyll – it is typical of the Arts and Crafts style.

The End of the Journey: Caversham

The Way next comes to Caversham Lock, where locks have been documented since the fifteenth century, and then arrives at the first primary site of pilgrimage on the last section of this route: Caversham Bridge.

CAVERSHAM BRIDGE

Caversham Bridge is sited across the River Thames between Caversham and the town centre of Reading. It is situated on the reach above Caversham Lock, and provides pedestrian access to the adjacent mid-river Pipers Island.

The first bridge on the site was built some time between 1163 and 1231. It was the site of a skirmish during the English Civil War in 1643 when Charles I and Prince Rupert of the Rhine led an attempt to relieve the Royalist forces, besieged for months in Reading, by storming the Parliamentary troops on the great bridge. It was subsequently left with a wooden drawbridge structure on the Berkshire side. The bridge was still in this state when it was depicted by J.M.W. Turner in 1806–7, in a painting entitled *Caversham Bridge with Cattle in the Water*.

In 1869, the entire bridge was replaced by an iron lattice construction. Then when Reading Bridge was completed in 1923, work began on replacing Caversham Bridge with the current structure, which is of concrete with a granite balustrade. It was opened in 1926 by Edward, Prince of Wales.

On the high ground above Caversham village stands Caversham Park, an eighteenth-century mansion, now home to the BBC world listening service. Finally, it is also the alleged site of Richard Neville's proposal to Anne, daughter of Richard Beauchamps, 13th Earl of Warwick. He later became the notorious Warwick the Kingmaker.

THE CHAPEL OF ST ANNE

Historically, a chapel of St Anne once stood here, the chapel's foundations having been discovered during the building of the new bridge. When another new bridge was built in the 1920s, stones from the foundations of the original bridge chapel were given to the parish to be incorporated into a restored shrine.

Pilgrims visiting the shrine from the south would first find a stopping place on Caversham Bridge. This was the function served by St Anne's Chapel.

ST PETER'S CHURCH

The medieval community of Caversham was clustered on the north side of Caversham Bridge, to the east of St Peter's Church.

The church now overlooks Caversham Court gardens. The oldest surviving building in Caversham, St Peter's Church dates from 1162 or earlier. Walter Gifford, Earl of Buckingham, gave the church to Notley Abbey, Buckinghamshire, but, following the Dissolution, its patron became Christ Church, Oxford. Rectorial rights were restored in 1916. Today, the flint-built, garish church consists of a chancel, north and south chapels, a north vestry, nave, aisles, south porch and west tower, of various dates ranging from the twelfth century, principally the fifteenth century and also the high Victorian era.

Royalists stationed troops in St Peter's Church during the siege of Reading in 1643, and situated a cannon on top of the tower. When the Parliamentarians used artillery to destroy the tower, the church itself was also ruined in the process. The tower was then rebuilt in 1878.

A Lady Chapel, or Chapel of St Mary, existed before 1189. This became dilapidated, but was rebuilt in the Perpendicular style using the north wall of the chancel, and the two were connected by arches, ornamented with unusual, curious panelled soffits and joints. The first shrine of Our Lady of Caversham was allegedly kept in this building, so when it was dissolved in 1538, St Peter's Church acted as a place of pilgrimage for a short time.

Caversham Court, alias 'The Old Rectory'

A house was built on the site of the old Chapel of Our Lady for the canon of St Peter's Church in the seventeenth century, but it was later leased to laymen who were responsible for providing a priest. In the nineteenth century, the church was enlarged, and the house remodelled into a neo-Gothic mansion. Now, the only remains of the original house and grounds are the garden pavilion/gazebo laid out between 1660 and 1681 by Thomas Loveday as a private retreat surrounding the house, together with the stable block, and the yew hedge along the raised east-west walkway.

The Victorian revival-style house was built around two courtyards, and its timber framing prompted its nickname the 'Striped House'. It had a 1638 staircase, with bullet holes from a Civil War attack, and an elaborate decorated plaster ceiling. Both survived an almost total rebuilding programme by Augustus Welby Northmore Pugin in 1840, under the patronage of the Simonds, a great brewing family. Pugin gave the house a castellated façade with fretwork balustrading, and a 'Norman' (revival) porch surmounted by a figure of Cardinal Wolsey. The house was renamed Caversham Court in the 1920s, but was demolished in 1933 as its state had gradually declined, and subsequently the Arts and Crafts-style toilet block was built (now the tea kiosk). The gardens are now a public park.

St Anne's Well, Caversham. STEVE DUNN

ST ANNE'S WELL

Still extant at the top of Priests' Hill, St Anne's Well was a popular draw for pilgrims, since its mineral spring waters were believed to possess miraculous healing properties. Its location had actually been lost following the Dissolution of the Monasteries until 1906 when a workman unearthed it. Transformed into a drinking fountain, the well was officially reopened on 19 April 1908, and can still be used for this purpose.

Originally, the well was situated on a small island that once formed the centre of the river; because the span of the bridge was so large, the island was thought to have been necessary. The well is now nicely preserved by the side of a suburban road, and has a brick surround of about five feet (1.5m), with an ornate birdcage-style grille covering the top. This holy well and the medieval chapel on the bridge were both dedicated to St Anne, the patron saint of women in childbirth.

FORMER PARISH ROOM, NOW ST JOHN THE BAPTIST CHURCH

This building, another interesting stop, was consecrated in November 1888 to serve the increasing population in Lower Caversham. In the twenty years between 1861 and 1881, the population of Caversham doubled, as people were drawn to the area to take advantage of Reading's thriving industries, including biscuit making, seed selling and brewing.

Our Lady and St Anne's Roman Catholic Church (shrine), Caversham. STEVE DUNN

The Parish Church of St Peter's and the chapel at Emmer Green were unable to cope with the numbers attending Sunday service, so the decision was taken to build a new church in Lower Caversham. A plot of land was chosen, a part of Bryant's Farm, and building work began in 1887, the year of Queen Victoria's Golden Jubilee. The church was built of flint with stone dressings in the Early English revival style, and was consecrated on 8 November 1888. The architect also designed the chancel screen, the font and the organ case.

OUR LADY AND ST ANNE'S ROMAN CATHOLIC CHURCH

Caversham village is mentioned in Domesday Book when, by that time (late eleventh century), a shrine chapel to the Virgin Mary, Mother of Christ, was already in existence beside the river; it was soon to become a major place of pilgrimage

A detailed history of the shrine and its restoration within the current church is detailed in the introduction to this chapter. As such, the following comprises a summary of the history and architecture of the present church only.

In the nineteenth century, a generous benefactor, Dr Cockran, purchased the land between South View Avenue and Gosbrook Road as a site for a new church, presbytery, school and convent. The first parish building, a school/chapel, was opened in 1899. The two-celled building served as a school during the week, and a centre for Mass at weekends. It is still in use as the infant block of St Anne's Primary School. However, with the aid of generous supporters, the building of a parish church was soon planned, and, in 1903, Bishop Ilsley formally opened the church. It was then a single-aisled building with a sanctuary and adjoining presbytery, but in 1907, the south aisle and tower were added, and then the north aisle in 1921. The church was consecrated by Archbishop Thomas Williams of Birmingham on 26 July 1933.

Since then, the major addition to the church has been the shrine chapel of Our Lady of Caversham, built in stone at its north-east corner.

Then, to celebrate the centenary of the church, the narthex (entrance area/vestibule) was extended, and the cenacle, an octagonal meeting and social room, was built on the south side of the church – it was opened by Archbishop Vincent Nichols in 2003.

Deans Farm

A final detour may be made to another of the further possible original sites of Our Lady of Caversham's shrine. Identified by Preece, Kift & Fallowfield, a field next to Deans Farm was called 'Capull (i.e. Chapel) alias Rayley' in 1633. The original manor house, which was pulled down in 1493 and the moat filled in, may also have stood here and thus all formed part of an overall complex. Fragments of an early Christian font dating from 360CE were uncovered in 1980, which then made way for the early manor house. The most prominent owner was William the Marshal, Earl of Pembroke and Regent of England, during the minority of Henry III. It then passed to the Earls of Warwick. The present building dates from the seventeenth and eighteenth centuries.

Many historians also suggest that the first Caversham Castle stood here prior to the manor house. Castles were often sited in close proximity to water mills, and as Caversham Mill was originally located on what is now Heron Island, Deans Farm may well have been the castle site. There has also always been a small harbour on the farm – allegedly, the original chapel had its own ferry.

Our Lady statue in Our Lady and St Anne's Roman Catholic Church, Caversham. STEVE DUNN

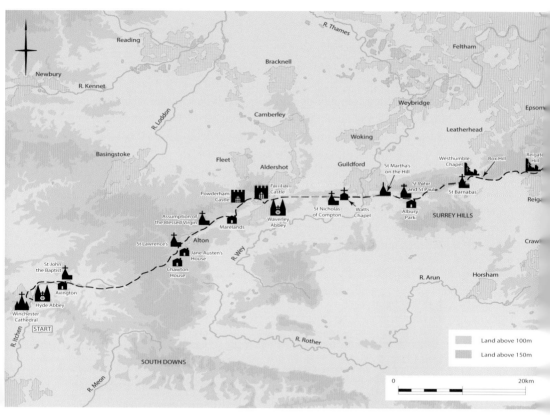

Map of south-east Pilgrims' Way: the west half. JIM BRIGHTMAN

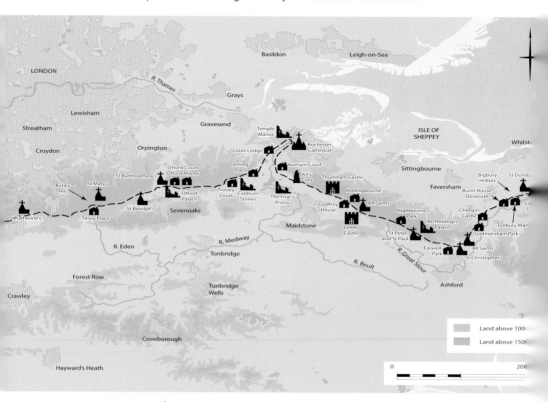

Map of south-east Pilgrims' Way: the east half. JIM BRIGHTMAN

CHAPTER FIVE

The Pilgrims' Way
(beginning as St Swithun's Way)

Reputed to be one of England's most ancient and infamous trackways, this Victorian interpretation of a medieval route winds its way from Winchester Cathedral (and the shrine of St Swithun) to the former site of St Thomas Becket's shrine/tomb at Canterbury Cathedral. Its notoriety was cemented in our memory for evermore thanks to its immortalization as the setting of Chaucer's *Canterbury Tales*, written in the fourteenth century (although only on occasions does the modern route coincide with Chaucer's), then again in 1893, when Julia Cartwright's first comprehensive account of the route was published, followed in 1904 by Hillaire Belloc's authoritative tome, *The Old Road*. Yet the latter text makes virtually no reference to the road as the Pilgrims' Way; instead Belloc prefers the Pilgrims' Road, or simply the Way.

The 112-mile (180km) pathway between Winchester and Canterbury was once perhaps the most important pilgrimage route in the country. There is no direct evidence to tell us the exact details of the route, but by following the ancient route to Farnham and the places associated with historical pilgrims and travellers, we can trace the course that most must have followed. It is thus possible to journey through the landscape they travelled, the settlements they passed, and the churches they visited.

The byway runs across the southern counties of Hampshire, Surrey and Kent, straddling the edge of/coinciding with much of the North Downs Way National Trail. Established as recently as 1978 by the Ramblers' Association/Countryside Commission, the Way is 131 miles (211km) long. It travels between Farnham and Dover, via Canterbury, and follows closely the route taken by Belloc's 'Old Road' of 120 miles (193km) in length. Over the last century, much of the Way was incorporated into the North Downs Way, which comprises fifteen national trails established by the Countryside Commission after World War II. Its ancient origins derive from its association with the landscape that lies a few miles south of Canterbury at the Channel coast near Dover and the great swathe of chalk land that connects Britain with the continent. This chalk route was used by Mesolithic and Neolithic hunters and traders, as well as in the Bronze Age, when the inhabitants of Kent maintained their links with mainland Europe via the Channel. Thus, the connection between the chalk coast and pilgrims is key, as the cliffs would have been an aid to migration for centuries.

Parts of the route have been eradicated over the subsequent 500 years since the height of its pilgrim popularity, so that pinpointing exactly which sections were taken by medieval travellers is somewhat challenging. Yet, sections of the old Pilgrims' Road to Canterbury are still clear and identified on modern mapping, and some also bear associative names. The memory of these pilgrimages survives in the wayside chapels and shrines that sprang up along the tracks, and in the churches restored for passing devotion, in addition to the local place names that have associations with pilgrims or religious customs. Particularly few traces can be found of the Way in Hampshire, for example, but early writing and probability suggests that the travellers' course would have taken the many who landed at Southampton through Winchester towards Canterbury. However, it is likely that Chaucer's fictional pilgrims travelled down from London along the old Roman road known as Watling Street, much of which is now overlaid by the London to Dover trunk road, the A2. Essentially, for the most part, the Pilgrims' Way follows the southern flank of the North Downs, whereas Watling Street follows its northern flank.

Previous to Belloc's publication, it was argued that the trackway was referred to as the Pilgrims' Way and, in fact, it is clearly marked as such on the Ordnance Survey map of 1873, though its name was apparently delineated in the previous decade. However, a century earlier, both Hasted's 1778 map of the Codsheath Hundred, and Andrew's Map of 1779, identify sections of road under the Downs as the Pilgrim's Road. Furthermore, references in the West Kent parish tithe apportionments of the early nineteenth century to 'woodlands south of the Pilgrims' Road [which] pay no tithe', may suggest there was a notable continuous track across the chalk hills, which later was referred to as the Pilgrims' Road.

Many of the gaps in the previous knowledge of the route were consciously filled by Belloc, and led him to make several alterations as to what had previously been marked out on the OS map. As he travelled, he too recognized that pilgrims often strayed from the line of the main route, which led to new tracks springing up and becoming gradually identified as parts of the Pilgrims' Way. The object of this chapter is to note the sacred sites and interesting aspects which arrest the pilgrim's notice, thus referring to the differences between the several versions of the route that are currently extant.

However, as there are simply so many interesting sites dotted along this route (and an abundance of literature already extant on it), the following chapter will cover only the most significant historical sites or notable pilgrim destinations, and will provide fewer detour options or stops of little relevance or association to the main Way or its histories.

The History of St Swithun and St Thomas Becket

As noted, the Pilgrims' Way follows the alleged medieval route of travellers largely from the south and west of England, starting at Winchester and culminating at Canterbury. The two primary saints associated with these cities are St Swithun and St Thomas Becket.

The body of St Swithun was located within Winchester Cathedral. Winchester was the old capital of Wessex, home of King Alfred and thus residence of the Anglo-Saxon and Norman kings. Within the cathedral was not only the tomb of Alfred the Great, but the golden shrine of St Swithun, the former bishop who was chaplain to Egbert, King of Wessex from 802–839CE. Egbert's son Ethelwulf, whom Swithun educated, made him Bishop of Winchester in 852. Swithun also allegedly tutored the young Alfred the Great. Swithun died on 2 July 862. According to tradition he had asked to be buried humbly, and so his grave was positioned just outside the west door of the old minster so that people would walk across it and rain would fall on it in accordance with his wishes.

However, on 15 July 971, Swithun's remains were dug up by Bishop Ethelwold and moved to a shrine in the cathedral – an act later seen as directly against the saint's wishes. Miraculous cures were associated with the event, and so Swithun's feast day was celebrated on the date of the removal of his remains (15 July), not the date of his death. The removal was accompanied by ferocious and violent rainstorms that lasted forty days and forty nights, and were said to indicate the saint's displeasure at being moved. This is possibly the origin of the legend that if it rains on St Swithun's feast day, the rain will continue for forty more days.

In the eleventh century, Swithun's relics were again moved. This time they were sited in the new cathedral built by the Norman invaders. His Anglo-Saxon reliquary was carried with great ceremony to its new position behind the high altar, where it remained until 1450.

His tomb became a major site for pilgrims, many seeking to be healed from illness. A short tunnel (the Holy Hole) allowed them to crawl right under his shrine, to get as close as possible to his miraculous healing powers. As a result, as was a common occurrence of popular shrines looking to keep attracting visitors, a new, even larger shrine was inaugurated at the far end of the church in 1476, and was festooned with gifts of silver, gold and jewels offered by grateful pilgrims.

Before its destruction in 1538, the shrine of St Swithun was perhaps the second most popular place of pilgrimage in medieval England, only following that of St Thomas Becket.

The murder of Archbishop Thomas Becket on 29 December 1170 is one of the most famous events of the medieval period. That evening, while Becket made his way to vespers, Henry II's four knights rushed upon the religious man with their swords, scalping and ultimately murdering him in the north transept of his own cathedral. He was canonized by the Pope three years later. The tragic circumstances greatly impacted on the population of the country, and his popularity as a religious man who dared to stand up against his sovereign for the rights of the Church was ubiquitous. From the moment of his death and as a result of its tragic circumstances, a growing belief in his holiness was confirmed by the many miracle stories that were increasingly being reported.

The next day, Becket's body was laid to rest in a Purbeck marble tomb behind Our Lady's altar in the undercroft of the cathedral. The miracle stories continued as a stream of devout pilgrims visited it to seek healing or to pay their vows of penance. Then, in 1174, the choir of the church was destroyed by fire. Its rebuilding was largely assisted by the offerings made at Becket's tomb and, as a result, the saint's body was transferred to a glorious new gilded shrine in 1220, surrounded by colourful stained glass windows depicting the miracle accounts carried out in his life and after his death, that were installed in the new apse or Trinity Chapel at the east of the cathedral. Various other relics associated with the Archbishop were housed in reliquaries and situated in various side chapels around the church to attract as many visitors as possible. Canterbury Cathedral thus became the most popular pilgrim destination in all of medieval England.

The History of the Pilgrims' Way

The literature surrounding the Pilgrims' Way is abundant. F. C. Elliston-Erwood wrote in a 1925 article in *Archaeologia Cantiana* that 'There is probably no other road or trackway in the whole of England that can boast such a literature as does this path, around which myth, legend, history, enthusiasm and tradition have combined to weave such a tangled web'. And it is this web that we seek to unravel.

Folklore, legend and perhaps even Victorian romanticism are largely to blame for the amount of stories relating to the trackway. Clearly a well-trodden path in the nineteenth century, as confirmed by Belloc, the claim that the path was taken by thousands of medieval pilgrims lies more in popular folklore, with some asserting that no pilgrims ever strode the trackway en route to Becket's shrine. While the prehistoric origins of the route are under no doubt, its use as a pilgrim route to Canterbury is very much disputed.

There is clear evidence that the path is far older than its medieval pilgrimage reputation. Some scholars have suggested it was an established merchants' highway for tin miners travelling from Cornwall to have their wares shipped across the seas. Furthermore, archaeological evidence excavated along the route has included Roman villas, bathhouses and pavements. Still, it perhaps cannot be disputed that at least portions of the Way served as a principal medieval thoroughfare from the west to the east of England.

The route was taken by Henry II after he landed at Southampton and then went eastwards for his penitential visit to Canterbury in July 1174 (following his regrettable orders to murder the archbishop), and there is no doubt that this event popularized and promoted the trail because lay pilgrims desired to literally follow in the footsteps of their sovereign. It is therefore likely that its notoriety stemmed from this period as well as its royal connection.

Belloc, however, speculated that both Winchester and Canterbury already possessed established urban positions prior to the influx of Christian visitors. He noted their positions in the hinterland of the coast, both towns being not far from any of the main ports. The construction of Watling Street from Dover to London in the Roman era also meant that Canterbury remained central to the kingdom of Kent, and was an established town on the map. In fact, Canterbury had been a site of pilgrimage long before Becket, as it possessed a multitude of early cults including Sts Augustine, Dunstan and Alphege, while Winchester was the monarchical capital of the Anglo-Saxon kings. Thus, the main route to the towns was already a major communication route prior to medieval pilgrimage, and so it is likely that it was created following improvements to Watling Street at the time of Edward the Confessor, which made such distant travel much simpler.

But you might then ask how the route survived as an ancient trackway, and then continued on as a pilgrimage route? By the time of Becket's martyrdom in 1170, Winchester had started to decline as London grew in importance. Fewer metals were forthcoming from the West Country, as the Sussex iron industry in the Weald had taken its place. Belloc's assertion therefore was that medieval pilgrimage saved the old road from falling into terminal decline. But while the theory is certainly valid, it is difficult to confirm. If the old trackway did become a pilgrimage route between Winchester and Canterbury, then it would have been used by pilgrims between the late twelfth century right through to the abolition of the pilgrimage in September 1538, when Henry VIII's commissioner, Dr Leyton, sacked the saint's shrine, tomb and reliquaries, and removed the bones of Becket, while the donations of pilgrims were removed and transferred to the king.

Therefore, if the number of pilgrims who visited Canterbury is correct – and indeed 100,000 visited for the Jubilee year in 1420 – then the route would no doubt have gained in popularity with pilgrims and, with it, a notable number of associative sites along the trail. For example, Boughton Aluph Church boasts a pilgrims' porch with a chimney and fireplace on its southern wall, and local folklore suggests that pilgrims gathered in this porch for warmth and security until their numbers were large enough to ascend into King's Wood in safety.

This brings me to another point of contention: notable shrine sites were approached via a number of different routes, dependent upon where people were travelling from. For example, several routes to Canterbury were in existence during the Age of Pilgrimage: firstly, there was the route taken by Chaucer's pilgrims from London through Deptford, Greenwich, Rochester and Sittingbourne; then there was the one taken by those journeying from the north. Yet the greatest number approached from the south, many of them foreign pilgrims who landed at Dover, while others who landed at Southampton travelled through Hampshire, Surrey and Kent. A stop at Winchester would certainly be made to visit the relics of St Swithun, where they would be joined by those coming from the west.

It is this latter route that was probably taken by Henry II on his pilgrimage to the city. And while it is this route upon which this book focuses, as noted earlier, it was not simply the public or Roman routes, or even royal routes, that pilgrims followed: many elements influenced pilgrims' journey choices, from the weather to the stability of the surfaces, and even to security.

An Overview of the Route

The North Downs Way national trail parallels the old Pilgrims' Way between Farnham and Canterbury. Much of the traditional route of the Pilgrims' Way is now part of the modern road network, and the Ramblers Association has previously advised walkers wishing to follow it to use St Swithun's Way between Winchester and Farnham, and the North Downs Way between Farnham and Canterbury as an alternative.

The route begins at St Swithun's shrine in Winchester Cathedral, and continues eastwards through the Itchen Valley, where several other named footpaths meet. It then follows close to the River Itchen until it reaches New Alresford, where it passes through the towns and villages that lie near the Watercress Line. From Alton, it continues through farmland and the villages of Froyle and Bentley, until it reaches the castle at Farnham. It runs from Farnham to Dover, past Guildford, Dorking, Reigate, Merstham, Chaldon, Godstone, Limpsfield and Westerham, through Otford, Kemsing and Wrotham, north of Trottiscliffe, and towards Cuxton (where it crosses the River Medway). South of Rochester, the Way travels through the villages of Burham, Boxley and Detling, and continues in a south-easterly direction towards the north of the villages of Harrietsham and Lenham. It then continues south-east along the top of the Downs past Charing to Wye, and then turns north to follow the valley of the Great Stour through Chilham and on to Canterbury.

The ancient trackway has been described as both a ridge walk and a terrace way that follows the chalk escarpment of the North Downs. For identification purposes, a good rule of thumb is that the old trackway usually kept to the lower southern slopes, which were less exposed than the upper ridges. The road kept just above the woods of the Weald or the cultivated land at the foot of the escarpment, and avoided the claggy clay found on the lower ground. Today, if one walks along the North Downs Way National Trail, sections signposted as the 'Pilgrims' Way' run along the foot of the North Downs escarpment, but are often just a few metres above the fields, and are therefore high enough to benefit from the better drainage of the chalk and flint underfoot.

Start of the Route: Winchester Cathedral

The route begins in the City of Winchester, situated at the western end of the South Downs, with a number of historic buildings dominating its skyline. Winchester Cathedral, begun in 1079 by Walkelin, the first Norman Bishop of Winchester, was ready for worship in 1093. It is the second longest cathedral in Europe. It also contains the shrine of St Swithun, and marks the beginning of the ancient Pilgrims' Way leading to Canterbury, making it an important pilgrim centre. As Winchester Cathedral also begins the Pilgrims' Trail – i.e. the route featured in Chapter Seven, and where it is described in detail – I will not repeat the same information here; however, the cathedral contains much fine architecture spanning the eleventh to the sixteenth centuries, and is the burial place for numerous bishops and later monarchs, such as King Canute and William Rufus.

If you wish to follow the few stops associated with Jane Austen sited along this route, then do visit her memorial in the north side aisle and the brass plaque erected in 1872; there is an illustrated exhibition detailing her life, work and death in Hampshire displayed beside her grave. There is also a stained-glass memorial window erected above the plaque.

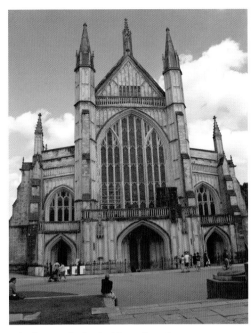

Winchester Cathedral (east front). STEVE DUNN

Hyde Abbey

The ruins of Hyde Abbey are situated along the banks of the River Itchen. Hyde Abbey was the last resting place of King Alfred the Great. The New Minster at Winchester, located very close to the Old Minster, was founded at the wish of King Alfred (died 899) – it was built by his son and dedicated *c*.903. This Benedictine abbey relocated from the New Minster in 1110 after the latter burnt down in 1094. The abbey was dissolved in 1538. A hospital for the sick and poor was connected with the abbey at this time.

The abbey was demolished following the Dissolution, and nothing of it now remains except the fourteenth-/fifteenth-century gatehouse, which is the only upstanding survival; material was reused in St Bart's Church nearby, and various farm buildings in the vicinity. Excavations on the site were carried out in 1972–4. The west precinct wall was located, and a ditch dating to about 1110 was found the following year, together with evidence of occupation earlier than the abbey. A medieval hall, possibly the almoner's hall, a length of the precinct wall, and a garderobe were also found. The City Bridewell (the city lock-up) occupied the site of the abbey church from 1788 onwards, but this has been removed and houses erected on the site. The cart shed adjoining the gatehouse has been converted into a row of houses, and the shed with rubble walls is now part of the Historic Resources Centre offices.

Avington

A short detour to the south, across the River Itchen and before you reach Itchen Abbas, will take you to Avington, where there is an interesting Georgian church, and Avington

Park. Now a luxury hotel, this seventeenth-century Palladian mansion features a classical portico surmounted by three statues built in 1670, and glass conservatories. The Restoration house is constructed of brick, with a giant Doric portico; it was built by John James (who assisted Wren in building Greenwich Hospital) for George Brydges, who died in the lake rescuing his pet dog. The sumptuous painted interiors, informal gardens and further elaborations are by the eighteenth-century Duke of Chandos. Charles II stayed at various times, as did George IV.

Itchen Abbas

Next, St John the Baptist Church can be seen at Itchen Abbas. The present building dates from 1863–83, but incorporates an original Norman chancel arch. It has been described as a modest, but thoroughly realized work of the Romanesque Revival by architect William Cole.

Chawton

Although there are certainly interesting sites to see after Itchen Abbas, the Pilgrims' Way heads straight through the village of Chawton, and it is worth taking a while to admire its many sites of interest. Firstly, there is Chawton House, an Elizabethan manor house which has been in the Knight family for over 400 years; it once belonged to Jane Austen's brother, Edward, who was adopted by childless Knight cousins. It is now a specialist and unique library of over 9,000 titles, focusing on women's writing in English from 1600 to 1830; it also contains the Knight family library, with some volumes that were known to Jane Austen. There are family portraits as well as those of women writers.

JANE AUSTEN'S HOUSE

The Jane Austen connection continues, as the village is also the location of Jane's house, now a museum. It is the only house where Jane lived and wrote that is open to the public. An eighteenth-century structure, it was formerly known as Chawton Cottage. Here, she revised the three manuscripts she had written previously but which had remained unpublished, and wrote three more novels; she also started one more, but this was destined to remain unfinished as illness overtook her. Jane left the cottage for the last time in May 1817 to take lodgings near her physician in Winchester. She died only two months later on the 18 July, and was buried in Winchester Cathedral (the first stop on the route, so if you are interested in Jane Austen, do visit her grave first).

Jane's mother and sister, Cassandra, continued to live at the cottage for the rest of their lives. When Cassandra died in 1845, the cottage was split into three dwellings for labourers on the Chawton estate, and it remained that way until it was sold in 1947.

Alton

The Church of St Lawrence in Alton is the next place of interest. It is likely there was a Saxon church here, but little appears to survive of this except, possibly, the old font and a small amount of remains at the bottom of the tower.

The church was enlarged in the twelfth century and again in the fifteenth century – its interior is a feast of sculptures. There is a chantry chapel, founded by John Champflour; the carvings at the top of the pillars depict a wolf, a cock and a pelican, amongst other things. Also, another of the fifteenth-century pillars depicts an interesting mural of three portraits: St Cornelius, a contemporary of St Lawrence after whom the church is dedicated; a king, possibly Henry VI who reigned from 1422 to 1461, at the time when this part of the church was rebuilt; and, at the bottom, a martyred bishop. It is suggested that this figure may be St Thomas Becket, due to the church's location on the Pilgrims' Way. The north chancel also possesses a set of intricate misericords. Though these are usually found in monastic churches, they may have simply been brought from Hyde Abbey after the Dissolution.

The expression 'Sweet Fanny Adams' originates from the village. It involved the abduction, murder and dismemberment of little eight-year-old Fanny Adams in Alton on Saturday 24 August 1867 by clerk Frederick Baker. In 1869, British sailors were served tins of mutton as the latest shipboard convenience food, and gloomily declared that the vile-looking butchered contents must surely be 'Sweet Fanny Adams'. It was gradually accepted throughout the armed services as a euphemism for 'sweet nothing', and so passed into common usage.

Passing the fourteenth-century Church of the Assumption of the Blessed Virgin at Upper Froyle, the next point of interest is the seventeenth-century Marelands House at Bentley. Then on to Powderham Castle, one of England's oldest family homes. Sir Philip Courtenay began building the fortified mansion in 1391, and it has remained in the same family to this day; it is currently home to the 18th Earl and Countess of Devon. The castle was expanded and altered extensively in the eighteenth and nineteenth centuries, most notably by James Wyatt in the 1790s.

Farnham

The route then swings round and into Farnham, where the castle, technically the Bishop's Palace, is one of the most important buildings in south-east England. It is generally accepted that construction of Farnham Castle began in about 1138 by Henry of Blois, Bishop of Winchester and brother of King Stephen, but it is a mixture of architectural styles – primarily early Norman, Tudor and Restoration. It is an impressive stone motte and bailey fortress, which has been in continuous occupation since the twelfth century. The original building was demolished by Henry II in 1155 after the Anarchy, and then rebuilt in the late twelfth and early thirteenth centuries. In the early fifteenth century, it was the residence of Cardinal Henry Beaufort, who presided at the trial of Joan of Arc in 1414. It is for this reason that the church in Farnham is dedicated to her. The castle was slighted again after the Civil War in 1648. Since then, more buildings have been constructed in the castle grounds, the most impressive being those built by Bishop George Morley in the seventeenth century.

Waverley

On a short detour to the south, not far from Compton, is Waverley Abbey. The first Cistercian house to be established in Britain, the abbey was founded in 1128 by William Gifford, Bishop of Winchester, with twelve monks and an abbot from Aumone in France. By 1187, the monastic population had risen to seventy, with a further 120 lay brothers in residence. In 1201, the abbey buildings were badly flooded. This became a common occurrence, and as a result the abbey was substantially rebuilt during the thirteenth century.

It continued to grow into the next century. The monks and lay brothers farmed the surrounding land and were active in the Cistercian wool trade; they provided shelter for pilgrims and travellers and an infirmary for the sick.

After its dissolution in 1536, the site passed to Sir William Fitzherbert, treasurer of Henry VIII's household. Much of the abbey was dismantled and some of the stone was reused to build Sir William More's house at Loseley, a few miles to the east, as well as the Georgian mansion known as Waverley Abbey House, which was built in 1723 in the northern portion of the former abbey precinct.

There are also many earthworks in the area known as The Sands, to the east of Crooksbury Hill, including Soldiers' Ring.

Along Puttenham Heath you will encounter the site of a Roman villa and fort; then a quick detour to the south takes you to Compton St Nicholas. The tower and part of the west wall of the nave are believed to be pre-Conquest, but the main body was built in phases between 1080 and 1180. The church has many historical features, including a unique double sanctuary and much medieval graffiti. It is available for pilgrims' use.

Watts' Chapel

Back along the main route is an interesting stop: Watts' Chapel, now also an artists' village. This red brick Arts and Crafts masterpiece was designed by craftswoman and social reformer Mary Watts (who is also buried here), and dedicated to 'the loving memory of all who find rest near its walls, and for the comfort and help of those to whom the sorrow of separation remains'. It is thus technically a mortuary chapel, but is simply a masterpiece of the Art Nouveau Celtic Revival style.

In 1895, Mary began to run evening terracotta classes at Limnerslease, the Watts' nearby residence and studio. At these classes, Mary would teach the local villagers how to model tiles from local clay with the beautiful and symbolic patterns she had designed to decorate the walls of the chapel, still seen here today. Through painting commissioned portraits, G. F. Watts financed the building of the chapel and presented it as his gift to the village of Compton. It also remains a working village parish church to this day.

The Church of St Martha-on-the-Hill

The route then bypasses Guildford to the south, and just before St Martha's Hill, a detour south takes you to Chilworth Manor and the Church of St Martha-on-the-Hill. The church occupies one of the most striking settings of any place of worship in Britain, perched on the crown of the hill, 573ft (175m) up, and with no road leading to it.

The first chapel on this site was allegedly built on the summit by the Anglo-Saxons but, dating back beyond this, Neolithic flints and Bronze Age earthworks suggest this was a spot venerated in prehistory. Although recorded in Domesday Book, no trace of the original Saxon chapel remains, and by the early thirteenth century, a Norman church occupied the site. This building was constructed between 1189 and 1204, and was dominated by a tall west tower.

By 1262, the church was taken over by the Augustinian monks of Newark Abbey, and being a monastic place of worship, was larger than a typical parish church. Unusually, it had five doors, to allow separate entrances for the monks and other worshippers.

Disaster struck St Martha's in 1745, when the church was wrecked by a huge explosion that rocked the hill and demolished the tower. This was caused by one of several accidental blasts at the gunpowder works under the southern slopes of the hill, in the Tillingbourne Valley. The rebuilding of St Martha's Church was inspired by the Norman style, incorporating the remaining walls into a new design, with a well-proportioned central tower to replace the large western tower of the original church.

The church had links with two ancient manor houses that lay one on each side of the hill. According to legend, both Chilworth Manor and Tyting House had secret passageways leading to the church, thus providing an escape route for any priest needing a swift escape during Henry VIII's Reformation.

St Martha's Hill

St Martha's Hill is frequently referred to in old documents as Martyr's Hill, and some historians have suggested it was dedicated to St Thomas Becket after his murder in 1170. However, the name seems to date from a much earlier period, and it is possible that the first martyrs were early Christians who met their deaths on the land.

The Way then goes back into woodland, following the contour at around 600ft (180m) and passing a series of World War II pillboxes, part of the defence against the expected invasion in the early 1940s. The route then passes by Newlands Corner, site of a Bronze Age bowl barrow. From here, pilgrims had their first extended view of the open chalk downland across the Weald, the ridge of the South Downs. The crime writer Agatha

Christie staged her disappearance from Newlands Corner in 1926; she was found days later in Harrogate, North Yorkshire.

Albury Park

A short detour south takes you to the magnificent Jacobethan Albury Park mansion, remodelled by A.W.N. Pugin in the mid-1800s, which is well worth a visit. More interesting still is the redundant old church of St Peter and St Paul, with parts pre-dating 1066. It features Saxon origins, with a twelfth-century Norman tower, a thirteenth-century chancel and south transept, as well as a fourteenth-century nave and south aisle, and an early sixteenth-century north porch. The south chantry chapel was also remodelled by Augustus Welby Pugin in the early 1840s, and there is a fine fifteenth-century wall painting of St Christopher sporting a curly red beard.

The route then goes through Netley Heath, and passes the Church of St Barnabas at Ranmore. This church is a large Gilbert Scott creation, completed in 1859, which stands in the middle of nowhere.

Westhumble

As you leave Ranmore Common, the route skirts to the south of the village of Westhumble. Just outside the village are the remains of a late twelfth-century chapel of locally quarried flint stones; by the fifteenth century, the chapel had been desecrated and had fallen into a ruinous state. It has been managed by the National Trust since 1937. It originally stood on land belonging to Merton Priory, so was likely built as a chapel-of-ease for their tenants.

Box Hill

The route now comes to Box Hill, a summit of the North Downs in Surrey. The hill takes its name from the ancient box woodland found on the steepest west-facing chalk slopes overlooking the River Mole. The earliest archaeological evidence of human activity here are two Bronze Age round barrows located close to Salomons Memorial. The larger barrow is 66ft (20m) in diameter and 7ft 3in (2.2m) high, although a slight depression in the top suggests that it may have been partially excavated or robbed. In the medieval era, the larger barrow was used as a boundary marker for the parish of Mickleham. Traces of prehistoric field boundaries are visible on Burford Spur, and the low flint banks on the steeper and more wooded White Hill may be contemporaneous.

Box Hill is also known for its association with witches. Covens of witches congregate at its summit and carry out spells, enchantments and other practices associated with Wicca and Pagan practices. The box trees that cover the area are said to enhance their connection to spirits on a level similar to the winter or summer solstice.

The route then passes Colley Hill, and beyond to Reigate Hill and an old fort. Sitting proud at the top of the hill is the nineteenth-century Reigate Fort. The fort commands a historic defensive position looking out over the Weald towards the South Downs. To the east Gatton Park, designed by Lancelot Capability Brown, nestles serenely into the North Downs. Also in the vicinity is the nineteenth-century Margery Hall.

Merstham

Moving on, the route then enters Merstham. The medieval Church of St Katherine is reached via a footbridge over the M25. The parish is mentioned in documents as early as 675CE, and it is therefore certain that an earlier pre-Conquest church stood on or near the present site. Fragments of Romanesque stone carving have been found within the current walls, and are now preserved. The tower, nave, aisles and chancel were built during the first half of the thirteenth century. Domesday Book states that the Manor of Merstham belonged to the prior and convent of Christ Church, Canterbury, the revenues being used to provide clothing for the brethren; an arrangement lasting until 1539. The gift of the living remains with the Archbishop of Canterbury, but the parish was transferred to the diocese of Winchester, then Rochester, and lastly Southwark in 1905. Fragments of medieval glass are included throughout the windows, while the tiles of the Lady Chapel are attributed to Constance Kent, who confessed in 1865 to the murder of her four-year-old brother. The story was accounted in Kate Summerscale's *The Suspicions of Mr Whicher*.

Moving east, Caterham is a short detour to the north. There are a few areas of outstanding natural beauty around this section of the route.

Botley Hill

The Way then passes Botley Hill, the highest point of the North Downs at 885ft (269.6m). The prime meridian crosses the hill. Botley Hill was a main surveying point for the Anglo-French survey of 1784–1790, which sought to measure precisely the relative positions of the Royal Greenwich Observatory and the Paris Observatory.

Titsey Place

The Way then skirts round and veers south to pass Titsey Place. This manor house has its origins in the sixteenth century, although the first impression is now of an early nineteenth-century house in a picturesque park. It was built by Sir John Gresham, a former mayor of London in the mid-sixteenth century, on the site of its predecessor. The predominately Tudor house was demolished and rebuilt in the eighteenth century, before being refronted in 1826. Finally, a tower was added in 1856.

A short southern detour here takes you to the site of a Roman villa near the Vanguard

Way. If you stay on the route, you will next encounter the Church of St Mary in Tatsfield, which is worth visiting: it is a small eleventh-century church with Norman windows and an unusual quatrefoil window in the south wall – perhaps a site for pilgrims to receive communion or a low-side window for ringing the scaring bell.

Knockholt

The route then heads towards Knockholt, where a short detour to the south takes you to St Botolph's Church at Chevening. There has been a place of worship on this site for nearly 900 years, and a consecrated churchyard existed before that. The church is one of sixty-eight churches in England dedicated to St Botolph, the patron saint of travellers (not coincidental given its location). The earliest remaining portion of the church is the south wall of the south aisle. The rest is largely thirteenth and fourteenth century, with repairs made in the early twentieth century. It is built mainly of local flint rubble mixed with Kent ragstone for strength. There are also a few fragments of Roman material, which may be from a ruined villa nearby to the east of the site.

Otford

Next is the large village of Otford. The parish church here was the first in the Rochester diocese. The flint and stone rubble building of St Bartholomew's Church is interesting for its eleventh-century nave, late twelfth-century tower, fourteenth-century chancel and sixteenth-century south aisle and chapel.

Otford is also interesting in itself, as the Archbishops of Canterbury held it from as early as the late ninth century. One of the more important of the smaller Anglo-Saxon estates in Kent was also at Otford. Otford Palace, also known as the Archbishop's Palace, was practically rebuilt between 1514 and 1518 by Archbishop Wareham, with the addition of a large inner courtyard and a set of lodgings. Otford became a vast Renaissance palace, and was clearly the inspiration for Cardinal Wolseley's (slightly later) Hampton Court.

Eight years after acquiring Hampton Court in 1529, Henry VIII acquired Otford from Archbishop Cranmer, and went on to enlarge them both. Following Henry VIII's death, however, the palace fell into ruin, and now all that remains is the shell of the north-west tower, which is connected by the ground storey of a gallery to one side of the gatehouse, the lower gallery, now converted to cottages, and a part of the Great Gatehouse.

A further Roman villa site is also located just to the south-east of the palace.

Further east is Otford Court, which is now St Michael's Preparatory School. The extensive Beechy Lees estate, as it was known, was built in the early 1880s. It is an unusual three-storey house of red brick with terracotta embellishments, stained-glass windows and a tower and cupola, which embodied the High Victorian style, together with the large rooms and the oak wood panelling/carving. The house is set into the side of the North Downs and enjoys views out over its terraces and parkland to a distant church. The house became a school in the 1930s, and some of the land was put to use for sports.

Next is Otford Manor, now known as Oak Hall, a 1920s building, now a residential Christian centre which runs adventure and overseas holidays. It was formerly the home of Mr Lyle of Tate & Lyle sugar refiners.

Trottiscliffe

Passing Wortham, Trottiscliffe (known as Trosley) and the country park is next encountered. It was initially part of a large nineteenth-century woodland estate built by Sir Sydney Waterlow to encircle Trosley Towers, demolished in 1936.

The Coldrum Long Barrow, also known as the Coldrum Stones and the Adscombe Stones, a chambered long barrow, is located just to the east of the village of Trottiscliffe. Constructed *c*.4000BC, today it survives only in a ruined state.

Birling

Moving on, just to the south of the route is Birling Place, a large red and blue brick house, home of the Nevill family since 1435. The fifteenth-century building stands prominently beneath the Downs escarpment. There has been a substantial dwelling here for several hundred years – at one time, it was a fortified medieval house. Records show that Elizabeth I paid a visit to Birling Place in 1573.

Cuxton

The route then heads north towards Cuxton, where Court Lodge is situated. Originally an eighteenth-century farmhouse, owned by the Earls of Darnley and used by the Pye family in the 1800s, it was taken over by the Short Brothers during World War II and used as a drawing office – the Stirling bomber was designed here. After the war it became RAF No. 4 Reserve Centre, and then a plastics factory, and in the 1950s it was extensively modernised and expanded.

Rochester

Next is the historic town of Rochester, which has an abundance of interesting historic places. The cathedral is England's second oldest, having been founded in 604CE by Bishop Justus. The present building dates back to the work of the French monk, Gundulf, in 1080. The glorious Norman architecture of the nave, parts of the crypt, as well as one of the finest Romanesque façades in England, make this a great site to visit. There is also a fine collection of medieval wall paintings and the first fresco painted in an English cathedral in almost 800 years.

Rochester Cathedral, west front.
CHARLOTTE STANFORD

There is also Temple Manor. This stone hall of the manor house of the Knights Templar lies to the west of the River Medway in Strood. Now surrounded by an industrial estate, it once stood in farmland, which provided it with a substantial income in the thirteenth century. Built in about 1240 by the Knights Templar, the manor was designed to provide suitable lodging for dignitaries travelling between Dover and London. In the years that followed, however, the building not only changed functions but, on many occasions, also changed hands, eventually falling into disuse and disrepair.

The imposing fortress, Rochester Castle, is also nearby. Built in *c*.1127, then rebuilt under Henry III and Edward I, there is much to see here.

Burham

Burham is next and features Burham Court. The red and blue brick house is largely sixteenth century, with later nineteenth-century additions.

Kit's Coty

The Way then goes directly passed Kit's Coty House and its neighbour, Little Kit's Coty House, which constitute the remains of two megalithic 'dolmen' burial chambers. The larger of the two monuments, Kit's Coty, has three uprights and a huge capstone, while the smaller, Little Kit's Coty (also known as the Countless Stones), is now a jumble of sarsens (sandstone boulders).

Although the origins of their names are unknown, long barrows such as these were initially constructed during the early Neolithic period to act as communal burial sites. The most distinctive surviving feature of this monument is the H-shaped arrangement of three large slabs of sarsen stone (a fine-grained, crystalline sandstone), capped by a further slab, which formed the main burial chamber of the barrow. The stones were originally buried at the eastern end of a long earthen mound, of which only traces survive.

Little Kit's Coty House is a group of around twenty clustered sarsen stones. They represent the remains of a burial mound which was, unfortunately, seriously damaged in 1690.

Medway Gap

This area, known as the Medway Gap, is filled with megaliths including the two described above and a further large sarsen dolmen, known as the White Horse Stone. Legend has it that the Saxon leader Horsa was buried under the stone. It has also been suggested that when brothers Horsa and Hengist landed in Britain in 449CE, the White Horse standard was draped across the stone. However, armorial emblems were not used until the twelfth century, so it is highly unlikely that there is any validity in the link between the white horse emblem and the Anglo-Saxons.

A short detour south-west takes you to Aylesford. The Friars Priory on the opposite bank is a thirteenth-century religious house of the Order of Carmelites. The Friars was always a traditional stop in the medieval era and, in fact, the Pilgrims' Hall, the oldest building at The Friars, is so named because it offered hospitality and accommodation for pilgrim travellers to Canterbury. This custom of hospitality to pilgrims continues to this day. The open-air shrine is dedicated to the Glorious Assumption of the Blessed Virgin Mary and St Simon Stock, Prior General of the Order in the thirteenth century. The building was originally reached by crossing the ancient bridge linking the old settlement with the northern edge of Maidstone.

Boxley

Making your way east and returning to the route takes you past the ruins of Boxley Abbey, a Cistercian monastery founded *c*.1146 by William of Ypres, leader of King Stephen's Flemish mercenaries, and colonized by monks from Clairvaux Abbey in France. The abbey was famous for a relic known as the Rood of Grace, a wooden cross, the figure upon which was said to miraculously move and speak, and would certainly have justified a stop during any pilgrimage in the area.

Thurnham

Next of interest is Thurnham Castle, a twelfth-century flint-built castle on a hill also known as Godard's Castle. The north side of the bailey wall still stands 10ft (3m) high, though the west wall has completely collapsed. There is no visible stonework on the large motte, although there were once two towers and an outer curtain wall. In the twelfth century, the fortress belonged to the de Say family, and then the de Thurnhams. One source indicates that Robert de Thurnham never returned from the Crusades, and the castle was left to decay. A charter of 1215 mentions the lands within the walls of the castle, which may indicate that it was already in ruins as reported in the early nineteenth century. The area is also known for its Roman remains.

Hollingbourne

Moving into Hollingbourne, a site worth visiting is the manor house. This Elizabethan building was the home of a prominent Kentish family, the Culpepers, for around 125 years. It was first acquired in 1590 by Francis Culpeper of Greenway Court in the county of Kent (1538–91). The L-shaped house was built in the late sixteenth century, and comprises the south and west wings of an incomplete E-shaped house; the north wing was not built, apart from the first few courses of brickwork. It is a two-storey house constructed largely of English bonded distinctive red brick with a tiled roof. It is now privately owned.

The church, dedicated to All Saints, dates from the fourteenth and fifteenth centuries, as well as *c*.1638. It was then restored in 1876 by George Gilbert Scott Jnr. Attached to it is a north chapel with a marble floor, containing a superb monument to the memory of Lady Elizabeth Culpeper, and the family's arms in the east window.

Godfrey House

A short detour to the south takes you to Godfrey House. Although privately owned, the late Elizabethan manor house is of local importance. An inscription above the front door reads 'Godfrey House built 1587, restored 1859'. This timber-framed house has an attractive front elevation with coved windows on the first floor and jettied gables above. It really is a must-see.

Leeds Castle

Leeds Castle is also only a short distance from the Pilgrims' Way. Leeds Castle has served numerous functions, including: a Norman stronghold; the private property of six of England's medieval queens; a palace used by Henry VIII and his first wife, Catherine of Aragon; a Jacobean country house; a Georgian mansion; an elegant early twentieth-century retreat for the influential and famous; and in the twenty-first century, it is one of the most visited historic buildings in Britain. The first stone castle was built by a Norman baron during the reign of William the Conqueror's son, Henry I, on an island in the River Len. In 1278, a century and a half later, it came into the possession of Queen Eleanor of Castile, first wife of Edward I.

The route then passes to the north of Harrietsham, and the wooden sculpture of a monkish pilgrim called Brother Perceval who sits overlooking the view south over the village. Harrietsham's late fifteenth-century parish church tower is also to your right.

Lenham

Lenham is then seen from the north, after passing the top end of the 'Marley Tile

Works' (still in business but focused on plastic of various types). Visit the church to see the war memorial: originally, it was placed at the foot of the 189ft (57.6m) chalk cross cut into the hillside in 1922, but in more recent years, it was brought back down to the village churchyard, together with a World War II memorial. The Christian-style cross now commemorates the casualties of the two world wars.

Highbourne Park

The route next passes Highbourne Park, built on the site of the old Lenham Chest Hospital. The hospital was founded in 1914 after it was thought the invigorating Kentish air would help tuberculosis sufferers.

Charing

The route then turns into the village of Charing, where you can see the remains of one of the old palaces of the Archbishops of Canterbury. The history of the palace and the manor of Charing can be traced back to the eighth century, when the land was presented to Christchurch Priory at Canterbury, and the records of the convent and cathedral then document the series of building works carried out by subsequent archbishops. The buildings, which date principally from the fourteenth century, include the Great Hall, part of the chapel, the gatehouse and the precinct boundary wall, part of the west range and the present farmhouse. Many are now private dwellings.

The Church of St Peter and St Paul stands at the heart of the village, next to the remains of the Archbishop's Palace. The west tower is over 600 years old, though the rest of the church was rebuilt in the sixteenth century. The church contains seventeenth-century chandeliers and a rare seventeenth-century vamping horn used to amplify the choir and make announcements. St Richard's Chapel is so named because St Richard (patron saint of Sussex) visited as he walked through on his way to Chichester. There are also remains of a holy water stoup by the entrance door.

Eastwell Park

Along the route further east is Eastwell Park, a large area of parkland and a country estate. Over time successive buildings have served as homes to Sir Thomas Moyle, the earls of Winchilsea and Nottingham, Prince Alfred, the Duke of Edinburgh, and others.

The estate is now mainly a farming concern. Part of the estate is landscaped to include a large shallow lake that can be fished, and the distinctive Eastwell Towers. The largest building on the site today is Eastwell Manor, a stately home that now operates as a country house hotel.

The original country house at Eastwell was built for Sir Thomas Moyle – commissioner for Henry VIII – between 1540 and 1550. One of the men employed on the estate was the bricklayer Richard Plantagenet, who claimed to be an illegitimate son of Richard III.

Much of Eastwell Manor was built in the Jacobethan revival style between 1793 and 1799 for George Finch-Hatton, 9th Earl of Winchilsea. A Victorian neo-Tudor wing was later added. In the mid-1860s, the 11th Earl of Winchilsea experienced serious financial difficulties, which eventually forced him to leave the property. Eastwell was next occupied by Prince Alfred, Duke of Edinburgh, the second son of Queen Victoria. During that time, Victoria was a frequent visitor. In the 1920s the main house was severely damaged by fire, but was rebuilt on the same site between 1926 and 1928.

The structure now known as Eastwell Towers stands a mile south-west of the manor. It was the original main gatehouse to Eastwell Park, and built in 1848. Next to the large shallow lake at Eastwell Park is the ruined Church of St Mary the Virgin, which is now cared for by the Friends of Friendless Churches. The church features little besides a fifteenth century tower. It fell out of use after World War I. Severe damage was sustained by a storm in 1951 when parts of the nave and the choir collapsed. A tombstone located in the grounds is alleged to be that of Richard Plantagenet.

Boughton Lees

St Christopher's Church, Boughton Lees, is known as the 'winter church'. Originally a medieval hall house, then a barn, followed by the village school, it was adopted as a chapel-of-ease in the 1950s and is used for weekly services from October to May. The 'summer church' is next along the route.

Boughton Aluph

Boughton Aluph's church (All Saints) is significant in terms of its historical pilgrimage connection: not only does it boast a pilgrims' porch with a chimney and fireplace on the southern wall, but there are many fine medieval features, fixtures and artworks.

Built in the thirteenth century to replace a Saxon church, it was enlarged in the fourteenth century by Sir Thomas Aldon, one of Edward III's courtiers. The main church building comprises a thirteenth-century chancel and chapel, with various fourteenth- and fifteenth-century additions and seventeenth-century porches, which may have been rebuilt, or may indicate that the pilgrim connection is indeed a myth. The church was restored in 1878. On the north transept east wall is a fifteenth-century wall painting of the Trinity. There is also a fourteenth-century wooden screen in the north chapel, as well as fragments of fourteenth-century glass in the chancel east window, which depicts the Coronation of the Virgin and representations of Edward III and Eleanor.

Local folklore suggests that pilgrims gathered in the porch for warmth and until their numbers were large enough to ascend up into Kings Wood without the risk of being robbed.

A few miles further along, the trail passes through Kings Wood. From here, one gets a similar view to the medieval pilgrims journeying to Canterbury Cathedral, as they looked across Godmersham Park and due north-east along the Stour valley. However, only pilgrims travelling in the last few decades of the sixteenth century would have glimpsed its Bell Harry tower, which was built between 1490 and 1498.

The route then passes by Godmersham Park: built in 1732, it was once owned by Jane Austen's brother, and thought by some to be the setting for *Mansfield Park*.

Hurst Farm and its oast houses are also interesting buildings to see along the way here.

Chilham

Now the way stretches the last 7.5 miles (12km) to Canterbury, and here it comes to the charming village of Chilham. There has been a castle at the site of Chilham, on the edge of a wood, for over eight centuries – perhaps even thirteen or more. Held from time to time by the kings of England, it was also once, briefly, in 1216, occupied by the Dauphin, heir to the French throne. Having captured Canterbury, he was on his way to London to claim the English throne, which had been offered to him by rebellious barons. However, he was forestalled by the death of King John: the barons changed their minds and decided to favour John's infant son Henry, so sent the foreign prince back home.

Today, the site comprises a manor house and the castle's keep that date from 1174. The Jacobean manor house, within sight of the 'Old Castle' (the keep), was completed in 1616 for Sir Dudley Digges on a hexagonal plan, with five angled ranges and the sixth left open.

Chartham Hatch

The route then runs towards Long Hill and into Old Wives Lees, and enters Chartham Hatch. Here, the dovecote at Burnt House Farm is notable, not only for its architectural merit, but also for its role in sending homing birds to and from important envoys such as the Archbishop of Canterbury.

Bigbury Camp

The Way then passes straight through the Iron Age hill fort at Bigbury Wood. Formerly Bigberry Camp, this univallate fort is the only confirmed Iron Age hill fort in east Kent. Bigbury Camp was abandoned in about 54BC, when it was stormed by Roman soldiers of the Legio VII Claudia under the command of Julius Caesar; after the battle the settlement shifted to nearby Canterbury. The fort has a single 16ft (4.8m) wide defensive ditch with a raised bank on the inner side and a lower counterscarp bank. The ramparts form an irregular shape, following the contour of the hill. The earthworks follow an irregular curvilinear plan. It has been suggested that the annexe may have been used as a cattle compound, although this is uncertain. There is an entrance in the eastern side of the hill fort.

A notable find at Bigbury was a slave chain with its lock, associated with the pre-Roman slave trade between Britain and Gaul. Parts of an iron wheel rim were also found, together with early Iron Age pottery, indicating the presence of a prosperous agricultural community during the Iron Age.

Harbledown

The Way then travels into Harbledown. Just before the village, it is worth making a detour south to Tonford Manor to see the remains of a fortified fifteenth-century house; this had four round towers and was built by Sir Thomas Browne, comptroller and treasurer to Henry VI. Henry VIII and Katherine of Aragon once spent three days here. It is believed that Harbledown is referred to as 'Bobbe-Up-and-Down' by Chaucer in *The Manciple's Tale*.

ST DUNSTAN'S CHURCH

After entering Harbledown, the last step for pilgrims on their way to Canterbury was likely St Dunstan's Church, where the head of Thomas More is buried. There is also the Old Leper Church, built as part of the original St Nicholas' Hospital – a leper hospital, probably the first in England, founded *c*.1084 by Lanfranc, Archbishop of Canterbury 1070–89, and in operation until the end of the fourteenth century. Henry II visited here on his penitential journey to Canterbury in 1174. After *c*.1400, the hospital became an almshouse for the poor; in 1562 it had sixty places for poor men and women. The foundation was reconstituted in 1565, and the domestic ranges rebuilt in 1685 and again in 1840. It is still an almshouse today, for retired people. The north aisle and the tower were added in the twelfth century, and the south aisle in the fourteenth. It was originally known as the Hospital of the Forest of Blean.

In the grounds of the church is 'The Black Prince's Well', which features the motto 'Ich Dien' ('I serve'). It is not a well as such but a small spring. The stone appears to have been derived from another structure, rather than carved especially for the well head. The well is reached by a series of stone steps between two courses of walling. The water emerges as a small trickle through a 5in (13cm) diameter red clay pipe, flowing to fill a circular basin. It is said to have had healing properties for eye complaints and also leprosy – which is not surprising, given its proximity to St Nicholas'.

Legend has it that the Black Prince visited and drank from the well in 1357, as he was said to have suffered from a mild form of leprosy. As he lay on his deathbed in Westminster, he asked that some water from the well be brought to him.

The End of the Journey: Canterbury Cathedral

The Way now runs through the west gate of Canterbury and to the gate of the cathedral, where the journey culminates.

The Mother Church of the world-wide Anglican Communion, and seat of the Archbishop of Canterbury, Canterbury Cathedral was one of the most important centres of pilgrimage in medieval England. There has been a cathedral at Canterbury since 597CE when St Augustine baptised the Anglo-Saxon king, Ethelbert. During the tenth century, it became a formal community of Benedictine monks, which continued here until the monastery was dissolved by Henry VIII in 1540.

Augustine's original building lies beneath the floor of the nave – it was extensively rebuilt and enlarged in the Anglo-Saxon era, and was then completely rebuilt by Archbishop Lanfranc in 1070, following a major fire. A staircase and parts of the north wall – in the area of the north-west transept called the Martyrdom (where Becket was murdered) – remain from that building.

There have been many additions to the building over the last 900 years, but parts of the choir and some of the windows and their stained glass date from the twelfth century. In fact, Canterbury Cathedral contains over 1,435sq yd (1,200sq m) of stained glass, including one of England's largest early medieval collections.

Its importance as a centre of pilgrimage greatly increased after the murder of Thomas Becket here in 1170. As a result, Canterbury itself had to be altered in order to accommodate the many pilgrims who came to visit the saint's remains within the cathedral. In 1220, Becket's bones were moved from a tomb in the crypt to a magnificent jewel-encrusted shrine within the Trinity Chapel.

Exterior of Canterbury Cathedral, south entrance. AUTHOR

Altar of the Swordpoint, Canterbury Cathedral. AUTHOR

Location of St Thomas Becket's tomb, crypt, Canterbury Cathedral. AUTHOR

Former site of St Thomas Becket's shrine, Canterbury Cathedral. AUTHOR

St Thomas Becket was widely revered throughout both England and Europe with Canterbury becoming a centre of national pilgrimage importance. Furthermore, Canterbury Cathedral possessed the prestigious shrine of Our Lady of the Undercroft, and a multitude of additional shrines that largely decreased in eminence following the martyrdom of Becket (notably Sts Alphege and Dunstan). Accurate figures for the number of pilgrims who went to Canterbury are not easy to gain but it is said that 100,000 pilgrims journeyed on their knees along the nave to the Pilgrim's Steps in 1420, which approached the choir, where Becket's shrine stood.

Medieval pilgrims could follow a route of many attractions around the church, akin to the modern theme-park attraction. These included the altar (of the Swordpoint) in the north transept, where Becket was martyred; the crypt, to visit his original tomb site; and then into the light-filled Trinity Chapel, which housed the shrine.

Surrounding this section of the route were twelve windows depicting healing miracles within the ambulatory of Trinity Chapel; nearby, at its apex, was the light-filled Corona Chapel, which featured the head reliquary of Becket.

Two of the windows in the ambulatory illustrated Becket's life, while ten depicted the posthumous miracles he performed in the immediate years following his martyrdom (between 1171 and 1173).

Corona, Canterbury Cathedral. AUTHOR

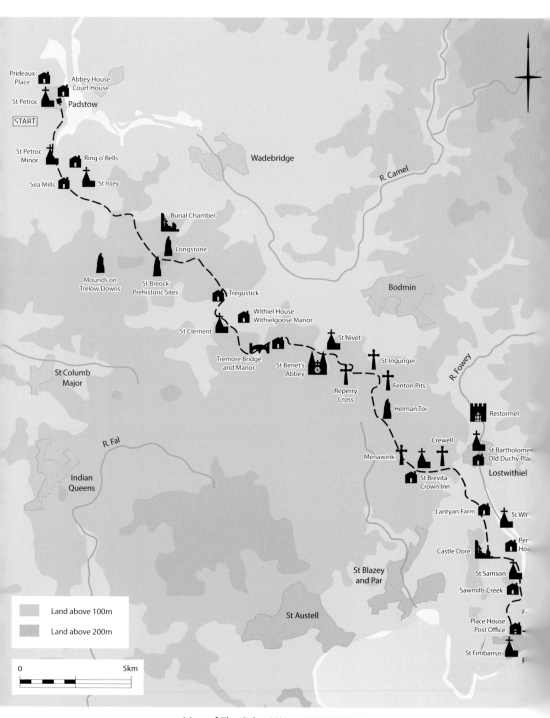

Map of The Saints' Way. JIM BRIGHTMAN

CHAPTER SIX

The Saints' Way, or Forth an Syns

This loosely ancient trail of 30 miles (48km) crosses mid-Cornwall from the harbour town of Padstow in the north, all the way across the county to the southern port of Fowey. The emphasis of the route lies in glorifying the landscape of the area known as the former kingdom of Dumnonia, at the same time as following sections of a trail thought to date from the Bronze Age, known as Drovers' Way. Essentially, this route exists as a series of connections between sacred shrines, wells, stones, chapels and churches, all linked together through the Cornish landscape, and used by traders and drovers from Ireland and Wales to avoid the waters around Land's End, and then later, in the medieval period, by pilgrims and missionaries en route to holy sites overseas, such as Jerusalem, Compostela and Lourdes.

The modern route ('Forth an Syns' in Cornish) was opened in 1986 and follows public footpaths and country lanes, thus making the most of the Cornish countryside as much as its sacred Celtic past. The route differs from the others in this book in that it is not a clear route from one starting location to a saint's shrine at another; rather, it consists of a plethora of intertwined and connected historic trails and sites that together form the overall Way.

Culminating at the Church of St Fimbarrus in the town of Fowey, the end to this route acts more like the beginning of another journey. It marks the end of land, but opens out into the harbour mouth and the open sea beyond, which led pilgrims to the next phase of their journey and ultimate destination overseas. Many travelled to Compostela from this port. Records show that in 1434, boats took passengers on the journey in groups of twenty-five to sixty – but Fowey was only one of many of these passage points: others included Falmouth, Landulph, St Michael's Mount, Penzance and Saltash. It is therefore very unlikely that there was a particular 'pilgrim's way' to a single point of departure; rather, there were many, and they were linked through connections to the historic, sacred landscape.

The unique situation of the saintly landscape of Cornwall versus the rest of the British Isles lies in the association of local saints with churches, whereas in England, most were dedicated to, or contained, well-known national or international saints. In medieval Cornwall, 185 saintly churches were in existence; this was about 140 saints in total, given that some had more than one site named after them. Furthermore, just over half were venerated in Cornwall alone, most at a single site. However, there were also places that honoured the infamous saints of the Christian Church, such as

St Michael and the Virgin. Many of them did possess relics associated with the patron saint, with some claiming to hold the body of the saint after which they were named. The variety of these dedications therefore shows just how complex the history of the sacred landscape of Cornwall really is.

The History of the Cornish Sacred Landscape

The Christian landscape of Cornwall is indeed ancient. Between *c.*550CE and 900CE particularly, a basic vocabulary of sites was established that existed until the Reformation, and included many churches, chapels and holy wells whose beginnings lay some 900 years earlier. Nonetheless, the historical narrative of the southwest is much sparser than, say, the writings associated with the north-east of England (for example, Bede). The history of Cornwall lies more in the practices hinted at in the accounts of Anglo-Saxon writers, but it would appear that early Christianity here came from Roman Britain, Wales, Ireland and continental Europe, possibly even the Mediterranean.

Accordingly, it is easier to speculate that many influences abounded in the earliest Christianity of the area, and therefore the link between these ancient sites and their medieval successors simply shows a continuance of practices that began elsewhere and had migrated into the culture of the Southwest. The most significant of these early churches provided connections to earlier landscapes, in perpetuating ancient burial sites, for example. Many of the names that since became saints of north, mid- and east Cornwall were largely Welsh, and believed to be the descendants of King Brychan of Brecon. These Celtic missionaries made pilgrimages throughout Cornwall and beyond, and their teachings became subsumed within the culture, societies and landscape, which became dedicated to their memory.

Yet, the earliest mention of the Cornish monasteries is in the seventh- to ninth-century *First Life of St Samson*. And the name of the ancient monastery of 'Docco' at St Kew is virtually all that is known of the earliest church site of the county. No churches dating to before the ninth century have been excavated or have survived, and no canonizations took place in Cornwall between the Norman Conquest and the Reformation. Still, the churches acted as foci for the surrounding communities, with the medieval landscapes emerging and developing around them from that time onwards.

By the eleventh century, many of these sites were enlarged and embellished, and with them, many place names appear to have been regarded as saintly, with the 'St' often prefixed to the church name, and providing modern place names such as St Neot or St Austell. Monasteries, churches, chapels, burial grounds, wells and crosses of various origins certainly dotted the landscape by this time, many of which had well-developed saintly cults. In addition, the numerous holy wells represented the quintessential 'Celtic' pagan survival. Some are amongst the earliest in the region, and may be very ancient sacred places that were given a makeover in the early medieval period.

When one thinks of sacred sites in Cornwall, the immediate image that most often springs to mind is the freestanding stone cross. The earliest such examples in this area survive from the late eighth and ninth century, up until about the fifteenth century, of which many may be linked to major ecclesiastical centres, but also fulfilled a variety of roles. These included churchyard crosses that identified boundaries (or sanctuaries) within an ecclesiastical complex, while in rural settings they were often waymarkers, as signs for chapels, fords or holy wells, preaching crosses, or were even used simply to mark out newly formed territories. In addition, some evidence suggests that in the medieval period they were simply used as foci for acts of religious piety and devotion, which became linked over time with associated saints and sites, and thus pilgrimage.

Though scholars have suggested that early medieval sculpture rarely strays far from its original site, issues arise if we begin to ask whether it is all in situ. However, it is clear that the crosses had a range of functions, which were established in the early Middle Ages and continued until the Reformation, including simply as waymarkers, especially in difficult and otherwise unmarked terrain. Over 350 wayside crosses are known nationally, concentrated in south-west England throughout Cornwall and on Dartmoor, where they form the most common type. In Cornwall, wayside crosses vary considerably in form and decoration. The most common includes a round, or 'wheel' head, on the faces of which various forms of cross or related designs are carved in relief or incised, while the spaces between the cross arms are sometimes pierced. Less common forms in Cornwall include the 'Latin' cross, and the simple slab with a low relief cross on both faces, though this design is much rarer.

Nevertheless, it is very difficult to show continuity of practice in these sacred Cornish sites, given the small amount of evidence there is, and as they may just as easily have gained religious associations during the conversion to Christianity. This conjectural point means that the Saints' Way must be treated as a very modern (and somewhat artificial) creation, bringing together these supposed links between the early pagan locations and those of the cult of saints, which collectively formed a developing network of Christian sites.

Finally, a quick note must be made regarding the impact of the Reformation on Cornwall, and thus why the majority of these sacred places appear to be so ancient in their origins. The activities of the church throughout the sixteenth century appear to have largely continued. There were numerous occurrences of rebuildings and money spent on installing stained glass, screens and seating. For example, much of the Church of St Neot's glass dates from the 1530s; chapels dedicated to various saints also continued in popularity, while pilgrimages to St Michael's Mount were still very frequent in the early sixteenth century – although John Leland, writing after visiting the county in 1542, implied that pilgrimage had ceased by that time.

The large majority of these sites were not dismantled or demolished, but rather fell out of use and therefore survive as ruins, or were turned into secular/civic sites. Smaller sites such as wells and crosses ultimately survived because they were less obtrusive, due to their popular support, or because they were thought not to be a threat to the new faith.

An Overview of the Route

Beginning from the town of Padstow at its parish church, the route heads inland from the harbour, leaving the Camel Estuary behind and then winding its way along the creeks through Little Petherick (or St Petroc Minor), following the A389 for a short distance, into the tiny hamlet of Mellingey.

After climbing out of the Mellingey valley, a detour may be taken to St Issey from the hamlet of Trenance. Following the main route, the path climbs to the highest point in the journey: the beacon on St Breock Downs, 700ft (213m) above sea level. The path then winds down from Longstone towards Hustyn Wood, and to a ford and two footbridges that cross the Ruthern river. Uphill, the Way then takes you through the parish of Withiel, and across the fields through the valley to Lanzota. Leading next to the tiny hamlet of Retire, it descends into Tremorebridge and past Tremore Manor. Proceed next to Higher Woodley and across the fields and lanes into Lanivet – this section of the route features a number of old cross stones, and Lanivet marks the halfway point.

The route then climbs out of the village and under the A30 to Reperry Cross. A mile further is St Ingunger and a further cross. Following the markers through Fenton Pits, a cross is sited at the end of the road: from this proceed to Trebell Green, and then on until Helman Tor Gate. The route skirts the Tor here and heads towards Lanlivery where a further cross, known as Menawink, stands. Follow the signs over Pennant Crossroads into the village. Here, a detour to St Bryvyth's Well is recommended, sited along the footpath to Luxulyan.

The route then leads away from the village, following the road to Lostwithiel, climbing through fields and emerging on to the B3269. From No Man's Land it continues down towards Lostwithiel along the A390, then branches through a farmyard towards Castle – a further detour into Lostwithiel is also advised here.

From Castle, follow the signs to Milltown. This is the last section of the Way and runs roughly parallel with the River Fowey. Heading south, the lane passes Lantyan and Woodgate Woods, and then ascends to the crest of the hill before continuing down to the Church of St Sampson and into Golant. The Way follows a footpath into the village, then shortly thereafter leaves it and runs into the Downs. Here the former monastic settlement of St Cadix may be visited, before the path dips down through the woods to Sawmill's Creek. The route heads towards the former Par to Fowey branch line and then into Fowey itself. At the end of Fore Street is the junction with Bull Hill, which it ascends to the last stop of the journey: the Church of St Fimbarrus.

Start of the Route: Padstow

The parish and town of Padstow (Cornish: Lannwedhenek) is situated in the Deanery of Pydar. It is bounded on the north by the sea and the entrance to Padstow harbour, on the east by the estuary of the River Camel and Tregonce Creek, which separates it from St Minver and St Issey, on the south by Little Petherick (alias St Petroc Minor), and on the west by St Merryn. The original meaning of the name 'Padstow' was 'the holy place of St Petrock', an important Cornish saint. In the fourteenth century this became confused with St Patrick, hence the present name, 'stowe' being the English for 'holy place'.

Possibly from as early as 2,500BC, Padstow has been used as a natural harbour linking Brittany to Ireland along the 'Saints' Way' from Fowey. Legend has it that St Petroc arrived from Ireland around 520CE and built a monastery on the hill above the harbour. The harbour developed in the Middle Ages as a trading port for copper, tin and lead ores, slate, pilchards and agricultural produce.

ABBEY HOUSE

This slate stone and rubble late fifteenth-century house, possibly with earlier origins, is the oldest secular building in the town; it was extended and remodelled in the eighteenth and nineteenth centuries, and was once the guildhouse of Padstow's merchants. It owes its name to a legend about a subterranean passage linking it with the early monastery that stood on the site of Prideaux Place, the castellated mansion of the Lord of the Manor.

Situated on the North Quay, it has a three-storey porch at the front with a reset Catacleuse, stone-moulded, four-centred arch. The upper storey is timber-framed and hung with rag slates. Initially, it had a first-floor hall, probably open to the roof.

COURT HOUSE

South of the harbour, Court House is said to be where Sir Walter Raleigh, as Lord Lieutenant, held his maritime courts as Warden of Cornwall. Now two private houses and a holiday cottage, the building dates from the late sixteenth century, but was then extended in the late seventeenth and nineteenth centuries.

Abbey House, Padstow. OLIVER HOWES

Prideaux Place, Padstow. OLIVER HOWES

PRIDEAUX PLACE

Since its completion in the sixteenth century, Prideaux Place has been the seat of the Prideaux family, an ancient Cornish clan. Their origins go back almost 1,000 years to the time of the Norman Conquest, when they were recorded as Lords of the Manor at Prideaux Castle, Luxulyan. Sir Nicholas Prideaux built Prideaux Place, completing it in 1592 with later eighteenth- and nineteenth-century additions. The Elizabethan E-shaped manor house still presides over the fishing port of Padstow, with views of the Camel Estuary. The north wing remains as it was the day the 121st Engineer Combat Battalion of the American Army marched from Prideaux to take up its role in the D-Day landings.

CHURCH OF ST PETROC

The first church here was built by Petroc in the sixth century as part of a monastery founded by him. All that survives from this early period are the head of a four-holed Celtic cross on a modern shaft outside the south door, and the base of a very large cross by the south-east gate.

Next to Padstow church there is also the site of a Christian cemetery of 850 to 950CE, and this may well be the date of the cross base that stands by the south churchyard entrance. St Petroc's bones were venerated here, and the church was one of the most important in Cornwall. However, in c.981 the church and monastic community were largely destroyed by the Vikings, and Petroc's bones were transferred to Bodmin. A further church was then built in the twelfth century – the lower half of the current tower dates from this period.

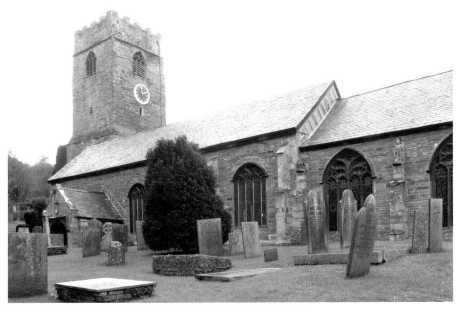

St Petroc Church, Padstow. OLIVER HOWES

The present grey Devonian siltstone church fabric dates to around the twelfth century, with the tower base and possibly the chancel being the earliest features; however, the majority is from the fifteenth century, with the Lady Chapel built as the chantry chapel of Sir John Nanfan, a knight, who died in *c*.1462.

The buttresses outside this chapel feature some of the finest stone carvings in Cornwall, including a young male figure in a short tunic carrying the arms of the Nanfan family, and on each side of this statue are a headless lion and a chained hart or unicorn, which show that Nanfan was in royal service.

Other treasures are the bench ends, which include Reynard the fox preaching to the geese, of 1530 date, and the pulpit, of the same date. All but one of the six pulpit panels are original. There are depictions of scallop shells at the top of the panels – the badge of pilgrims. Padstow was possibly the port of embarkation for Europe's most popular shrine site, that of St James at Santiago in Spain, and their offerings no doubt helped to build this church. To the right of the altar, in the wall, is a holy water stoup with a crude carving of St Petroc in a monk's habit. This is the earliest representation of him.

To the west of the tower, a wall encloses the entrance to the Prideaux family vault (of Prideaux Place), which features a reset medieval cross taken from the grounds of the manor house and erected in memory of Charles Prideaux-Brune in 1833. The church was restored *c*.1855, and again between 1888 and 1889, by S.D. Sedding.

Sea Mills, Little Petherick Creek

Sea Mills, a house on the banks of the creek, was formerly a gristmill in the late eighteenth and early nineteenth centuries. It was powered by flood tidal water, which then drove a waterwheel when the tide was on the ebb. The sea walls can still be seen, including the sluice gate, but the wheel is long gone.

Little Petherick (or St Petroc Minor)

Little Petherick was developed as a subsidiary settlement to St Issey parish by the Welsh missionary St Petroc, who arrived in the early sixth century and was active in the neighbourhood for about thirty years. The parish of Little Petherick (Cornish: Nansfenten, meaning 'the spring in the valley') is more properly known as St Petroc Minor. The name 'Little Petherick' comes from the ancient name for Little Padstow: Pedroc-stowe, which means 'Petroc's Place'. This parish was originally 'Sanctus Petrocus Minor', meaning Little St Petroc or St Petroc Minor, to distinguish it from Padstow, which was also a parish dedicated to St Petroc.

Little Petherick had several mills – there are visible remains of the mill's old sea wall which served to trap the tides, and both the Old Mill and Mellingey Mill still have working waterwheels.

Old Mill, now a hotel, is an eighteenth-century building with nineteenth-century additions. The rear has been altered, however, with the introduction of twentieth-century mock bow windows and casement-style openings.

The house adjacent to the Mill House was the home of Dr Marley. He was a close friend of Charles Dickens, who borrowed his name for the character in *A Christmas Carol* – a memorial tablet to the doctor is sited on the north wall of the Church of St Petroc.

ST PETROC MINOR

The elevated position of the Church of St Petroc Minor is typical of many in the area, and is indicative of the site's original function as a preaching point and place of religious assembly. It has fourteenth-century origins, but was largely rebuilt in 1745, and was then completely restored in 1858 by William White, when it was taken down almost to its foundations and rebuilt with its old materials, and using much material from the ruinous church at St Merryn. The chief alterations took place in the north aisle; this was originally cut out of the living rock, which was left as the north wall, and from which water had been continually dripping.

It has a squat Victorian tower with carved granite pinnacles and a pyramidal slate roof. The remainder of the church is more domestic in scale than most Cornish churches, with gabled dormer windows and leaded lights. A Royal coat of arms, 1741, is inlaid in the floor.

In 1908, the church was again restored, this time by Sir Ninian Comper, whose work can be seen in the rood screen, the reredos and the high altar. Comper was employed by a great benefactor of the church, the antiquarian Athelstan Riley, who played a major role in the Anglo-Catholic movement in the early twentieth century. He lived in the house called St Mary's, which features a carving of the Virgin and Child on its front elevation.

Nearby was a chapel at Trevibban, and another, dedicated to St Ide, near where the church now stands. Some of the carved stones from the latter chapel are reputedly scattered throughout the village, though little else is known of the sites.

Along the way, the route passes through the hamlet of Mellingey (from which Mellingey, the 'mill house', gets its name) with its impressive five-storey, eighteenth-century former mill. It then passes by the very small hamlet of Trenance, meaning 'valley farm', where you can take a detour to the village of St Issey.

St Issey

The parish takes its name from St Yse or Ida, who was born in Ireland around 480CE as one of the twenty-four children of St Brychan, a fourth-century Welsh saint and king. Its Cornish name 'Egloscruk' means 'the church on the tumulus'. Until 1199, the parish formed part of the manor and peculiar of Pawton, belonging to the Bishop of Exeter; it was then appropriated by the bishop to the Chapter of Exeter Cathedral.

The parish church is partly Norman but was enlarged in the fourteenth and fifteenth centuries when the south aisle and tower were built. It was originally dedicated to St Issey, but has also been dedicated to St Filius. The first church at St Issey was built during the seventh or eighth century, and stands within a pre-Christian burial mound. The tower has been rebuilt twice, in *c.*1680, and again in 1872 after it had been struck by lightning and collapsed. Features of interest include the reredos and a Pietà of Catacleuse stone, which may be fragments of a late medieval monument. According to local tradition, the stonework was originally in the chapel at Halwyn, an estate of the Hamelys.

THE RING O'BELLS

Situated opposite the church is the Ring O'Bells Inn, known locally as 'The Ringers'. Dating from the seventeenth century, it is one of the oldest inns in the area and still retains many of its original features.

ARCHAEOLOGICAL SITES

There are a number of archaeological sites within the parish: an Iron Age settlement, known as Trenance Rounds; nine round barrows near Cannalidgey; a menhyr/menhir, known as the Magi Stone or the Fiddler, also near Cannalidgey; three barrows on Trelow Downs; and the Nine Maidens stone row. Trelow Downs is also a Site of Special Scientific Interest for the dry and wet heaths and scrub.

No Man's Land

Passing through the crossroads hamlet of No Man's Land takes you along the Way. Most of the land that did not fit into stitches was the poorer ground, which remained common; some of it became hay meadows for the landowner, and the least valuable often went under the name of 'noman's land'. This description also included smaller areas of disputed land between parishes, and has also been attributed to unhedged land set aside by the Normans to appease their gods. In 1929, Charles Henderson instead linked the name Noman's Land with Nine Maidens and Noon Maen. His suggestion that the various stone circles, each usually having more than nine standing stones, and various heaths that had a standing stone, were originally called Noon Maen, meaning the heathland stone(s), was subsequently corrupted into Noman's Land and Nine Maidens may well be the case.

Men Gurta

The view here is punctuated by the beacon on St Breock Downs – a menhir or prehistoric longstone, which was originally about 16ft (5m) high, known as 'Men Gurta'. It is now called St Breock Longstone. Weighing about 16.5 tons, it is still the heaviest standing stone in Cornwall. There are also two round barrows on St Breock Downs.

A menhir is a large upright standing stone found singly as monoliths, or as part of a group of similar stones, and generally uneven and squared in shape, yet often tapering towards the top. They date from the late Neolithic and Bronze Age periods, roughly from 3000 to 1200BC, but their purpose remains unclear. Over the centuries, there have been many conflicting theories, but most archaeologists accept that they either marked the boundaries of territory; were meeting points; grave markers; or fulfilled a religious/ceremonial role. The one here dates from the Bronze Age.

In association, from this vantage point, the distinctive outline of Castle-an-Dinas, one of Cornwall's largest prehistoric hill forts, can be seen to the west, sited on the summit of Castle Downs. In Cornish legend it is one of the seats of the Duke of Cornwall, and folklore has it that Cador, Duke of Cornwall, and Igraine, King Arthur's mother, were killed here.

St Breock

The village and parish of St Breock (in Cornish, the saint is also referred to as Lansant or Nansant, meaning Holy Valley) is a landscape peppered with archaeological remains. Another smaller menhir, similar to Men Gurta, can be seen on St Breock Downs.

Near Pawton is a burial chamber of the Penwith Chamber Tomb type dated *c*.3200–2500BC, and is often known as Pawton Quoit or the Giant's Quoit. Many round barrows are also sited in St Breock parish itself: several tumuli near Pawtongate on St Breock Downs, three round barrows near Pawtonsprings, and three barrows northeast of St

Breock Beacon. At Nanscow, west of St Breock, there is an inscribed stone dating from the fifth or sixth century. It reads 'Ulcagni Fili Severi' or 'the body or monument of Ulcagnus son of Severus'.

At Whitecross, north of Nanscow, is a medieval granite white-washed cross which gives the hamlet its name, standing on the grass verge of the A39. There was also formerly a chapel dedicated to St Katherine at Hustyn in 1379, although no remains appear to survive.

The path then leads down from High Tregustick into the Tregawne Valley and along the ancient rocky track to Tregustick, a mid-nineteenth-century, slate-stone rubble farmhouse.

Withiel

The next main place the Way enters is the village of Withiel. The name 'Withiel' has links with a fourth-century Irish saint, St Uvel, and is derived from a word meaning 'a place of trees'. At the time of Domesday Book, and probably long before that, the church and manor of Withiel belonged to the monastery of Bodmin, from which they were alienated in 1538.

ST CLEMENT'S CHURCH

The historic granite buildings of the village include the medieval Parish Church of St Clement. Withiel church was located elsewhere at the time of Domesday, but was

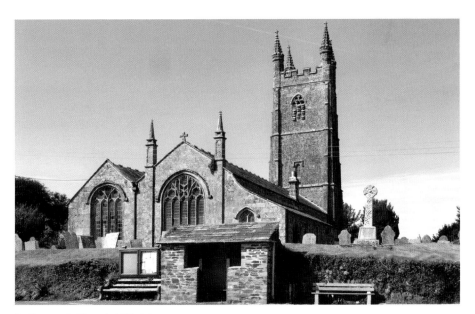

St Clement's Church, Withiel. OLIVER HOWES

built in the thirteenth century. At first, it seems to have comprised simply a nave and chancel, and in the fifteenth and sixteenth centuries was rebuilt in granite. A fine south aisle and tower were added, then a curious lean-to north aisle chapel. It is dedicated to St Clement, third Pope of Rome.

To the right of the door as you enter the church is a list of rectors dating from 1297. The most notable of these is Prior Thomas Vyvyan, who became rector of the then-derelict church in 1523 and began to rebuild it. The main building remains largely from this period.

The octagonal font of quartz-porphyry is *c*.1520. On its pillar are carvings that depict St Clement, martyred on an anchor in the Black Sea. The panelling in the baptistery is painted with texts that refer to baptism, dating from about 1660, while the neo-Gothic pinnacles were added to the church in about 1819 when it underwent a major makeover after years of neglect. Finally, there is an angel holy water stoup in the porch.

THE OLD RECTORY

Opposite the church stands the Old Rectory, built *c*.1520 by Prior Vyvyan. The rectory was replaced in the Victorian era by Withiel House, when it was extended, remodelled and re-fronted in the neo-Gothic style in *c*.1815, but also features twentieth-century alterations. It was known at Domesday as 'Berneves', and belonged for several centuries to Bodmin Priory.

Originally a two-room plan, with a larger room to the left and a smaller room to the right, each was heated from a gable-end stack. In *c*.1815, a one-room plan was added to the left end, heated from a fireplace backing on to the original gable-end fireplace. The house sits within a seventeenth-century estate that is the site of a Celtic wheel-headed cross, on a modern base, probably moved and re-erected in *c*.1860 from outside the rectory entrance gate.

The manor here is now denominated Withielgoose. The name 'Withielgoose' derives from the Cornish 'gwyth' (trees), 'yel' (origin unknown), and 'coes' (wood), suggesting the clearance of woodland to create agricultural land. Withielgoose belonged to Bodmin Priory, and previously to William I via the Earl of Cornwall. It was leased by the crown in 1539 to Richard Kendall, and in 1588, granted in fee-farm to Richard Branthwayte and Roger Bromley. It was then occupied by the Coswarth family, followed by the Vyvyan family, who still owned it in the early 1800s, as noted above. A mill also stood here, its millstone now incorporated into the wall of nearby houses.

Leaving Withiel, the route passes a place in the valley known as Lanzota, interesting because the name may have marked the site of a Celtic settlement called Zota, as 'Lan' means 'church site', and 'Zota' is a saint's name.

The route now descends and crosses Tremore Bridge, an eighteenth-century granite clapper bridge over the River Ruthen. The bridge carries the medieval road from

Tremore Cross. OLIVER HOWES

Lanivet Cross. OLIVER HOWES

Bodmin – the major ecclesiastical centre – to Padstow, and also the market town of St Columb.

The Way then continues past Tremore Manor, a former farmhouse built *c*.1815, with a gatehouse/lodge dating from *c*.1840, perched right on the road side.

Not too far along the Way, at Tremore crossroads, is a decorated, well-preserved twelfth-century round-headed cross set in a hedge. It probably once stood on the wastrel at the crossroads.

Lanivet

This next section of the route features a number of old cross stones. Lanivet marks the halfway point of the Way.

The name 'Lanivet' means the 'church site (lann) at neved'. As 'neved' means 'a pagan sacred place', it must have been a pre-existing name. Situated in the geographical centre of Cornwall, Lanivet previously had eleven copper mines, now all closed.

ST NIVET CHURCH

The church at Lanivet is dedicated to St Nivet, and originally dates from the early fifteenth century. The bells in the tower are particularly interesting, largely dating from the sixteenth century onwards; now a full octave set to the key of F. There is also an inscribed pillar stone in the south aisle with Roman capitals, likely fifth or sixth century.

In the churchyard are two ancient stone crosses, and a rare example of a Viking tenth-century hogback tombstone. In the nineteenth century there were four more stone crosses in the parish. The wheel-headed cross is the most elaborately carved in Cornwall, with its figure of a man with a 'tail' being most unusual.

ST BENET'S ABBEY

A short detour of roughly ten minutes' walk, or about a quarter of a mile south from the church, brings you to another interesting building that contains the remains of St Benet's Abbey, a monastery of the Benedictine order, built in 1411. It is said to have been subordinate to Monte Cassino, Italy, or Clairvaux in Burgundy, and is now a guesthouse. Initially founded as a lazar house (leper colony) in 1411, during the later fifteenth century, a chapel with a tower and an adjacent longhouse were built. There is also an emblem of St John of Jerusalem on the corner of the building, which is perhaps no surprise as the English house of this Military Order, the Hospitallers, was founded in 1144 to care for pilgrims – St Benet's was a hospital for the poor, and no doubt administered to pilgrims travelling the Saints' Way.

After the Reformation it became the seat of the Courtenay family, then a hospice for troops returning from the Crimean War. Further alterations in the nineteenth century gives the present house a Victorian look, though adorned with fifteenth-century windows. At a later date, stone from the cloisters and the top of the tower was taken to build a farmhouse.

In the front gardens is a small wheel-headed cross mounted on to a modern shaft, which may have been a gable cross from the roof of the chapel – the shaft looks like part of a crocketed gable.

Amongst other functions, the chapel lands have been used to produce bamboo, supplying the pandas of London Zoo.

Reperry Cross

The route then climbs out of Lanivet and past the wayside Reperry Cross, situated at the top of the hedge bordering the old turnpike road from Bodmin to St Austell. Dating from the pre-Conquest era, the upright granite cross was restored in the nineteenth century by Sir Robert Edgcumbe, Bt. About 3ft (1m) high, it is a wheel-head, re-set on a nineteenth-century shaft and a raised Latin cross carved on each face. It is now in its original location, having been lost under a hedge

Close by is also the granite guide stone, which points the way to Lanivet. This is where Thomas Hardy reminisces in his poem 'Near Lanivet, 1872'.

St Ingunger and a Further Cross

A mile further along the road is another wayside cross at St Ingunger – this was the site of an important Christian centre where a chapel and holy well (300m from the cross) once stood, dedicated to a St Ingunger resident: the hermit, St Congar of Congresbury, in the early sixth century. Churches dedicated to him may also be found in Brittany and Cornwall.

The St Ingunger cross is an upright granite cross set in a large groundfast granite boulder. It has a wheel-head decorated on both principal faces by a low-relief cross but has been cemented to its shaft. It is situated on the northern side of a road junction on a major ancient route across central Cornwall linking the Camel and Fowey estuaries.

Use of this route is considered to extend back into the prehistoric period, as it is marked by several other surviving medieval wayside crosses. Thus, the position of the St Ingunger Cross on the Saints' Way demonstrates the continuity of such major routeways, and the relationship between wayside crosses and early thoroughfares, as it

Reperry Cross. OLIVER HOWES

is also sited on a route to the Lanivet parish church.

Fenton Pits Cross

Fenton Pits Cross has survived well. Though formally relocated, it still sits on its original route. A good example of a wheel-headed cross, complete with head, shaft and base. In 1896, historian Langdon recorded its base and lower shaft in a nearby hedge. The cross was reassembled and erected in its present position in 1926 by workmen from the neighbouring Lanhydrock estate.

Helman Tor

Moving on past the historic hamlet of Trebell Green takes you next to Helman Tor Gate, where the two southern arms of the Saints' Way divide. The route skirts the tor itself, but it is worth a detour to the top to

Fenton Pits Cross. OLIVER HOWES

see the granite ridge where there is a logan, or rocking stone. There is also a prehistoric hill fort and a stone hut circle settlement, dating from the Neolithic period, and further flat platforms alleged to be dwellings

The landscape shows evidence of past tin streaming.

Lanlivery

The Way then follows towards Lanlivery, and, where it joins the road, there is a further cross, known as Menawink. The medieval wheel-headed cross was discovered in a field in 1990 being used as a gate post. It was rededicated in 1991 by the Vicar of Lanlivery and sited in its present location.

CHURCH OF ST BREVITA

In the village itself is the Parish Church of St Brevita, which has a tower of 100ft (30m); one of the finest landmarks in Cornwall, it is considered the third highest church tower in the county – it reputedly acted as a landmark for ships entering Fowey harbour. The present building largely dates from the fifteenth century, while a Norman capital in the chancel was said to have come from Bodmin Priory. It is unclear when the first holy building was sited here. The remains of a Norman tower were found in the 1990s. Also, the near circular enclosure of the ancient churchyard (as indicated by the prefix 'lan' in Lanlivery) suggests that it was an important site even in the pre-Christian era.

Although today the church's patron saint is Brevita or Bryvyth, there is little known about the female saint in earlier histories, but her cult appears unique to the parish. It has been suggested that the parish was named after the almost unknown St Vorck, hence the derivation of Lanlivery as Lan-le-Vorck, meaning St Vorck's holy place, but this is a mistake.

THE CROWN INN

The Crown Inn pub dates from *c*.1130, but the present longhouse building is largely from the early seventeenth century. It acted as the last stop for drovers taking their stock to boats sailing from Fowey (and for pilgrims along the Way). This way, animals would not lose condition, and the hazardous sea passage round Land's End was avoided. Instead, drovers could find board and lodging for both themselves and their animals at the inn.

ST BRYVYTH'S WELL

Here, a detour to St Bryvyth's Well is highly recommended. Sited along the footpath to Luxulyan, the stone-clad holy well is hidden in a tiny wood and well worth a visit – although it is not too easy to find. This little-known site was mentioned in the will of the vicar in 1539. In 1841, it was referred to as Briber's Well.

St Bryvyth's (Brevita) Well. OLIVER HOWES

Crewel Cross

Next is the village of No Man's Land with its historical cottages and the medieval Crewel Cross. The granite cross is well preserved and is a good example of a wheel-head cross – one of the largest wayside crosses in Cornwall. The changing form between the lower and upper shafts is unusual, as is its interlace decoration. It has been moved a short distance from its original location at the junction of two ancient routeways.

From here, a further detour into Lostwithiel is advised.

Lostwithiel

The name Lostwithiel is believed to come from the Old Cornish 'Lostgwydeyel' meaning 'the place at the tail of the forest'. Once the capital of Cornwall and the first stannary town where tin ingots were brought to be assayed, Lostwithiel was actually founded by the Norman lords who built nearby Restormel Castle. The town was developed to become a major port for seagoing ships, exporting tin to Europe and the eastern Mediterranean. The castle was rebuilt in the late thirteenth century by Edmund, Earl of Cornwall, who was also responsible for building the town's Great Hall (where affairs both Cornish and stannary were administered), the bridge and the square tower of St Bartholomew's Church with its Catherine Wheel on the side facing the bridge.

St Bartholomew's Church, Lostwithiel. OLIVER HOWES

The Great Hall later became known as the Duchy Palace, and is worth a trip to see. It was constructed in 1272 by Edmund, Earl of Cornwall. In 1337 the Black Prince became the first Duke of Cornwall and made the palace his administrative centre. It then it became a Freemasons' temple in 1878, and remained as such until 2008.

ST BARTHOLOMEW'S CHURCH

The present church at Lostwithiel was mainly built *c*.1300, though first mentioned a century earlier. Before its construction, Lostwithiel's inhabitants had to climb the steep hill to Lanlivery, or journey downriver to St Winnow to worship. St Bartholomew, patron saint of tanners, was chosen as the dedication for this town church, which was built in the Early English style, at the top of a medieval triangular market place. The Duchy Palace and river crossing were sited at the lower end. While most Cornish churches were enlarged in the late medieval and Tudor period when the tin industry started to generate wealth (as the town itself did), oddly not Lostwithiel. A new churchyard lantern cross was commissioned for the churchyard, however.

In the north-east corner there is a late medieval alabaster of the martyrdom of St Bartholomew; even while being flayed he is wearing his bishop's hat and raising a hand in blessing for the skinner. Carved on the earlier fourteenth-century font is a green bishop (with leaves sprouting from his mouth), and a knight out hunting wearing

Restormel Castle (the interior ruins). DAVID ROSS

fashionable prick spurs. Sepulchral recesses, originally for the tombs of the Cardinhams (original Lords of the Borough) can be seen on the outside of the church.

RESTORMEL CASTLE

The great thirteenth-century, circular shell-keep of Restormel encloses the principal rooms of the castle and stands on an earlier Norman mound surrounded by a deep dry ditch beside the River Fowey. Twice visited by the Black Prince, the castle finally saw action during the Civil War in 1644. It is notable for its perfectly circular design, and is well worth a detour to visit.

The route then heads toward the village of Castle.

Milltown

From Castle, follow the signs to the tiny hamlet of Milltown with its two former flourmills and the pub located inside 'Merlin' cottage.

St Winnow Church, near Lantyan. OLIVER HOWES

Lantyan

The next place of interest is the historic Lantyan Farm. The farm is the presumed site of King Mark's (uncle of Tristan and husband of Iseult) palace, with some of the fabric possibly dating from the thirteenth century – the Anglo-Norman poet Béroul set the story at 'Lancien'.

ST WINNOW CHURCH

Along the Way's descent are glimpses of the creekside Church of St Winnow. The church is at the riverside, next to a quay at the limit of navigation of the River Fowey. Its name may be connected with that of either Winnoc or Winwaloe, and is probably sited upon the original seventh-century oratory of St Winnoc.

The church is of twelfth-century foundation, but the present building is almost entirely fifteenth century. Traces of the original stonework are evident on the north side. The chancel was restored by J. H. Seddon in the nineteenth century, retaining the sixteenth-century east window, while the west tower is of standard Cornish Perpendicular style. The sixteenth-century rood screen survives, carved with leaves and flowers (restored by Violet Pinwell in 1907), and there is some interesting stained glass. The granite font, carved with angels bearing shields, is fourteenth century; the pulpit is of *c*.1600 and richly carved; there are also carved bench ends of various dates from 1485 to 1630 including a sixteenth and seventeenth-century Cornishman in a 'kilt' and an elaborate ship. A burial plot with Celtic-style headstones for the Vivian family occupies the north-west corner of the churchyard.

CHAPEL OF ST NECTAN

The Chapel of St Nectan (also called St Nighton's) nearby is also worth a visit. Originally a chapel-of-ease dating from 1281, most of the current building is actually from the fifteenth century; the north aisle was then added in 1825. The tower lost its upper stages in the Civil War. The medieval parish was larger and also included Boconnoc and St Bradoc: the chapels of St Nectan and St Martin's at Respryn were quasi-parochial.

Castle Dore

A short detour takes you to Castle Dore, another alleged site associated with King Mark (his chief residence in Cornwall), although now this seems to have been proved incorrect. The defended hillfort is of Iron Age date, described by William of Worcester (1415–82) as 'a dilapidated castle by the name of Dirford, near Golant'; the sixteenth-century antiquarian, John Leland, identified it as 'Castledour'.

Penquite

The Way then climbs up through the fields, and halfway along is Penquite House, a nineteenth-century Italianate mansion. Built between 1848 and 1850, the property has seen a number of interesting and historical occupants. The home of John Whitehead Peard (1811–80), colonel in the Royal Army of Savoy and known as 'Garibaldi's Englishman'; when the Italian revolutionary Garibaldi made his triumphant visit to England in 1864, he stayed with Peard at Penquite. It has also been suggested that Edward VIII enjoyed parties here. In 1948 the land was sold off, and in 1969 the YHA bought Penquite House and opened it as a youth hostel in 1970.

From here, Golant is the next village on our route.

Golant

Golant is a small coastal village where some of the famous Troy boats are built. It has two historical connections that make it unique: that of the life (and church) of St Sampson, and the tragic tale of Tristan and Iseult.

Tristan was a nephew of King Mark of Cornwall, who was based at Castle Dore, and Iseult was an Irish princess betrothed to King Mark. Due to the hazards of travel in the sixth century, Tristan was sent by his uncle to accompany Iseult. On the journey

St Sampson's Church, Golant. OLIVER HOWES

back from Ireland to Castle Dore she and Tristan fell for one another and, inevitably, were discovered in compromising circumstances. Tristan fled to France where he married the daughter of a local chief, another Iseult – but he could not forget his first love. While out hunting, he was wounded and became seriously ill, so sent a ship to Cornwall with a message for Iseult to come to France to nurse him. He instructed his sailors to hoist black sails if their journey had been in vain, and white if she was aboard. His wife, discovering the plan, reported to Tristan that the sails were black, whereas they had been white.

Tristan died, followed soon after by Iseult. She was buried beside her lover. Out of the graves grew two saplings, the branches of which became intertwined, and it is said that 'in death they were united, although parted in life'.

St Sampson's *Life* (hagiography – his story) states that he travelled to Cornwall and established himself where the church now stands, having erected a shelter near the holy well which can be seen by the south porch and door.

The current granite-rubble well structure is late fifteenth century. It is a small, single cell building, about 1m high, with a sink in the bottom. An opening in the west side of the church porch gives covered access to the well.

St Sampson's Well, Golant. OLIVER HOWES

The link between the Church of St Sampson and King Mark and Iseult is that he and his wife made their devotions in state here, and that Iseult gave her best dress to the church. The current building was annexed to the priory at Tywardreath, recorded from 1281; it was extensively rebuilt between about 1450 and 1500, and was consecrated as a separate church in 1509; there was then a further restoration in 1842. The church is of a traditional Celtic design, with parts dating from 1200, and features interesting stained glass and much wood carving such as the bench ends – decorated with apostles, coats of arms and one large carving of St Sampson – the pulpit and the roof timbers, which were provided by the local guilds and carry inscriptions also dating from 1509. The Royal Arms displayed are of James II, and the Lord's Prayer in Cornish, *Pader Agan/ Arloedh*, is on the north wall.

The route then continues across the Downs, but on the opposite side is Penpol Hill, leading to the former monastic settlement of St Cadix, which is definitely a site to visit.

St Cadix

A small cell or priory was built by the side of Penpol Creek. Today it is referred to as St Cadix's Priory, but it has also appeared as St Ciric, St Carroc, St Cadokys, St Carrett and St Karroc. There is some uncertainty as to which saint the Benedictine priory was dedicated to: either the sixth-century Celtic St Cadoc, or Cyricus, son of Saint Julietta, to whom the parish church is dedicated. In 1100, the priory was granted to the Benedictine Cluniac Montacute Priory in Somerset by William, Count of Mortain. Before that a small cell or holy well had existed. It remained the priory's until the Dissolution of the Monasteries in 1536. Just one monk and prior lived there for the majority of its existence.

Little of the priory survives, and a farmhouse was built on the site in 1710, but there are some remains of dressed stone, tracery, column bases and mullions in the garden that date from 1150 onwards.

Sawmills Creek

From here, the path dips down through a wood to Sawmills Creek and what is now known as the Old Sawmills. The location is unique in that it can only be accessed by boat or via the railway line that runs directly past the studio. The area is mentioned in Domesday Book, and evidence of medieval activity can still be observed, such as the remains of a quay clearly visible at the head of the creek. The creek is still referred to as Bodmin Pill – 'pill' is an old West Country term meaning a creek or landing place.

From 1729, the site was owned by the Fortescue family of Boconnoc House as part of a large estate. The sawmill was formerly a thriving business – barges regularly came into the creek to fetch loads of freshly sawn timber. The building of a railway across the entrance to the sawmill occurred around 1860. As compensation, the railway company provided a replacement quay on the main river, from which the sawmills could carry on shipping their timber.

Opened in early 1974 as one of the very first residential recording studios in the UK, Sawmills Studio is a unique recording environment, with a long list of successful clients to its name, including Robert Plant, Stone Roses, Oasis, Muse and Jessie J.

Crossing the former Par to Fowey branch line, now a private road for transporting china clay, the route heads into the town of Fowey.

The End of the Journey: Fowey

The name 'Fowey' comes from the river which flowed here, and the two watermills, which were recorded as early as 1272. This medieval port town ran from a north gate near Boddinnick Passage to a south gate at what is now Lostwithiel Street; the town extended a little way up the hillside, and was bounded on the other side by the river,

Ferryside, Fowey. OLIVER HOWES

where merchants' houses backed onto the waterfront. The harbour allowed trade to develop with Europe, and local ship owners often hired their vessels to the king to support various wars, although the town also developed a reputation for piracy and smugglers.

In the fourteenth century, the harbour was defended by 160 archers; after these were withdrawn, two blockhouses (or small forts) were built, one on each side of the harbour entrance. Despite these defences, the town was attacked by French forces in 1457; Place House, by the church, was successfully defended against the French, but was subsequently strengthened. This building still exists, though much remodelled. A small castle was built on St Catherine's Point, the western side of the harbour entrance, around 1540.

Fishing became more important as the fortunes of the harbour declined as trade moved to Plymouth and elsewhere. A beacon tower was erected on the Gribbin Head by Trinity House to improve navigation into Fowey and around Par Bay.

Caffa Mill was also known for ship building and maintenance: Nickels, Brokenshaw and Heller had shipyards here, but trade declined as the area gradually became silted up. The site is now the main place for the car ferry crossing. Fowey station was sited here before the railway was closed to passenger traffic. In 1972, the whole area was infilled and redeveloped to provide car parking.

The Old Post Office, Fowey. OLIVER HOWES

FERRYSIDE

The ferry today, recorded in operation since 1344, crosses the River Fowey to Bodinnick. This area is very much Daphne du Maurier country: opposite the Old Ferry Inn at Bodinnick is du Maurier's family home, where she lived from 1926 until 1943, and where she wrote *Jamaica Inn*, *Rebecca* and *Frenchman's Creek*; it is also where Arthur Quiller-Couch spent much of his time, tending the gardens along Hall Walk. Ferryside, perched on the Fowey estuary, was locally known as Swiss Cottage, and the property was once a shipyard where many famous sailing ships were built. Daphne du Maurier first saw the house when she was nineteen, when in Cornwall on holiday. The du Maurier family still live there.

THE OLD POST OFFICE

Other buildings of interest in Fowey include The Old Post Office, with its fine stuccoed ornamental porch hood topped by the symbol of the pilgrim: the scallop shell. The building stands on the site of a medieval resthouse for pilgrims en route to Santiago; hundreds sailed across from Fowey in the fourteenth and fifteenth centuries. This former private residence dates from the early eighteenth century; it was subsequently adapted to a Post Office in the 1930s, although it no longer serves this purpose.

THE CHURCH OF ST FIMBARRUS

Finally, the last leg of the route climbs Bull Hill, leading to the culmination of the Saints' Way: the Church of St Fimbarrus, or St Nicholas. The dedication of this ancient church has caused some confusion as the church was originally dedicated to St Barry. By the late thirteenth century, documents referred to the saint as Fimbarrus in Latin (yet local people appeared to prefer the initial name). The form of the two names led to many people confusing him with the Irish saint, Finbarr, the first Bishop of Cork. Although there are other 'Barry' saints, which make determining his authenticity difficult (including the Welsh version), St Barry was reputed to be buried at Fowey and may have been unique to the location. A man with this name appears in a stained-glass window at St Neot Church as Neot's servant, and a connection is likely as St Barry of Fowey and St Neot shared the same feast day.

The original Celtic church was replaced by a Norman structure that was itself entirely rebuilt and rededicated in 1336 to St Nicholas, the patron saint of sailors; however, the new name failed to replace that of St Finbarr. At this stage the church was served by Benedictine monks from Tywardreath Priory (a few miles away), but a resident vicar was appointed in 1260. Only the font has survived from the early church – it features a round bowl and striking palmette leaf design, typical of eleventh-century fonts in south Cornwall and Devon.

The present building of slate-stone rubble with freestone and granite dressings was constructed shortly before 1336. It features simple octagonal columns, lean-to north and south aisles, and a clerestory. In a reprisal for raids on the French coast by Fowey sailors, the town was attacked in 1456 and the church was partially destroyed; it was restored in c.1460 with the help of the Earl of Warwick, Lord High Admiral of England, and lasted until the next century – the tower and roof carvings date from this period. Warwick's badge (the ragged staff) can be seen on the second string-course of the tower. In 1876, further restoration took place.

Features of interest include the fifteenth-century waggon roof over the nave with carved principal trusses, including angels with long Tudor hairstyles – this may suggest that a re-roofing of the church occurred a century after its first installation. There is also a fifteenth-century rood stair with its original doorways on the north side of the original rood position. The Treffry Chapel dates from c.1500. Finally, other notable features are a twelfth- or early thirteenth-century round Catecleuse stone font with star and anthemion decoration, a fine carved oak pulpit of 1601, and a painted letter above the south doorway from Charles I written and sent from his camp at Sudeley Castle in 1643.

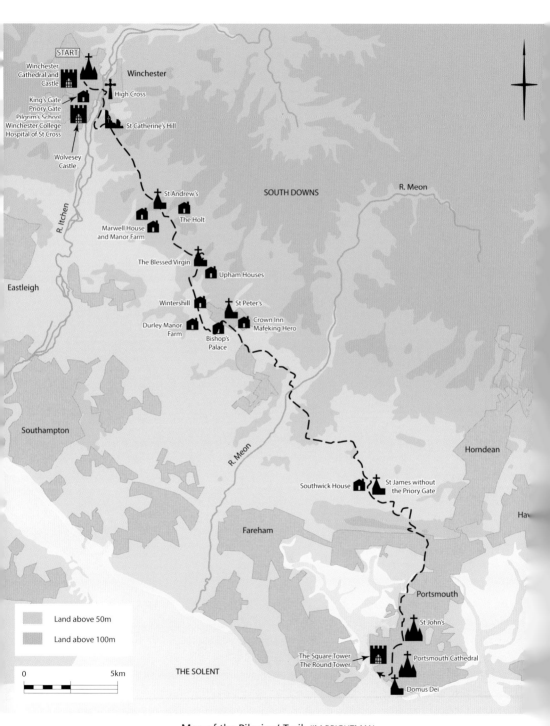

Map of the Pilgrims' Trail. JIM BRIGHTMAN

CHAPTER SEVEN

The Pilgrims' Trail
(Hampshire to Normandy)

K nown also as the Hampshire Millennium Pilgrims' Trail, this route forms part of
a longer trail, St Michael's Way, between Winchester and the island Mont-Saint-
Michel in Normandy, France. The Pilgrims' Trail – 28 miles (45km) in England but
155 miles (250km) in total – was opened in 1999 by Hampshire County Council as a
nod to the medieval route from the shrine of St Swithun at Winchester Cathedral, by
way of Bishop's Waltham and Southwick, and on to Portsmouth. Pilgrims would then
cross the Channel and make the long journey to worship at the medieval sanctuary of
St Michael in Normandy. Today, travellers have the advantage of special waymark
signs for the route – green in Hampshire and blue in France.

The History of St Michael and the Trail

Located in the bay where Normandy and Brittany merge, the granite island of Mont-
Saint-Michel is sacred due to its associations with the Archangel Michael, and because
a community of Benedictine monks settled there. For over 1,000 years, Mont-Saint-
Michel was one of the most popular pilgrim destinations in Europe, attracting pilgrims
from as far afield as Scandinavia, Italy and Germany, as well as from England. Most
pilgrims used it as a station on the way to Santiago de Compostela in northern Spain;
landing at Barfleur, near Cherbourg (France), they would walk to the Mont and then,
after visiting the holy monastic site, continue on to Santiago.

But one might ask why St Michael was celebrated in Britain, and why pilgrims
journeyed such a distance to seek his intercessory power. The cult of St Michael,
the protector of Christians and the Church, was actually widespread throughout the
British Isles from the ninth century, and by the Reformation in the sixteenth century,
there were more than 600 churches in England dedicated to the saint – his reputation
therefore crossed oceans. He was most often depicted brandishing a sword and clad
in protective armour, which symbolized his purpose: to be present at the Judgement,
as the weigher of souls to sort the condemned and the saved and, most importantly,
to lead the saved souls up to heaven and protect them from satanic intervention. It
was therefore very common that his shrines were built in the highest, most strategic
positions – and so it is no coincidence that at both Normandy and Cornwall his cult

sites crown the summit of conical islands just off the coast.

Le Mont-Saint-Michel was, in the sixth and seventh centuries, a stronghold of Romano-British culture and power until it was sacked by the Franks, thus ending the trans-channel culture that had stood since the departure of the Romans in 45CE.

Before the construction of the first monastic establishment in the eighth century, the island was called Mont Tombe.

In 709CE Aubert, bishop of the nearby hill-top town of Avranches, claimed that he had experienced a vision wherein Archangel Michael pressured him into building an oratory atop the island in his honour. Soon after the church was built, an extraordinarily high tide reconfigured the coastline, leaving Mont Tombe over a mile (2km) from land. These unprecedented events increased the sanctity of the site, as did the presence of St Michael's relics (a piece of red cloth that he had touched, and a marble slab on which he had sat) which had been brought from Mount Gargano, the focus of his cult in Italy. Miracle stories then began circulating, attracting pilgrims to the island from all over Europe.

In 966CE, the dukes of Normandy, followed by the French kings, commissioned a Benedictine abbey on Mont-Saint-Michel. This was then replaced by a grander abbey in 1023 and, by 1058, most of the Romanesque structures had been completed — they still stand to this day. An Italian architect, William de Volpiano, designed the Romanesque church of the abbey in the eleventh century, daringly placing the transept crossing at the top of the mount. Many underground crypts and chapels had to be built to compensate for this weight. Robert de Thorigny, a great supporter of Henry II of England (who was also Duke of Normandy), reinforced the structure of the buildings and constructed the main façade of the church in the twelfth century.

The abbey became a renowned centre of learning, attracting some of the greatest minds and manuscript illuminators in Europe. Vast numbers of pilgrims also visited, despite warring cross-Channel royals. As such, following his annexation of Normandy in 1204, the King of France, Philip Augustus, offered Abbot Jourdain a grant for the construction of a new Gothic monastery, which included a refectory and cloister. Due to its daring architecture, this monastery was termed 'La Merveille' (or 'The Marvel'). It was this church that attracted the majority of the medieval pilgrims, and so important were these visitors, they were called 'miquelots'.

The wealth and influence of the abbey extended to many daughter foundations. In 1067, the monastery gave its support to Duke William of Normandy in his claim to the English throne. The abbey was rewarded with properties and grounds on the English side of the Channel, including a small island located at the west of Cornwall which, modelled after the Mont, became the Norman priory on St Michael's Mount.

Mont-Saint-Michel's popularity and prestige as a centre of international pilgrimage waned with the Reformation. By the time of the French Revolution there were scarcely any monks in residence, so the abbey was closed and converted into a reformatory, initially to hold clerical opponents of the republican regime. Though the prison closed in 1863, the island was declared a historic monument in 1874, then was added to the list of World Heritage Sites in 1979, according to criteria such as being of cultural, historical and architectural significance, as well as natural beauty.

An Overview of the Route

The route begins at Winchester Cathedral's west door, continues to the south of the cathedral, and passes through the passage into the cloister and then through the Priory Gate into St Swithun's Street. It then goes to Winchester College, passing the ruins of Wolvesey Castle, follows the road, continuing over the River Itchen and along the Itchen Navigation until it meets the road. Crossing over here, taking the path through the car park, it follows the path to 'Plague Pit', then up the valley to the M3 crossing.

It then continues over the footbridge, crossing the M3 and leaving St Catherine's Hill behind you. Once across, it follows the well-defined track over Twyford Down and down to Hazeley Road, passing Hazeley Down's gallops and a war memorial to the troops stationed on Hazeley Down during World War I.

Crossing over Hatchers Lane to Whites Hill, and after twenty or so yards (20m), it takes the footpath on the left to Owslebury. The trail continues through the churchyard, then crosses open fields before going downhill to cross Lower Baybridge Lane. Walk across this lane to the lane opposite, following the gravel track to the edge of Austin's Copse. Within the coppice, the Roman road survives as an earthwork.

Follow the trail through woodland until you reach Upham, then continue until Church Street; pass the church and carry on, following the trail to the road and down to Winchester Road. Cross over to the footpath, following the line of the ancient Roman road.

The trail continues along the line of the old earth road to Wintershill Farm, crossing several stiles until Winters Hill road. Passing Tangier Farm, the trail follows the field's edge and under electricity lines towards Brooklands Farm, past the dismantled railway line, and then on to the ruins of the Bishop's Palace at Bishop's Waltham. From here, head to Bishop's Wood, North Boarhunt, then Goathouse Copse and on towards Mitchelland.

Southwick is next on the agenda, passing through the High Street and the church. At the intersection with the major road, turn sharp left to the path towards the woods, then climb the hill on the road, passing the entrance to Pigeon House Farm. Continue along the road, and descend the hill on Southwick Hill Road, London Road, then continue straight ahead on Northern Road and head beside the M27. Follow the route on until the underpass; cross the motorway slip road and bear left towards Portsmouth ferry terminal.

The trail can be continued to Mont-Saint-Michel by taking the ferry from Portsmouth to Cherbourg, and following the waymarked route southwards through the Normandy countryside (see Appendix for details).

Start of the Route: Winchester

The Pilgrims' Trail starts at the cathedral in the City of Winchester. A detailed description of the cathedral can be found in Chapter Five, as it also forms the starting point for the Pilgrims' Way to Canterbury; it will therefore not be repeated here. However, a brief overview of the rest of the city will be provided, and the significant and historic buildings that dominate its skyline.

The city lies at the western end of the South Downs with the scenic River Itchen running through it. Once England's ancient capital, and the former seat of King Alfred the Great, the first permanent residents of Winchester appear to have arrived in the Iron Age, around 150BC, establishing a hill fort and a trading settlement on the western edge of the modern city.

The Romans built their own 'new town' at Winchester, known as Venta Belgarum, or 'market place of the Belgae'. This new town developed over the centuries of occupation to become the region's capital.

From 597CE, the new Christian faith began to spread through southern England, and in the middle of the seventh century the first Christian church, the Old Minster, was built within the Roman walls here. A few years later, in 676, the Bishop of Wessex moved his seat to Winchester, and the Old Minster became a cathedral.

Although born at Wantage in Berkshire, Winchester is most associated with Alfred 'The Great'. Alfred (Aelfred) became ruler of the West Saxons after he and his brother defeated the Danish Vikings at the Battle of Ashdown. In 871, Alfred was crowned King of Wessex and established Winchester as his capital. Saxon Winchester was therefore rebuilt with its streets laid out in a grid pattern; people were encouraged to settle there, and soon the town was flourishing again.

Shortly after 1066, William the Conqueror ordered the rebuilding of the Saxon royal palace and the construction of a new castle to the west of the town. The Normans were also responsible for demolishing the Old Minster cathedral and starting the construction of the present church on the same site in 1079.

The early Middle Ages saw Winchester's importance as a significant cultural centre continuously reaffirmed (and again in the nineteenth century – *see* below), as witnessed by the number of royal births, deaths and marriages that took place in the town. But during the twelfth and thirteenth centuries, Winchester's fortunes began, once again, to decline as power and prestige gradually shifted to the new capital, London, which included the relocation of the royal mint.

The novelist Jane Austen died in Winchester in 1817 and is buried in the cathedral. While staying in Winchester from mid-August to October 1819, the Romantic poet John Keats wrote *Isabella*, *St Agnes' Eve*, *To Autumn*, *Lamia* and parts of *Hyperion*, as well as the five-act poetic tragedy, *Otho the Great*.

The High Cross

The High Cross, also known as the City or Butter Cross, dates to the fifteenth century. It is a tall, pinnacled cross on a stepped plinth with five octagonal steps. The Grade II Listed monument was used to sell produce, hence the name 'Butter Cross'. Twelve figures adorn the monument: each face features a large figure surmounted by two smaller ones in niches. The eight figures at the highest level represent the Blessed Virgin, and the saints Bartholomew, John, Lawrence, Maurice, Peter, Swithun and Thomas. Other figures depicted are William of Wykeham, Lawrence de Anne (an early Mayor of Winchester) and Alfred the Great. The oldest statue (facing the nearby building) is of St John the Evangelist; however, evidence also indicates that this figure may be St Amphibalus, one of the first English martyrs. (Winchester Cathedral was under his patronage before it was dedicated to St Swithun, so there is possibly a connection to support this hypothesis.)

In 1770, Thomas Dummer purchased the Butter Cross from the Corporation of Winchester, intending to have it re-erected at Cranbury Park, near Otterbourne. When his workmen arrived to dismantle it, they were prevented from doing so by a small riot inflicted by the people of the city; the workmen were forced to abandon their task. The Butter Cross was then restored by George Gilbert Scott in 1865, and still stands in the High Street.

Winchester Cathedral

Originally built in the eleventh century, Winchester is the second longest cathedral in Europe. It contains the shrine of St Swithun and is the beginning of the Pilgrims' Way, making it a centre of importance for pilgrims for the past millennium. However, the current building has its roots in the seventh century, when England's pagan monarchy first became Christian.

In 635CE, Cenwalh, son of Cynegils (King of West Saxons) built the first Christian church in Winchester. This small, cruciform church became known as Old Minster – its outline can still be traced in red brick, just north of the nave of the present building.

Old Minster then became a cathedral, housing the throne (*cathedra*) of the bishop who oversaw a large diocese stretching from the English Channel to the River Thames. Now the most important royal church in Anglo-Saxon England, it became the burial place for some of the earliest kings of Wessex.

Here, too, King Cnut, who ruled England and Denmark in the early eleventh century, chose to be buried, and was joined by his wife Queen Emma on her death in 1052. The church was enlarged and aggrandized by the tenth-century Bishop Aethelwold. The bones of St Swithun were dug up and placed in a splendid new shrine, attracting pilgrims from far and wide.

By the year 1000, Old Minster was a multi-purpose building – a great cathedral, a thriving priory church, a healing place of pilgrimage, and the final resting place of

Winchester Cathedral (north transept). STEVE DUNN

West Saxon kings. After 450 years it was then demolished and its stones reused in the new building, consecrated in 1093 by Bishop Walkelyn (or Walkelin). However, the tower fell in 1107 and was later rebuilt, the Early English retrochoir and Lady Chapel date from the early thirteenth century, and the nave was completely remodelled by Bishop Edington and William of Wykeham in the fourteenth and fifteenth centuries by master-mason William of Wynforde: this involved a Perpendicular recasing of the Norman nave.

The Norman elements of the present cathedral are still visible in its round-arched crypt, as well as in the transepts.

By the early 1900s there were fears that the east end would collapse after centuries of subsidence. Deep-sea diver, William Walker, worked under water in total darkness for six years to stabilize it.

Winchester Castle

All that now remains of Winchester Castle is one of the finest surviving aisled halls of the thirteenth century, containing the greatest symbol of medieval mythology and legend: King Arthur's Round Table. The hall was built between 1222 and 1235 by Henry III, while the infamous Round Table has hung in the hall from c.1348. The names of the Knights of the Round Table are written around its edge, surmounted by King Arthur on his throne. It is likely that it was created in about 1290 for a tournament to celebrate the betrothal of one of Edward I's daughters. When the table was taken down from the wall and examined in 1976, tree-ring evidence and carbon dating placed it in the thirteenth or early fourteenth century, thus upholding this suggestion.

The oak table originally stood with twelve outer legs and a central support. It measures 18ft (5.5m) in diameter, weighs 2,646lb (1,200kg). It has hung on the west wall of the Great Hall since 1873, when it was moved from the east wall where it had hung since the fourteenth century. The present painting of the table was carried out on the order of Henry VIII's in 1522. It features the Tudor Rose at its centre, and is thought to portray Henry as King Arthur on his throne, surrounded by twenty-four places for his knights.

The castle was originally constructed for William the Conqueror in 1067 to help secure his hold on the city after the Norman Conquest. Important aspects of government such as the Treasury and the Exchequer were housed inside. By the end of King John's reign in 1216, the castle and its royal palace required extensive repair, and so were replaced by the present building. In 1302, Edward I and his second wife narrowly escaped death when the royal apartments were destroyed by fire.

The castle was held by the Royalists during the English Civil War until it was captured by the parliamentary forces in 1646. Oliver Cromwell eventually ordered its demolition, but the Great Hall was kept as a venue for assemblies and the County Assizes. Sir Walter Raleigh stood trial here in 1603, and the notorious Judge Jeffreys condemned supporters of the Duke of Monmouth to death here as part of the Bloody Assizes in 1685.

Winchester College

The College is a public school founded in 1382 by William of Wykeham, Bishop of Winchester and Chancellor of England. In 1382, he obtained a charter to found Winchester; the buildings were begun in 1387. Though they were immediately occupied, they were still incomplete in 1394.

In 1740 the then Headmaster, Dr Burton, bought up the leases and later the freehold of the old Sustern Spital, a women's hospital situated on the site of the (present) Headmaster's offices, and altered it to provide boarding accommodation for commoners.

The school comprises two courtyards, a gatehouse, cloister, hall, a college chapel and also the Water Meadows, through which part of the River Itchen runs. Some of the first-established buildings of the late fourteenth century include the outer court, chapel and chantry. Further interesting architectural elements include Victorian revival-style classrooms designed by James Butterfield, and the War Cloisters that were originally built in commemoration of certain members of the school killed in the First World War.

Situated on the south side of Chamber Court, the chapel is part of the original college complex and retains its wooden fan-vaulted ceiling. Little of its original medieval glass, designed by Thomas Glazier, survives as, in the 1820s, cleaning of the glass led it to badly deteriorate and so the panels were copied, while most of the original glass was scattered or destroyed. Some pieces have been recovered.

Situated to the west of the playing fields or 'Meads', the College War Cloister now serves as a memorial to the Wykehamist dead of the two World Wars. It was designed by Sir Herbert Baker, and dedicated in 1924 and again in 1948. A bronze bust of Air Chief Marshal Lord Dowding, commander of Royal Air Force Fighter Command during the Battle of Britain in 1940, also sits on the west side.

The Pilgrims' Trail starts at the west door of the cathedral, continues to the south and through the passage into the cloister. It then passes the deanery and continues into the close, passing the medieval priory's storehouses.

The Pilgrims' School

A number of schools founded to educate the choir boys of Winchester Cathedral have existed since Anglo-Saxon times, most significantly the Alta Schola, which was established in Winchester around 676. The current Pilgrims' School is a boys' preparatory and cathedral school. It moved to its present site in 1931 for choristers and non-choristers alike.

The main building was redesigned in the seventeenth century and sits on the site of former Roman and medieval buildings such as the Pilgrims' Hall (c.1308), once the priory guest house, and was used to accommodate pilgrims travelling to the cathedral; it boasts the oldest surviving timber double-hammerbeam roof.

The Priory Gate and Porter's Lodge/Cheyney Court

The route leaves the close by the main entrance, through the fifteenth-century Prior's Gate. This has a plain four-centred arch, its original traceried doors, a castellated parapet, and a coat of arms over the arch. Cheyney Court, also fifteenth century, was once the seat of the bishop's secular power in Winchester and thus his court house. The ground floor is constructed of stone, with an oversailing three-gabled timber frame and plaster infill above.

Kingsgate

The route then passes under Kingsgate, one of two surviving medieval gates to the city of Winchester (the other is Westgate). The name was first recorded in 1148, but is situated on, or near to, the site of one of the Roman gates to the city, and was the entrance to the royal palace before the Cathedral Close was enclosed in the tenth

Kingsgate, Winchester. STEVE DUNN

century. The present gate likely dates from the fourteenth century, with eighteenth-century walkways.

Above the gate is the small Church of St Swithun-upon-Kingsgate. St Swithun was built in the medieval Early English style, and is unusual as it forms part of the fabric of the old city walls. It achieved some literary fame under the fictional name of St Cuthbert's in Anthony Trollope's novel, *The Warden*. The chapel likely served the medieval abbey's lay workers. The interior is rather plain, with whitewashed walls and an unadorned wooden ceiling. It was badly damaged by fire in the thirteenth century when the citizens of Winchester, who were locked in a dispute with the Prior of Winchester Abbey, set it alight.

The route follows College Street, passing the home in which Jane Austen died in 1817. Now a private house, Jane spent her final days in No. 8 College Street, which she rented.

Wolvesey Castle

Wolvesey has been a residence of the bishops of Winchester since the Anglo-Saxon period. Sited adjacent to Winchester Cathedral, the extensive surviving palace remains date largely to the twelfth-century period of Henry of Blois, grandson of William the Conqueror and younger brother to King Stephen of England. The castle was erected by Henry, who was the Bishop of Winchester, between *c.*1130 and 1171, possibly reusing material from the earlier palace destroyed in 1141. The

Wolvesey Castle. STEVE DUNN

castle featured a courtyard house with keep, remodelled *c*.1160 by the addition of a hall, north range and gatehouse, and further remodelling by the addition of a range along the north side of the courtyard late that same century. On the south side of the courtyard was also a chapel.

The site was the scene for the Rout of Winchester. Empress Matilda made attempts to consolidate her position as Queen of England by assaulting Bishop Henry in 1141, during a period known as the Anarchy. The besieged castle defenders set fire to the city, destroying most of the old town of Winchester and holding off Matilda's forces until she arrived with reinforcements from London.

The last great occasion here was on 25 July 1554, when Mary I and Philip of Spain held their wedding breakfast in the East Hall, and the castle was destroyed during the Civil War in 1646. A new palace was built for Bishop Morley in 1684 by Sir Christopher Wren, incorporating the fifteenth-century chapel.

St Catherine's Hill and 'Plague Pit' Valley

St Catherine's Hill is a small but dramatic chalk hill to the south-east of Winchester, owned by Winchester College and largely managed as a nature reserve by the Hampshire and Isle of Wight Wildlife Trust. The top of the hill is ringed by the ramparts of an Iron Age hill fort. In the centre, a copse of beech trees contains the site of the twelfth-century Chapel of St Catherine. There is also an old turf maze, cut between

Pilgrim route earthwork. STEVE DUNN

St Catherine's Hill (fort). STEVE DUNN

1647 and 1710. On the south side of the hill is Plague Pits Valley, where victims of the 1666 plague were buried.

The Hospital of St Cross and the Almshouse of Noble Poverty

England's oldest charitable organization (and almshouse still in use), founded by Henry of Blois; its church dates from the Norman period, while the Brothers of St Cross still worship in it daily.

The medieval almshouse complex was founded between 1133 and 1136. Legend has it that the hospital's foundation originated in a walk that Henry took in the Itchen Meadows. He was allegedly stopped by a young peasant girl, who begged him to help her people, who were starving because of the civil war. The parallel with the Virgin Mary was not lost on Henry. So moved was he by the girl's plight that, when a little further along the river he discovered the ruins of a religious house, and used the site to establish a new community to help the poor. Whether the story has its basis in fact, Henry was the Bishop of Winchester in 1129 at the age of twenty-eight, and founded the Hospital of St Cross during his incumbency.

The hospital was founded to support thirteen poor men, so frail that they were unable to work, and to feed 100 men at the gates each day. The thirteen became the Brothers of St Cross, yet it was/is not a monastery but a secular foundation. The

Hospital of St Cross from St Catherine's Hill, Winchester. STEVE DUNN

hospital still provides accommodation for a total of twenty-five elderly men known as 'the Brothers' under the care of 'the Master'. They belong to either of two charitable foundations: those belonging to the Foundation of the Hospital of St Cross wear black robes with a silver cross and square caps, while those belonging to the Order of Noble Poverty (founded in 1445) wear claret red robes and trencher hats. The hospital also continues the tradition of the 'wayfarers' dole' – a small horn cup of ale and a piece of bread. The dole was started by a Cluniac monk and can be obtained by anyone who asks at the porter's lodge.

The stone building itself surrounds two quadrangles: the smaller outer northern quadrangle comprises the outer gate, which is sixteenth century, and the fourteenth-century brewhouse. The guest wing and kitchen are from the fifteenth century, while the porter's lodge to 1503 and the Beaufort Tower date to c.1450; the latter features a niche containing a weathered statue of Cardinal Beaufort, former Bishop of Winchester.

The tower's arch takes you to the inner quadrangle. The north range includes the fourteenth-century Brethren's Hall, with its timber screen and gallery, arch-braced timber roof, a central hearth and a dais where the Master dined with the Brethren in the main part of the hall. The main lodgings are on the north-west and west sides of the quadrangle. A corresponding range stood on the south side and was joined to the church, but was demolished in the 1760s. The east range is a sixteenth-century long gallery for the use of the Master. It is raised on a cloister open to the quadrangle, and leads into the church.

Hospital of St Cross (quadrangle), Winchester. STEVE DUNN

St Faith's Church, Hospital of St Cross, Winchester. STEVE DUNN

Hospital of St Cross (gateway), Winchester. STEVE DUNN

The Norman, twelfth- and thirteenth-century Church of St Faith in the south-east corner is more like a miniature cathedral. The building is stone-vaulted throughout, with transepts and a central tower. Begun in 1135, the Norman-style chancel is the oldest part, with typical round-headed windows, chevron ornamentation, and also medieval encaustic tiles. There are also traces of medieval wall paintings. The stained glass is largely Victorian. Allegedly, the font and bell came from the nearby parish church, which was demolished in 1507. The church was restored by James Butterfield in 1864–5.

The route continues over the footbridge crossing the M3, leaving St Catherine's Hill behind. Once across, the medieval or earlier 'Dongas' trackways can be seen, a series of ancient parallel hollows on Twyford Down. The herding of thousands of animals over many centuries caused these deep hollows, named after a technical term for eroded gullies. When wet, the chalk becomes very slippery, and it is thought that when one track became too difficult to negotiate, it was abandoned in favour of a new route. The trackway was well established when the Romans occupied the area, and they built a road alongside it.

Owslebury

Approximately 5 miles (8km) outside Winchester, Owslebury is a village of medieval origin, through which pilgrims would have passed; it is the highest village in Hampshire. The village is one of the many settlements situated on the Roman roads that radiate from Winchester – this one led to the south coast near Porchester.

It is still not known if the village takes its name from Shakespeare's ousel cock, or from the Anglo-Saxon gentleman by the name of Osla. The ring ousel is an April to October visitor, similar to a blackbird but with a white crescent breast. Speculation is that Owslebury is from 'osle' – Old English – and 'ouzel', a blackbird.

The village is located high on the hills and is surrounded by ancient woodland, with long barrows just across the hill. Iron Age and Roman earthworks were also discovered here in the 1960s.

1830 saw the Owslebury riots. Due to the discontent of agricultural workers, a mob broke the threshing machines and other farm machinery. The Owslebury vestry minutes show that widespread poverty had forced the local farm labourers to take action, giving rise to the Swing Riots. They demanded a series of resolutions: essentially, minimum wages for various age brackets, supplemented by doles of bread for families above a certain size. They also urged the provision of cottagers' gardens so they could supplement their food supply and 'for the encouragement of industry'.

The rioters' ally, a local farmer named John Boyes, petitioned for higher wages for the farm labourers – he was convicted and transported to Australia as a result. 245 men were arrested and sent to Winchester for trial. Two of the prisoners were executed at the gallows.

St Andrew's Church, Owslebury. STEVE DUNN

There are many buildings of interest in the parish dating from the seventeenth century or earlier, which gives Owslebury a certain cohesiveness. There are also two farmsteads, both on the north side of Main Road: Owslebury Farm is at the north-east end of the settlement, whilst Boyes Farm (seventeenth century) is at the south-west extreme. Just east of Boyes Farm is the sixteenth-century Ship Inn; it faces southwards across a triangular plot of land that was probably once a common or green.

CHURCH OF ST ANDREW

The medieval Church of St Andrew features examples of Early English architecture (the chancel and lancets), although it was extensively renovated during the seventeenth century. It dates primarily from the fourteenth century and was built in two phases: the chancel, followed by the nave; the transepts are fifteenth century, the tower was rebuilt in the seventeenth century, and enlargement and restoration work was carried out in the nineteenth century.

Particularly interesting are two stained-glass windows, which inspired a young Vincent van Gogh. He saw the designs while working in London, and wrote passionately about them to his brother, Theo. The windows were commissioned by William Carnegie, the 8th Earl of Northesk, in memory of his wife and daughter who both died before him. Both are depicted as the Virgin Mary, in her youth and in old age.

The entrance door frame originates from the original Marwell Hall, the manor house nearby, and a hole in the wall behind the left side of the altar is said to be where a bullet stopped, after passing through the vicar who continued to practise the Latin Mass, thus disobeying orders to change to the Protestant Holy Communion.

Marwell

On the outskirts of the village some interesting detours can be made to the former residence of the bishops of Winchester. The bishop had a park at Marwell from the thirteenth to the mid-seventeenth century, where timber was cut, cattle were pastured and animals were hunted. The Manor of Marwell passed to the Crown in 1551, and was granted to Sir Henry Seymour later that same year, who already had a house at nearby Marwell Woodlock. When Mary I came to the throne, the Manor of Marwell was restored to the bishopric of Winchester, but by 1577, it had passed back to the Seymour family. At Marwell Park, Bishop Henry of Blois founded a small college of secular priests; this building and the nearby bishop's house were surrounded by a moat.

MARWELL MANOR FARM

Now a Grade II Listed building, Marwell Manor Farm stands on the site of a much older building, which was destroyed by fire in the sixteenth century. The current property represents a mid-nineteenth-century rebuilding of the sixteenth-century farmhouse, using materials from the fourteenth-century abbey grange, and a surviving moat.

MARWELL HALL

Marwell Hall was built *c*.1320, on the site of an earlier building. This medieval country house forms the core of the present building, which was originally an episcopal manor house of fourteenth-century date that was remodelled for Sir Henry Seymour in 1551, and then later again for Sir William Long in 1816. Elements of the old building still surviving include the Seymour crest in the entrance hall, and the Royal Arms and initials 'ER' above a fireplace, thought to refer to Edward VI.

The old house was the alleged scene of the secret marriage between Henry VIII and Jane Seymour in 1536.

The Hall was also a scene of mystery and tragedy. Lady Anne, the bride-to-be of Lord Lovell, was dancing on the night of her Christmas wedding when she requested a game of hide and seek with her groom. She hid in a large old oak chest, and its spring lock closed on her. Years later, she was found with a sprig of mistletoe beside her. This prompted Thomas Haynes Bayly (1797–1839) to write the ballad 'The Mistletoe Bough'.

Walk across Lower Baybridge Lane to the lane opposite, following the gravel track to the edge of Austin's Copse. Within the coppice, the Roman road survives as an earthwork. The trail meanders through the copse to open land and a track. Turn left, then right, until you meet another track: this will take you across high open farmland, before descending to a hedge.

Upham

The Pilgrims' Trail partly uses the course of the former Roman road from Winchester to Portchester near Portsmouth, which passes between Upham and Lower Upham.

The village has two centres. The original hamlet lies on the higher ground in the centre of the parish, and contains the church, the village recreation ground, the village pond and The Brushmakers Arms. Lower Upham lies about a mile (2km) to the south-west on the main road from Winchester/Colden Common to Bishop's Waltham.

At the time of Domesday Book it is believed that there was a church in Upham. Parts of the church date from the thirteenth century, although it was extensively remodelled in the nineteenth century by architect G. E. Street (who designed the Old Bailey).

The medieval road from Winchester to Bishop's Waltham also passed through Upham, and the name of Stephen's Castle Down a mile to the north-east represents the struggle between local supporters of Henry I and Matilda, and those of King Stephen.

Relics of a Roman villa on the outskirts of Upham were found in 1849.

THE HOLT

The Holt, a Grade II-Listed William and Mary country house, was the longtime seat of the Leavett-Shenley family, and the home of John Alfred Leavett-Shenley DL, High Sheriff of Hampshire in 1985–6. The Holt is situated to the west of Preshaw House, on high chalk downland backing onto Dur Wood.

The Holt was rebuilt around 1689, incorporating an older Tudor structure. The initials 'A.F.', together with the date 1689, were found carved in a pediment, and a William III coin dated 1696. The pedimented front has traces of the warm ochre wash prevalent in the eighteenth century, while the contrasting back of the house has a sizeable later wing with an intrusive water tower. The latter was reduced and the wing remodelled during alterations undertaken by the architects Trenwith Wills & Wills in 1955.

A second tower-like projection looks like part of an older house, while internal evidence of 'post-and-pan' oak partitioning could have been the screen of an early Tudor hall that was then moved when the house was rebuilt in the seventeenth century, and installed at the head of the staircase. Finally, the architectural style of the hall is also interesting as it is most often attributed to the lesser gentry and served as the prototype for many Colonial houses in the USA.

UPHAM HOUSE, WINTERSHILL AND DURLEY HALL FARM

Upham House is the most central of three large houses standing in a commanding position at the point where the medieval road left Upham to descend to Waltham. The estate was passed down generations until 1921, when it was broken up and the farms of Newlyn, Bigpath and Ower sold.

In the south-east corner of the parish is the hill known as Wintershill, with the house that bears its name. The original manor house was actually the farmhouse now known as Durley Hall Farm, which is about a quarter of a mile away from the upper lodge of Wintershill Hall, within the parish of Durley. This house has no connection with the Wintershill estate. The original manor house of Durley Hall Farm is now the sixteenth-century ruin within the boundary of Durley parish. Wintershill Hall was built by Mr G. H. Stares in 1852, and a large portion was then rebuilt in 1902 by Mr J. S. Moss. The main Roman road from Winchester to Porchester goes through the farm at Wintershill.

THE CHURCH OF THE BLESSED VIRGIN MARY

It is not known precisely when the Church of the Blessed Virgin Mary was built, but Domesday Book records two churches in the manor of Bishop's Waltham, of which one is thought to be Upham. It was referred to in the Charter of the Hospital of St Cross, Winchester in 1132, and again in 1284, in the letters patent of the priory and convent of St Swithun.

The current building largely dates to the thirteenth century. In 1598, the church was described as having a squat tower, a nave, a chancel and a south aisle. The original tower was rebuilt in 1700, of blue and red chequer brick, and in the Victorian era, the church was extensively restored and the north aisle added, the latter being completed in 1881.

The stained glass is mostly Victorian and later, while a small medieval window, high above the altar, is shaped like a lamb's head and contains the arms of the Plantagenet kings. These were also the arms of Henry, Cardinal Beaufort, Bishop of Winchester, who built the Beaufort Gatehouse at St Cross in the fifteenth century, so there may be a connection with him.

The Bishop's Palace (exterior), Bishop's Waltham. STEVE DUNN

The Way follows the road down to Winchester Road, and then along the line of the ancient Roman road. The surrounding land at Wintershill provided agricultural support to the Bishop's Palace in Bishop's Waltham in the medieval era.

Bishop's Waltham

The route next enters Bishop's Waltham. The name is comprised of three parts: 'walt', meaning 'forest'; 'ham', meaning 'settlement'; and 'Bishop's'. Beginning as an Anglo-Saxon village, it steadily grew into one of Hampshire's larger settlements, despite being burnt to the ground by Danes in 1001. In 904, it was given by the king to the Bishop of Winchester.

THE BISHOP'S PALACE

The medieval palace (together with later additions) was used by the bishops and senior clergy of Winchester – the richest diocese in England – on their travels throughout the diocese.

In 1136, Henry of Blois built Bishop's Waltham Palace. Little remains from this first phase of building, besides the doorway in a pit just south of the cloister; but Henry of Blois then seems to have rebuilt the palace in the 1160s or 1170s, having returned from exile in 1158. The outer walls of the south and west ranges incorporate much

Gatehouse, The Bishop's Palace, Bishop's
Waltham. STEVE DUNN

masonry from this second period. The Romanesque chapel crypt could date from either of the twelfth-century phases. The palace hosted a royal council in 1182, when Henry II asked his nobles for supplies and to plan a crusade. Later visits were by Richard I, Margaret of Anjou, and Henry V.

Much of what can be seen today is the work of William Wykeham, Chancellor to Edward III and Richard II, via his chief mason, William Wynford, who also supervised the building of Winchester College, New College Oxford, and the nave of Winchester Cathedral. It was then remodelled and extended in the fourteenth and fifteenth centuries.

Cardinal Bishop Henry Beaufort, half-brother to Henry IV, often resided at Waltham, and carried out further enhancements. He raised the west tower by a storey in c.1408, and built a new chapel between 1416 and 1427. Between 1438 and 1443 a new inner gatehouse and a range of lodgings along the northern side of the inner court were also erected.

Richard the Lionheart also stayed here, Mary I waited for King Phillip to arrive from Spain for their wedding in 1554, and Henry VIII and the Holy Roman Emperor, Charles V, signed a treaty at Waltham pledging an alliance against Francis I, King of France, in 1522. The palace was largely destroyed by Oliver Cromwell during the English Civil War, then general deterioration set in thereafter – it was a private dwelling for a time, before becoming a ruin.

THE CHURCH OF ST PETER

The Parish Church of St Peter is another place of historic interest. A building was first present on the site in 1136, followed by various changes, restorations and repairs over the intervening centuries. It was predominantly remodelled in the late fourteenth or fifteenth century. Although its earliest features date to the late medieval era, it is best noted for its post-Reformation, late-Perpendicular Elizabethan Gothic-style alterations.

The current building comprises a chancel, nave with aisles and south porch, south-west tower, and at the west end of the north aisle a vestry with gallery over. There is also a large gallery in the west bay of the nave. The capitals and arches of the nave's north arcade date from the beginning of the thirteenth century, as does the chancel.

Chapel, The Bishop's Palace, Bishop's Waltham. STEVE DUNN

Bakery, The Bishop's Palace, Bishop's Waltham. STEVE DUNN

The tower fell on 31 December 1582 and was rebuilt in 1584–9; this began a series of seventeenth-century rebuildings. The west end of the nave was also rebuilt in 1849 due to the west wall being in danger of collapse.

The church was then lightly restored in 1864–8, followed by a more substantial restoration in the 1890s, which transformed the building into what it is today. Work included the installation of a modern arcade in fourteenth-century style, while the south aisle gallery and windows were entirely removed and rebuilt, as was the north aisle arcade. The Anglo-Saxon font was discovered in 1933 and now stands in the church.

THE CROWN INN

The Crown Inn Hotel, parts of which date to the 1500s, was once a coaching inn with stables and brewhouse. It billeted captured French sailors after the Battle of Trafalgar, including the Admiral of the Franco-Spanish fleet, Vice-Admiral Villeneuve. It was also a site of cockfighting and figured in the town's Beer Riots of 1884.

THE MAFEKING HERO

The Mafeking Hero on Bank Street was originally a brick-built seventeenth-century coaching inn known as The White Hart. It was renamed in 1900, following the end of the 217-day siege of Mafeking, in South Africa: the pub name honoured men from the village who survived the siege. The building has a large L-shaped wing to the west side and rear, a carriage arch, and a main block with a smaller rear wing; the yard at the rear exposes a varied set of vernacular structures – formerly stables.

Southwick

Southwick is next on the agenda, and the village is particularly interesting to visit as it is full of timber-framed thatched cottages, occupied entirely by tenants as it was in the medieval era – they were all owned by the Southwick Estate. Subsequently, all the houses, except manor houses, have dark red-painted front doors – a condition laid down in the tenancy agreements. The only exceptions to this are the White House, the residence of the vicar and the Church Lodge. Southwick means 'south dairy farm', but at some stage, this farm grew into a small village.

In the twelfth century, Southwick was initially the site of the Augustinian Southwick Priory. It is certainly worth a detour to the priory, a medieval site of pilgrimage; however, only part of the refectory wall survives today. Originally founded in Portchester Castle on Portsmouth Harbour, it was later transferred 2 miles (3.2 km) north of Southwick. By the early thirteenth century, the priory is referred to as Southwick Priory. It thus moved to the current site in Southwick c.1145–53. In 1445, Henry VI was married to Margaret of Anjou here. Towards the end of the Middle Ages, the priory became a renowned centre of pilgrimage: in September 1510, Henry VIII passed through and made an offering of 6s. 8d. to Our Lady of Southwick.

Southwick Priory. STEVE DUNN

Following its dissolution in 1538, the priory came into the possession of John White, a servant of Thomas Wriothesley, 1st Earl of Southampton. He dismantled the church and converted the prior's lodgings into a private house known as Southwick Park, which became the family seat of a branch of the Norton family. In October 1551, Mary of Guise, Regent of Scotland and mother of Mary, Queen of Scots, stayed in the house. Little remains of the priory, besides a wall.

SOUTHWICK HOUSE

In the early seventeenth century, a Mr Daniel Norton built a new house on or near the site of the priory; however, that house was demolished at the beginning of the nineteenth century following a fire, and a Thomas Thistlethwayte built a new house on higher ground close by. The present Southwick House is in the Palladian revival style and is known as the 'White House'. The British Navy took over the house in 1941 and, in June 1944, Eisenhower made the decision to invade Normandy from within.

The house is distinct for its two-storey foyer lit from a cupola, and a series of elliptical rooms. A hemi-circular portico is centred on the house's colonnade of paired Ionic columns. It was also important during World War II: in 1940, the estate owners allowed the Royal Navy to use the house to accommodate overnight pupils of the Royal Navy School of Navigation, HMS *Dryad* in Portsmouth Naval Dockyard. In 1941, after heavy bombing of the dockyard, the house was requisitioned and became the new home of HMS *Dryad*.

The Church of St James Without-the-Priory Gate, Southwick. STEVE DUNN

THE CHURCH OF ST JAMES WITHOUT-THE-PRIORY GATE

The church is so called because it was situated outside the boundaries of the former priory. It is described as a 'peculiar', meaning that it is privately owned and exempt from the jurisdiction of the diocese in which it lies.

It is not certain when the original parish church of St James was built, but there was likely a chapel in existence before the priory came to Southwick, and possibly even before the Norman Conquest.

The church was restored and virtually rebuilt by John Whyte during the 1560s, reusing material from the priory. The lower part of the tower features ornamental chequering of knapped flint and stone, while the upper part is plain, nearly all flint, and 1566 in date. It is likely that the panelled west doorway entrance is fourteenth-century.

Preserved in the arch between the north aisle and chapel is an elegant Purbeck marble double capital with foliage, which must have come from the priory. The windows in the north aisle of the nave are fourteenth-century, while medieval roof tile fragments have been set into the base of the north wall. The font is also Purbeck marble, and dates to c.1200.

Between the north chapel and the chancel is the tomb of John Whyte, the builder of the church. Two eighteenth-century family pews also remain. The three-decker pulpit is unusual as it forms part of one of the pews, but with its own window – it dates to 1605.

Blocking most of the fifteenth-century Perpendicular east window is an unusual painted wooden reredos of the eighteenth century, with a classical painting of cherubs and doves in a pilastered surround. On the outside of the east wall is an inscription recording the rebuilding of 1566, and it is likely that the windows of the north chapel contain fragments of glass from the priory. The communion rail is Jacobean, and the altar table is Elizabethan.

The culminating location of the trail is Portsmouth.

Portsmouth

Although references to Portsmouth occur in the early twelfth century, they almost certainly allude to the anchorage at the top of the harbour at the mouth of the estuary of the Wallington river. Portchester Castle and the village of Portchester stood nearby on the northern edge of this area, and were referred to in an Anglo-Saxon chronicle, which stated 'in 501 A.D. Port and his two sons Bieda and Maegla came to Britain with two ships in the place called Portesmutha and killed a young British man, a very noble man.'

Portsmouth itself was founded by wealthy Norman landowner and merchant, Jean de Gisors, in c.1180 on Portsea Island. A small inlet in the south-west of the island called the Camber, it was a sheltered place for ships to land, so de Gisors chose it as the site of a new town. He divided up the land into plots for building houses and started a market, which then attracted craftsmen and merchants. In 1185, a parish church was built – it became Portsmouth Cathedral in the twentieth century.

By the early thirteenth century, Portsmouth was one of the most important English ports, the main exports being wool and grain. The main imports were wine, woad for dyeing, wax for candles and iron.

In 1527 Henry VIII enlarged Portsmouth dockyard then, when he closed the monasteries in 1539, he also closed the Domus Dei; it was turned into an armoury and later a house for the military governor. Henry also built a castle in 1544, east of Portsmouth, overlooking the sea: Southsea Castle. Then, in 1545, Henry watched as his warship, *Mary Rose*, sank in the Solent.

In 1729, the Royal Naval Academy was established at Portsmouth, and it continued to train officers and cadets until 1872, when it transferred to Greenwich. In 1770, the ramparts and moats that encircled the town of Portsea were begun. Two gates were erected to give access to the town: Lion Gate and Union Gate. Union Gate was moved to become the entrance to the new Anglesey Barracks, then again to become the base of the present Semaphore Tower in the dockyard.

Charles Dickens was born in Commercial Road, now Old Commercial Road, on 7 February 1812.

Portsmouth Town Hall was built at a cost of £137,098 and was opened on 9 August 1890 by the Prince and Princess of Wales.

Old Portsmouth

Old Portsmouth was where Portsmouth first began, and it has many historic buildings that are very much recommended as small detours along this route.

In 1704, royal permission was given to build houses near to the dockyard and so a new suburb called Portsmouth Common grew, which changed its name to Portsea in 1792. It soon outgrew the original town, which became known as Old Portsmouth. Old Portsmouth, located on the south-western tip of the island, was known as Spice Island, where the spices entered the city. The old defences are still in situ and it is possible to walk along what are known as the Hot Walls (or Coastal Battery Wall) – part of the fortifications for the harbour entrance and the site of the saluting platform – so termed as they were the reputed location at which hot shot was prepared during the Spithead Mutiny of 1797.

Prior to this, in the sixteenth century, the town was very small and Portsea Island was mainly farmland. The dockyard grew in importance after 1625 due to the necessary defence of the realm and, through this prosperity, by 1685, many new buildings were erected, such as those in Lombard Street and the High Street in Old Portsmouth. These terraced streets are particularly significant for architectural survivals. Lombard Street, for example, contains many seventeenth-century houses featuring Dutch gables. Also, while The Parade acquired its rendering in about 1833, the rear elevation is still much as it was when completed in 1719. The Commissioner's House dates from the 1780s and was one of the first in the country to be fitted with a flush toilet. It has been very little altered and now provides accommodation for the Commander-in-Chief, Naval Home Command and Second Sea Lord.

THE HIGH STREET

The High Street in Old Portsmouth is part of the original city and has many historic buildings. No. 11 High Street is an important landmark: it was known as the 'Spotted Dog' and owned by Captain John Mason, and was where George Villiers, the Duke of Buckingham, was assassinated by John Felton on 23 August 1628. The Duke was later buried in Westminster Abbey. There is also a house numbered with a ½.

George Court, now a block of flats, was formerly The George Hotel. This was where Nelson spent his last night before boarding the *Victory* to sail for Trafalgar. The George Hotel was actually destroyed along with a great part of the city in a German air raid on 10 and 11 January 1941. Also, in the High Street, is the Keppels Head/Sally Port, where Commander Lionel 'Buster' Crabb spent his last night before mysteriously vanishing during a diving operation in 1956.

Near the High Street is a memorial garden with a monument to John Pounds. John Pounds (1766–1839) was a shoemaker whose work for the poor of the district inspired

St John's Cathedral, Old Portsmouth. STEVE DUNN

the Ragged School Movement. Pounds fell into a dry dock as a boy and was crippled for life. Unable to follow his chosen trade, he became a shoemaker, and by 1803 had his own shop at No. 78 St Mary Street (now Highbury Street), Old Portsmouth. A re-creation of his shop has been built in the High Street.

ST JOHN'S CATHEDRAL

St John's Cathedral is located in Bishop Crispian Way and was built successively throughout the late nineteenth century, replacing a chapel built in 1796 in Prince George Street to the west of the current church (before 1791, it was illegal for Catholics to have chapels in towns of borough status). The cathedral is of the French neo-Gothic style, and was designed by John Crawley to have a tall spire at the south-west corner; however, the geology of the land made this impossible. The design was taken over by Joseph Hansom when John Crawley died, and it is built in Fareham red brick and Portland stone.

Most of the stained-glass windows sustained some bomb damage in 1941, especially those over the high altar. The round window in the south transept was the only one not damaged. An elaborate baldacchino surmounting the high altar was removed in the 1970 re-ordering. The last part to be built was St Patrick's Chapel in 1924.

PORTSMOUTH CATHEDRAL

Located in Old Portsmouth, just off the High Street, the Cathedral Church of St Thomas of Canterbury, commonly known as Portsmouth Anglican Cathedral, was built in c.1180 by Jean de Gisors, the founder of Portsmouth. It became a parish church in 1320, and a cathedral in 1927. The medieval building was cruciform with a central tower, which was used as a lookout point and lighthouse over the crossing. Only the choir and the transepts remain of the original twelfth-century building.

In 1591, Elizabeth I worshipped in St Thomas' Church. In 1642, during the civil war the church was bombarded by Parliamentarian forces.

The restoration of the monarchy in 1660 led Charles II to authorize a collection in churches across the country to raise the £9,000 required to rebuild the tower and nave. The nave was built in the neo-Classical style, galleries were added in 1708 to cater for growing congregations, and then were extended in 1750.

Between 1902 and 1904, the church was closed for restoration work, and in 1927 the diocese of Portsmouth was created. Sir Charles Nicholson then enlarged it in the neo-Byzantine style, yet the outbreak of World War II meant that work on the extension scheme stopped. Thus, from 1939 until 1991, Portsmouth had the only incomplete cathedral in England. In 1990, work was started to finish the scheme and, in 1991, the completed building was consecrated in the presence of HM Queen Elizabeth, the Queen Mother.

There is a dedicated Navy aisle where bones recovered from the *Mary Rose* lie. Finally a trefoiled arched recess in the north transept displays the remains of a thirteenth-century wall painting of the Last Judgement, in a small vesica (oval).

Portsmouth Anglican Cathedral (St Thomas). STEVE DUNN

Portsmouth Anglican Cathedral, wall painting (north transept). STEVE DUNN

THE DOMUS DEI

The Royal Garrison Church is the oldest British garrison church in the world and has been called 'The British Military Cathedral', but it actually dates back to 1212. The Domus Dei, or God's House, was founded in Old Portsmouth by Bishop de Rupibus in the thirteenth century as a hospitium, to shelter and help pilgrims bound for the shrines at Canterbury, Chichester and Winchester, and beyond.

Originally, it comprised a long, vaulted hall, divided on each side into bays to accommodate patients, with a chapel at one end. In the hall, the aged, sick and homeless were tended by six brethren and six sisters. As the importance of Portsmouth grew as a garrison town, so did the Domus Dei. The chancel was the chapel of the old Domus Dei, and the nave acted as the hospital.

In 1449, Henry VI sent the Bishop of Chichester to the church to pay the sailors and soldiers of the garrison. Due to a disagreement in the amount, the bishop was taken outside and murdered. The town was subsequently excommunicated, and remained so until 1508. The church was closed in 1540 as a result of the Dissolution. The buildings were then used for a brief time as an armoury. Charles II married Catherine of Braganza here on 21 May 1662.

Later, the south side of Domus Dei was converted into a residence for the governor of Portsmouth, called Government House. It was demolished in 1826. Two decades later, the interior of the church was refurbished, followed by reconstruction work betwen 1866 and 1868. The oak stalls were then dedicated to the memory of famous men including Lord Nelson, the Duke of Wellington, Sir John Moore, Lord Raglan and Outram of India.

On the night of 10 January 1941 a fire-bomb raid on Portsmouth gutted the nave but the chancel was saved by the verger, Mr J. Heaton, assisted by soldiers and airmen.

THE SQUARE TOWER

The Square Tower at the bottom of the High Street was erected in 1494 by order of Henry VII; so too was the adjacent platform. As well as a fort, the tower also served as the home of the governor of Portsmouth. It still retains a number of its original Tudor features and is therefore well worth a visit.

After 1540, the tower was used as a magazine so the governor was provided with quarters in the old Domus Dei. Then, in 1779, it was converted to store meat for the Royal Navy's ships. The coat of arms in the larger room are the past governors of Portsmouth. The central brick wall and brick vaulting were added at this time. Its use as a meat store continued until $c.1850$, when this store was moved to Gosport. The Square Tower was manned during the two World Wars, and has also been used by sea scouts and harbour pilots.

The tower was restored to its present condition between 1979 and 1986. An archaeological examination revealed historic features such as windows and Tudor fireplaces on the ground floor. On the first floor, the large window by the stairs is one of the original Tudor windows. The hooks may relate to the Tower's use as a meat store.

The Square Tower, Portsmouth. STEVE DUNN

THE ROUND TOWER

At the time it was built, the Round Tower was actually sited outside the town walls, on the small peninsula known as The Point. The nearest gate into Portsmouth – Point Gate, later known as King James' Gate – was roughly halfway along Broad Street between the Round Tower and the nearby Square Tower. Due to the importance of controlling the Point and thus Portsmouth harbour, the first permanent defences were erected here. In 1418, work on the Round Tower began, and was completed in the 1420s – at this time plans refer to it as 'King Edward's Tower', and it was later known as 'Master Ridley's Tower' after its sixteenth-century controller. Like most fortifications, the Round Tower has been modified many times in its history.

The long-vaulted casemates that face the parade were known as Eighteen Gun Battery. Henry VIII first established a battery here during the French invasion crisis of 1545. Originally, this battery was a single-storey narrow building backing on to a row of houses, where the parade ground is now situated. To gain access to the beach, a small S-shaped sally port in the wall at the south end of the battery was built, where the moat ran across the road; the outer wall was the work of Charles II's chief engineer, Sir Bernard de Gomme. The tower was raised in height twice – in 1815 and 1850 – bringing it to its present 35ft (11m).

The Round Tower, Portsmouth. STEVE DUNN

Between the fortifications and Broad Street, walls were erected in 1850, so the area became Point Battery and Barracks for the soldiers who manned these guns. An outline of the soldiers' barracks rooms is marked out with bricks on the ground, and visible today.

The End of the Journey: Cherbourg to Mont-Saint-Michel

Finally, from Portsmouth, the Pilgrims' Trail can be continued onwards to Mont-Saint-Michel in Normandy, France, by taking the ferry to Cherbourg and following the waymarked route southwards through the beautiful Normandy countryside (*see* Appendix for the journey details).

Postscript

And smale foules maken melodie,
That slepen alle night with open eye,
So priketh hem nature in hir corages;
Than longen folk to gon on pilgrimages

Canterbury Tales, Prologue

In emulation of the pilgrims discussed in this book, I also arrive here at the culmination of my peregrination, in reality and metaphorically. The final stage of this journey requires a retracing of my steps in order to consider what they have uncovered.

It is now almost 500 years since Henry VIII's Reformation, which saw the end of pilgrim culture. In the injunctions of 1536, pilgrimage was outlawed in England, as were all associated superstitious distractions – what William Gray of Reading termed 'fantassies of idolatrie' – that were thought to create an inappropriate setting for worship. A new private relationship between God and man was put forth, meaning that the role for intermediaries, the saints, was no longer required. All memory of them – including their official celebrated holy days, relics and shrines – was eradicated and thus the need to journey to them was gone.

Still, the essential nature of pilgrimage – making a transformative journey to a sacred site – remained a powerful metaphor for the spiritual life of Christians everywhere. It is this form of pilgrimage that was so popular throughout medieval Europe, and yet both concepts (the physical and spiritual) remain a staple of pilgrim tourism today.

In theory, anywhere can be a pilgrimage destination, can it not? What is it, then, that makes these routes so special? Why have they, at least in part, survived or held resonance for so many centuries? Or, is that our answer: is there simply something within us that wants to travel to places that have been significant to many people for a very long time?

While pilgrimage has been, since time immemorial, an expression of Christian devotion that was believed to purify the soul and perhaps even produce miraculous healing benefits, an instinctive longing to move with the seasons has been with us since the very beginnings of human nature. The call to pilgrimage can thus be profound, but it is not a solitary call – on pilgrimage we enter into a relationship with landscape, architecture, time and place, which hallows both Way and wayfarer in a manner that can only be understood through personal experience. A pilgrimage can deepen our relationship with such places. For example, following many of the trails featured in this book, the traveller will, at times, be struck by the sense of isolation and distance from the world, the quality that first attracted the early saints to these landscapes, upon which the routes were founded and formed.

Nonetheless, as noted earlier, the reason behind the longing to embrace the experience may be complex – for the modern traveller it may stem from a devotional desire to learn about a deity associated with a particular place, or simply just a slow-growing idea that takes shape over months or even years due to a desire to get away, or just to 'see' a place owing to an interest in architecture, history or culture. Whatever the intention, today's 'pilgrim' is assured of a rich and rewarding experience.

As this book has shown, many of Britain's routes have a supporting infrastructure of associated sites, or even a pre-Christian history for those who wish to find it. Walking them is a powerful way to connect with the archetypal wanderer, the past pilgrim, and through the tangible remains – the sites – one can 'connect' with the past in numerous ways. For example, the symbolic attributes of the pilgrim – staff, broad-brimmed hat, scrip and gourd – have long been associated with sacred wanderers of numerous cultures, and many of these symbols are reflected back at you from the iconography of the buildings along the routes (such as the scallop shell). And while pilgrimage churches were constructed with special features to make them particularly accessible to visitors, as the goal was to get as many people to visit the relics as possible, today the sites located along the routes featured act in a similar manner – as 'draws' along the Ways, enticing people towards the main attractions.

The routes collected here show how the sites of which they are comprised have been constructed by devotees and supporters as strings of important cult places that interconnect with the dynamics of British history, areas of picturesque countryside and broader material culture. Each shrine is not simply significant unto itself: the rich cultural impact of these monuments has been, and remains, indicative of broader trends in history, religion and travel. The narratives and counter-narratives concerning the routes over the past millennia in some respects encompass key issues in our identity that have hung over Britain since the Middle Ages, highlighting that we are an empire of deep memories and rich cultural reinventions, as well as a nation that enjoys clinging to the historic traditions, myths and legends that make our surroundings feel both more interesting and blessed.

As I hope to have shown in this book, even for many people who have never wished to make a pilgrimage, each route and its stories has been (even if largely out of sight now due to the little surviving evidence of their presence) far from out of mind, from the Middle Ages to modernity.

Whichever route you choose to follow, of utmost importance is that the destination is significant and meaningful for you; the primal experience of pilgrimage is a personal contact with the landscape and its various sites, which lies beyond the principles of any one faith.

Curiosity does, no less than devotion, pilgrims make.
Abraham Cowley

Further Reading

Abou-El-Haj, B. (1997) *The Medieval Cult of Saints: Formations and Transformations* (Cambridge: Cambridge University Press).

Black, C. (2010) *The Saint Andrew's Way: The Modern Restoration of a Medieval Pilgrimage Walk from Central Edinburgh across the Forth Road Bridge to St. Andrews* (Cameron Black).

Blick, S. and Tekippe, R. (eds.) (2005) *Art and Architecture of Late Medieval Pilgrimage in Northern Europe and the British Isles*. 2 vols. (Leiden: Brill).

Bradley, I. (2009) *Pilgrimage: A Spiritual and Cultural Journey* (Oxford: Lion Hudson).

Bright, D. (2011) *The Pilgrims' Way: Fact and Fiction of an Ancient Trackway* (Stroud: The History Press).

Brown, P. (1981) *The Cult of the Saints: Its Rise and Function in Latin Christianity* (Chicago and London: University of Chicago Press, SCM Press).

Candy, J. (2009) *The Archaeology of Pilgrimage on the Camino de Santiago de Compostela: a landscape perspective*. BAR International Series 1948 (Oxford: Archaeopress).

Cartwright, J. (2013) *The Pilgrims' Way: From Winchester to Canterbury* (Book on Demand Ltd).

Coleman, S. and Elsner, J. (1995) *Pilgrimage Past and Present: Sacred Travel and Sacred Space in the World Religions* (London: British Museum Press and Cambridge MA: Harvard University Press).

Crook, J. (2000) *The Architectural Setting of the Cult of Saints in the Early Christian West c.300–c.1200* (Oxford: Oxford University Press).

Crook, J. (2011) *English Medieval Shrines* (Woodbridge: The Boydell Press).

Cusack, C. M. (2013) 'History, Authenticity, and Tourism: Encountering the Medieval While Walking Saint Cuthbert's Way', in Alex Norman (ed.) *Journeys and Destinations: Studies in Travel, Identity, and Meaning* (Newcastle: Cambridge Scholars Publishing), 1–22.

Davidson, L. K. and Gitlitz, D. M. (2002) *Pilgrimage: From the Ganges to Graceland: an Encyclopedia* (California: ABC-CLIO, Inc).

Davies, P., Howard, D. and Pullan, W. (eds.) (2013) *Architecture and Pilgrimage, 1000–1500: Southern Europe and Beyond* (Surrey: Ashgate).

Dickinson, J. C. (1956) *The Shrine of Our Lady of Walsingham* (Cambridge: Cambridge University Press).

Duffy, E. (1992) *The Stripping of the Altars: Traditional Religion in England 1400–1550* (New Haven and London: Yale University Press).

Eade, J. and Sallnow, M. J. (eds.) (1991) *Contesting the sacred: the anthropology of Christian pilgrimage* (London: Routledge).

Farmer, D. (2011) *The Oxford Dictionary of Saints, Fifth Edition Revised* (Oxford: Oxford University Press).

Finucane, R. C. (1977) *Miracles and Pilgrims: Popular Beliefs in Medieval England* (London: Dent).

Hall, D. J. (1965) *English Mediaeval Pilgrimage* (London: Routledge and Kegan Paul).

Lasansky, D. M. and McLaren, B. (eds) (2004) *Architecture and tourism: perception, performance, and place* (Oxford; New York: Berg).

Lewis, H. and Lewis, G. (2012) *The Saints' Way Guide: Forth an Syns* (Cornwall: The Pelican Studio).

Locker, M. (2015) *Landscapes of Pilgrimage in Medieval Britain* (Oxford: Archaeopress).

Low, M. (2000) *St Cuthbert's Way: A Pilgrim's Companion* (Glasgow: Wild Goose Publications).

Macfarlane, R. (2013) *The Old Ways: Journeys on Foot* (London: Penguin).

Merrill, J. (2011) *Our Lady of Caversham Pilgrimage Walk* (Pilgrim Ways Series) (John Merrill Foundation).

Merrill, J. (2003) *The Walsingham Way: Ely to Walsingham* (Pilgrim Ways Series) (John Merrill Foundation).

Merrill, J. (2003) *The Walsingham Way: King's Lynn to Walsingham* (Pilgrim Ways Series) (John Merrill Foundation).

Morris, C. and Roberts, P. (eds.) (2002) *Pilgrimage: The English Experience from Becket to Bunyan* (Cambridge: Cambridge University Press).

Orme, N. (2000) *The Saints of Cornwall* (Oxford: Oxford University Press).

Orme, N. (2007) *Cornwall and the Cross: Christianity, 500–1560* (Cornwall: Phillimore).

Rees, E. (2003) *Celtic Sites and Their Saints: A Guidebook* (New York; London: Burns & Oates).

Rollason, D. (1989) *Saints and Relics in Anglo-Saxon England* (Oxford: Blackwell).

Selwyn, T. (ed.) (1996) *The Tourist image: myths and myth making in tourism* (Chichester; New York: John Wiley).

Shaw, R. and Smith, R. (2014) *St Cuthbert's Way: Official Trail Guide* (Edinburgh: Birlinn Ltd).

Stephenson, C. (2008) *Walsingham Way* (Norwich: Canterbury Press).

Stopford, J. (1999) *Pilgrimage Explored* (York: York Medieval Press).

Sumption, J. (1975) *Pilgrimage: an image of mediaeval religion* (London: Faber and Faber).

Sumption, J. (2003) *The Age of Pilgrimage: the Medieval Journey to God* (Mahwah, NJ: Hidden Spring).

Turner, V. and Turner, E. (1978) *Image and Pilgrimage in Christian Culture* (New York: Columbia University Press).

Turner, S. (2006) *Medieval Devon and Cornwall: Shaping an Ancient Countryside* (Macclesfield: Windgather Press).

Vail, A. (2004) *Shrines of Our Lady in England* (Bodmin: MPG Books).

Webb, D. (2000) *Pilgrimage in Medieval England* (London: Hambledon).

Wells, E. J. (2013) '"...he went round the holy places praying and offering": Evidence for Cuthbertine Pilgrimage to Lindisfarne and Farne in the Late Medieval Period', in J. Ashbee and J. M. Luxford (eds.) *Newcastle and Northumberland: Roman and Medieval Art, Architecture and Archaeology* (Leeds: Maney), 214–31.

See also the informative website (and DVD resources) of the University of York's Centre for Christianity and Culture: http://www.york.ac.uk/projects/pilgrimage/index.html

Cartographic Information for Routes

There are various possible courses and associated maps for each of the routes featured in this book. Below are listed the primary and most detailed maps which can be used alone or in conjunction with the others to create the best route for you. Many of these are available as PDF documents which may be printed out from the websites. However, the corresponding Ordnance Survey maps are also listed. Additional publications on the routes are also featured in the Further Reading section.

St Cuthbert's Way

Start: NT548341: Melrose Abbey, Borders (Scotland)
Finish: NU126418: Lindisfarne, Northumberland

OS Landranger: 73, 74, 75
OS Landranger Active: 73, 74, 75
OS Explorer: 16, 338, 339, 340
OS Explorer Active: 16, 338, 339, 340

OTHER PAPER MAPS
Harvey Map (Stripmap): St Cuthbert's Way (Harvey Maps 2010)

See also: http://stcuthbertsway.info/ walking-the-routes

St Andrew's Way

Start: NT257735: St Giles' Cathedral, Edinburgh
Finish: NO513166: St Andrews Cathedral, St Andrews, Fife

OS Landranger: 58, 59, 65, 66
OS Landranger Active: 58, 59, 65, 66
OS Explorer: 350, 367, 370, 371
OS Explorer Active: 350, 367, 370, 371

See also: http://www.thewayofstandrews. com/route/routes-and-photos/

North Wales Pilgrim's Way

Start: SJ194774: St Winefride's Well, Basingwerk Abbey, Holywell
Finish: SH173264: Aberdaron, Gwynedd (although technically Bardsey)

OS Landranger: 114, 115, 116, 123
OS Landranger Active:
114, 115, 116, 123
OS Explorer:
117, 253, 254, 263, 264, 265, 266
OS Explorer Active:
17, 253, 254, 263, 264, 265, 266

See also: http://www.pilgrims-way-north-wales.org/maps.html

Our Lady of Caversham Pilgrimage Walk

Start: SU967768: Windsor Castle, Windsor, Berkshire
Finish: SU715737: Reading Station, Reading (although technically the Church of Our Lady and St Anne)

OS Landranger: 175, 176
OS Landranger Active: 175, 176
OS Explorer: 159, 160, 171, 172
OS Explorer Active: 159, 160, 171, 172

See also: Revd John N. Merrill (2011)
*Our Lady of Caversham Pilgrimage
Walk* (John Merrill Foundation). ISBN:
9780956804464.

The Pilgrims' Way

Start: SU482292: Winchester, Hampshire
Finish: TR151579: Canterbury, Kent

OS Landranger: 177, 178, 179, 185, 186,
    187, 188, 189
OS Landranger Active: 177, 178, 179,
    185, 186, 187, 188, 189
OS Explorer: 132, 133, 137, 144, 145,
    146, 147, 148, 149, 150, 163
OS Explorer Active: 132, 133, 137, 144,
    145, 146, 147, 148, 149, 150, 163

OTHER PAPER MAPS

Harvey Map (Stripmap): North Downs
    Way (West): Farnham to the Medway
    (Harvey Maps 2001).
Harvey Map (Stripmap): North Downs
    Way (East): Dover to Medway
    (Harvey Maps 2001).

See also: http://www.
    pilgrimswaycanterbury.org/the-way/

The Saints' Way

Start: SW915754: Padstow, Cornwall
Finish: SX125516: Fowey, Cornwall

OS Landranger: 200, 204
OS Landranger Active: 200, 204
OS Explorer: 106, 107, 109
OS Explorer Active: 106, 107, 109

See also: Ginny and Heulyn Lewis (2012)
    Saints' Way/Forth an Syns (The Pelican
    Studio). ISBN: 9780957234000.

The Pilgrims' Trail

Start: SU481293: Winchester Cathedral,
    Hampshire
Finish: SU639018: Ferry Port, Portsmouth

OS Landranger: 185, 196
OS Landranger Active: 185, 196
OS Explorer: 29, 119, 132
OS Explorer Active: 29, 119, 132

See also: http://www3.hants.gov.uk/
    longdistance/pilgrims-trail.htm
http://www.walkandcycle.co.uk/
    trail?trailcode=hamptr0157

Appendix: Travel Information for Overseas Routes

St Cuthbert's Way: Mainland to Holy Island

The final section of the route leads from the mainland across to the Holy Island/ Lindisfarne. You can take the causeway on to the island, or follow the posts of the historic Pilgrims Path across the sands. Whichever option you choose, you must allow two hours to cross during the safe crossing times at low-tide (and again back to the mainland if you have not booked overnight accommodation on Holy Island).

The times provided are for those people who wish to use the Lindisfarne causeway road to access (or return from) Holy Island only. The times should be treated with caution, as local weather conditions (such as high wind) can change them. Always allow thirty minutes extra to compensate for these variables.

There is also a marked walking route over the sands, but these times do not apply to it. If you intend to use this route, please do so during daylight hours and *never cross during a rising tide*. You should therefore aim to have completed this walk *before* the mid-point of the safe-to-cross time period.

See the Northumberland County Council website for the causeway safe crossing times:
http://www.northumberland.gov.uk/www2/holyisland/HolyIsland.asp?dt=0115
Northumberland County Council, County Hall, Morpeth NE61 2EF
0845 600 6400 | Fax: 01670 511 413
ask@northumberland.gov.uk

North Wales Pilgrim's Way: Aberdaron to Bardsey Island

There are many companies offering boat trips to Bardsey, and virtually all require you to pre-book. The main company is Bardsey Boat Trips.

You are advised to wear waterproofs for the crossing.

Weather permitting, crossings take place on Saturdays for weekly visitors from Porth Meudwy (near Aberdaron). If crossings are delayed because of the weather, you will cross on the first possible fine day following.

Please check boat arrangements prior to your visit.
Mordaith Llyn Ltd, Cae Hen, Aberdaron, Pwllheli, Gwynedd LL53 8BY
07971 769895
www.bardseyboattrips.com

The Pilgrims' Trail (Hampshire to Normandy): Portsmouth to Cherbourg

There are two ferry operators running from Portsmouth to Cherbourg. Cherbourg does not have a great deal to offer today, so it is recommended that after disembarking from the ferry, you head straight out of the town and look for a more picturesque place to take a break.

Brittany Ferries: eleven crossings weekly, 2hr 45min sailing.
Brittany Ferries, The Brittany Centre, Wharf Rd, Portsmouth, PO2 8RU
Tel: 0044 870 536 0360
www.brittany-ferries.com

Condor Ferries: one crossing weekly, 5hr 30min sailing.
Condor Ferries Ltd, Continental Ferryport, George Byng Way, Portsmouth, PO2 8QN
Tel: 0044 239 266 4676
www.condorferries.co.uk

GETTING TO BARFLEUR FROM CHERBOURG

Arriving in France, there are essentially two routes to Mont-Saint-Michel: the inland route from the port at Barfleur, or the coastal route from the port of Cherbourg. Barfleur is 15½ miles (25km) east of Cherbourg, where the ferry lands. If following from Barfleur, the easiest option is to take the bus from Cherbourg to Barfleur as trains run only from Valognes, a distance of 17 miles (27km) from Cherbourg. However, this is following the exact Pilgrims' Trail way-marked route, which does start you further away from the Mont. Instead, you could hire a car to get straight from Cherbourg to Mont-Saint-Michel.

TIDE TIMES FOR MONT-SAINT-MICHEL

The highest tides in continental Europe take place at Mont-Saint-Michel, and there is up to 49ft (15m) difference between low and high water. Despite the high tides, the island can be accessed via the causeway at any time of the day and all year round. Even at extremely high tides, the car parks are the only areas subject to flooding. At high tide, the coach stop beside the tourist office is not accessible and coaches stop on the causeway. For full details of the tide times, *see:* http://www.ot-montsaintmichel.com/en/horaire-marees/mont-saint-michel.htm

The best way to discover the bay safely is to take one of the many guided tours on offer near the Mont and around the bay. For further information, contact Mont-Saint-Michel tourist office: http://www.ot-montsaintmichel.com/index.ht

Index